Happiness

In cooperation with the council of the Center for Economic Studies of the University of Munich

Happiness

A Revolution in Economics

Bruno S. Frey
in collaboration with Alois
Stutzer, Matthias Benz,
Stephan Meier, Simon
Luechinger, and Christine
Benesch

CES

The MIT Press
Cambridge, Massachusetts
London, England

First MIT Press paperback edition, 2010
© 2008 Massachusetts Institute of Technology

For information on quantity discounts, email special_sales@mitpress.mit.edu.

Set in Palatino by SPi Publisher Services, Puducherry, India. Printed and bound in the United States of America.

Library of Congress Cataloging-in-Publication Data

Frey, Bruno S.
Happiness : a revolution in economics / Bruno S. Frey, in collaboration with Alois Stutzer... [et al.].
p. cm. — (Munich lectures in economics)
Includes bibliographical references and index.
ISBN 978-0-262-06277-0 (hc. : alk. paper)—978-0-262-51495-8 (pb. : alk. paper)
1. Happiness—Economic aspects. 2. Economics—Psychological aspects. I. Title.
BF575.H27F74 2007
    01—dc22

                                        2007038248

10 9 8 7 6 5

Contents

•

Series Foreword

Every year the CES council awards a prize to an internationally renowned and innovative economist for outstanding contributions to economic research. The scholar is honored with the title Distinguished CES Fellow and is invited to give the Munich Lectures in Economics.

The lectures are held at the Center for Economic Studies of the University of Munich. They introduce areas of recent or potential interest to a wide audience in a nontechnical way and combine theoretical depth with policy relevance.

Hans-Werner Sinn
Professor of Economics and Public Finance Director of CES
University of Munich

Preface

Economics is undergoing a remarkable new development, which may even be called revolutionary. This development is likely to change economics substantially in the future. Our discipline has, at the same time, a conservative bias, due to its well-established body of knowledge. To this day, the core of economics is universal; the same principles of economics are taught everywhere in the world. This enables scholars to communicate easily. But an unfortunate consequence of this enshrined knowledge is that it is difficult to introduce new ideas not in line with received theory.

Happiness research is, to some extent, an exception. Its findings are slowly being taken into account in standard economics. Indeed, research on happiness has already become a hot topic, particularly among young economics scholars.

The economics of happiness is arguably revolutionary in three respects:

Measurement The measurable concept of happiness or life satisfaction allows us to proxy the concept of *utility* in a satisfactory way. It proposes the opposite of something that was considered a revolution in the 1930s, when Sir John Hicks, Lord Lionel Robbins, and others claimed that utility cannot and need not be measured. This was a great advance, and it opened the way to a fruitful application of microeconomics to economic issues, and more recently to issues far beyond economics. But the situation has changed dramatically since the 1930s. Psychologists have taught us how to measure happiness and thus to fill the concept of utility with life. Although these measures are certainly not ideal, they can usefully be applied to economic, political, and social problems. At the same time, the ways of measuring experienced utility are continually being improved.

Approximating experienced utility by using measures of subjective well-being allows us to extend economic theory into new areas. In particular, it enables us to analyze errors in decision making. Standard economic theory equates the utility expected when deciding between consumption bundles with the utility experienced when consuming them. Individuals always maximize their utility and only make errors in a random way. In contrast, happiness research demonstrates that individuals tend to make systematic errors when choosing between alternatives. For example, they often mispredict the utility gained by future consumption. They overestimate the satisfaction they derive from having a higher income in the future, and they underestimate the utility gained from immaterial aspects of life, such as friendship and social relations. As a result of these errors in judgment, they find themselves less satisfied with life than they could be according to their own evaluation. Similarly, individuals' utility is lower when they are subject to significant self-control problems, such as when they are induced to watch more television than they think they should.

Some economists have pointed out that such deviations from standard economic theory may exist, but this insight has not affected the principles of economics. Happiness research enables us not only to acknowledge these behavioral features but also to analyze them empirically. This was not possible in standard theory based on "revealed preference," which presumes that observed behavior is the result of a utility-maximizing calculus in which individuals do not make any mistakes.

New insights Happiness research teaches us how human beings value goods and services, as well as how they value social conditions. This applies, in particular, to the effects of income, unemployment, and other economic factors on well-being. The new insights go beyond economics to include non-material values such as the value of autonomy and social relations in the family and beyond.

Happiness research suggests that individual evaluations are much broader than those enshrined in standard economic theory. Most importantly, it shows that individuals derive utility not only from income (as is implied in much of received theory) but also from highly valued social relations and from self-determination, as well as using their own competence. Moreover, individuals derive utility from *processes*, not just from outcomes.

Policy consequences Happiness research suggests many policies that deviate significantly from those derived in standard economics. With respect to *current* economic policy, the research on happiness reveals that the goal of increasing income (or, at the aggregate level, growth in gross national product)—often implicitly or even explicitly assumed in received economics—is not an effective way of increasing utility in a sustainable way. Much of the initial utility increase from higher income dissipates rather quickly. Individuals adapt quite rapidly to higher income, and that leads to higher income aspiration. They also tend to compare themselves with others. Therefore, people do not evaluate income in absolute terms, but rather in relative terms.

Happiness research emphasizes the importance of employment and leisure for individual well-being much more than standard economics does. Moreover, it explicitly takes into account the genetic, socio-demographic, cultural, and political determinants of happiness. As a consequence, individuals can gain many different insights into how government policies affect the well-being of individuals. Proposals for increasing individuals' life satisfaction include increasing leisure time by raising the minimum vacation entitlements from two weeks to four weeks a year and other specific policies, such as curbing advertising on television and reducing excessive geographical mobility. At the level of *constitutional* design, happiness research helps to build institutions that enable individuals to achieve their highest level of well-being. It has been suggested that extending individuals' political participation rights and decentralizing political decision making have positive influences on life satisfaction.

This book advances the idea that a revolution in economics is under way by substantiating the three claims that have been made. Considerable emphasis is placed on going beyond purely theoretical conjectures and providing empirical evidence.

Part I traces the major developments in economic happiness research: Why is its study worthwhile? What is the relationship to utility as used in standard economic theory? It is demonstrated that we have gained major new insights into how income, unemployment, inflation, and income distribution affect human well-being.

Part II pushes the field ahead by looking at topics that so far have been neglected or have been studied in a much different way. Among the topics treated are democracy and federalism, self-employment and voluntary work, and watching television (one of the major activities of modern man). Moreover, it is shown how the concept of utility can be given life by considering procedural utility (beyond the outcome utility used in standard economics), the tendency of individuals to mispredict future utility of various types of consumption (the utility is sometimes overpredicted and sometimes underpredicted), and a new approach to empirically measuring the value of public goods (as a complement to the traditional willingness-to-pay approaches).

Part III deals with the policy consequences of happiness research. The media and the "positive psychology" movement have drawn on these insights. However, care must be taken not to fall prey to a "benevolent dictator" approach of telling individuals how to reach happiness, or forcing them to take the corresponding actions. Rather, governments should only provide the conditions that allow people to become and remain happy. A crucial role is played by adequate political institutions, particularly decentralized public decision making and a right to direct political participation.

The final chapter concludes that economic happiness research is revolutionary. Though much has been achieved, the field is wide open for future research.

This book does not survey happiness research; that has been done elsewhere. Nor is it possible to give a full account of the revolution we are witnessing. It is too early for that, and the participants are too engaged in the topic to be objective enough. Rather, the book demonstrates what can be achieved by the happiness research undertaken in economics.

The book is, to a significant extent, based on the work of the research group connected to my chair at the Institute for Empirical Research in Economics at the University of Zurich. It is therefore appropriate that the members of the group are listed as co-authors. I was a joint author of all but one of the papers on which the book is based. The following features characterize the work of the Zurich Group:

• It is highly interdisciplinary. In particular, many insights from psychology have been introduced. But political science and sociology also play substantial roles.

• Its members are willing to depart from standard economics if they find the departure useful.

• The work is empirical in orientation. Although theory is important, it is not enough.

• The members are prepared to draw policy conclusions, even when the evidence (as will always be the case) is only preliminary.

Leading the Zurich Group has been an extraordinarily exciting experience. I am particularly grateful to my long-time co-worker Alois

Stutzer, a master of applied empirical work in happiness research. He was kind enough to go through the whole manuscript. But I alone am responsible for any errors.

Parts of this book have been presented at many conferences and lectures around the world. The main ideas were developed in connection with the lecture given on the occasion of my being appointed Distinguished Fellow of 2005 by CESifo at the University of Munich. I benefited greatly from the discussions at an interdisciplinary conference on happiness held at Schwarzenberg, Austria, under the sponsorship of the Progress Foundation.

In writing this book, I was skillfully supported by Christine Benesch. I am most grateful to Rosemary Brown, Rosemary Fitzgerald, Silja Ang, and Isabel Ellenberger for improving my English and for checking the text.

Bruno S. Frey

Happiness

I   Major Developments

Chapter 1 argues that happiness research is important because the ultimate goal of most human beings is to be happy. Research on individual well-being contributes to many aspects of life, but it is particularly useful for these purposes: to study what conditions contribute to individual well-being, to understand human behavior and test alternative explanations for it, to study changes in preferences and social interaction, to analyze the consequences of happiness on behavior, to inquire whether happiness is a cause or an effect (for instance, does unemployment make for unhappy people, or are unhappy people more likely to be unemployed?), or to explain empirical observations at variance with standard economic theory (such as why increasing per-capita income does not necessarily increase happiness). Finally, happiness research is useful for economic policy. For current decisions, it is useful (e.g., when the choice is between higher inflation and lower unemployment) to know the relative importance of the many determinants of happiness. Happiness research is even more important in helping to determine which institutions enable individuals to increase their life satisfaction.

Chapter 2 rejects the view of standard economics that it is neither possible nor necessary to measure utility. Today there are many ways to proxy utility by measuring subjective well-being, the most prominent being global evaluations via surveys of life satisfaction. Methods range from evaluating happiness experiences in everyday life to brain scanning.

Chapter 3 is devoted to the relationship between income and happiness. Among individuals in a society, higher income is related to significantly higher subjective well-being. Higher income, however, is particularly important in relative terms but not in absolute terms. This can be attributed to the processes of social comparisons and adaptation, whereby higher income leads to upward adjustments of aspirations.

As a consequence, higher per-capita income has little or no effect on happiness over time. Desires tend to be insatiable. Between countries, higher average income is associated with higher average happiness. There is, however, substantial variation in subjective well-being across equally poor countries, and there is only a weak positive correlation between per-capita income and subjective well-being above some threshold of per-capita income.

Chapter 4 looks at the relationship between unemployment and happiness. One of the strongest and most ubiquitous findings is that unemployed people tend to be much less happy than employed people. This holds even if a related lower income level is taken into account, and it suggests that psychic costs and social norms are important. People's overall happiness suffers even if they themselves are not unemployed; unemployment has more general effects on the economy and society.

Chapter 5 deals with the effects of inflation and inequality on happiness. International cross-section and time-series studies suggest that rising prices have a negative effect on people's happiness. There is an interesting finding with respect to the effect of differences in income inequality: the happiness of Europeans decreases with income inequality, but the happiness of Americans does not. This can be attributed to Americans' belief (probably an illusion) that there is a greater amount of upward social mobility in their society, so that even poor people hope to benefit from higher income in the future.

Research on Happiness

Happiness is considered by many to be the ultimate goal in life; indeed, virtually everyone wants to be happy. The American Colonies' Declaration of Independence takes it as a self-evident truth that the "pursuit of happiness" is an "inalienable right" comparable to life and liberty. In the late 1980s, the fourth king of Bhutan, Jigme Singye Wangchuck, enunciated "Gross National Happiness" as the principle guiding force in his country (Ura and Galay 2004).

Economics is—or should be—about individual happiness. In particular, the question is: How do economic growth, unemployment, inflation, and inequality, as well as institutional factors such as good governance, affect individual well-being?

For a long time, economics has taken income as a suitable though incomplete proxy for human welfare. Happiness research shows that reported subjective well-being is a far better measure of individual welfare. "Reported subjective well-being" is the scientific term used in psychology for an individual's evaluation of the extent to which he or she experiences positive and negative affect, happiness, or satisfaction with life. They are separable constructs, and the precise terminology will be used whenever specific empirical research is reported. In general, however, as in the literature, the terms 'happiness', 'well-being', and 'life satisfaction' are used interchangeably.

1.1 Why Study Happiness?

There are various important reasons for economists to study happiness, in addition to intrinsic interest in the subject.

Identifying the Determinants of Happiness

Why do people experience a particular level of satisfaction with the life they lead? Happiness depends on a large number of determinants. Therefore, one of the most important tasks of happiness research is to isolate what conditions affect individual and social well-being, and to what extent.[1] It is important to emphasize that economic happiness research is not restricted to the influence of economic factors on subjective well-being. Indeed, one of the most important findings has been that non-material aspects of a person's life—in particular, social relations among family members, friends, and neighbors—are important.[2] Happiness research endeavors to determine quantitatively the relative importance of genetic, personality, socio-demographic, economic, cultural, and political factors. The genetic and personality factors that determine subjective well-being are largely outside the scope of economics. But they are nonetheless important, not least because the precision of the econometric estimates of the effects of the other determinants depends on the possibly confounding role of personality differences. However, research—e.g., that of Helliwell (2006b)—suggests that the influences of demographic, economic, and political factors on happiness are not greatly affected by personality differences. Nevertheless, it is important to keep in mind that there are specific cultural definitions of happiness, and that the motivations and predictors of happiness may differ between cultures (Uchida, Norasakkunkit, and Kitayama 2004). The same holds for possibly different interpretations of numerical scales in different societies.

Understanding the Nature of Happiness

The idea that individuals have happiness as their ultimate goal in life is not undisputed. Happiness is not necessarily the only goal that matters. For instance, Social Production Function Theory (Lindenberg 1986, 1990; Lindenberg and Frey 1993) identifies two ultimate goals

---

1. This is a major theme throughout the book. Particular emphasis is placed on income (chapter 3), unemployment (chapter 4), inflation and inequality (chapter 5), democracy and federalism (chapter 6), self-employment and voluntary work (chapter 7), marriage (chapter 8), television viewing (chapter 9), and terrorism (chapter 12).

2. On "relational goods," see Bruni and Porta 2007 or Gui and Sugden 2005. A higher level of such social capital (Putnam 2000) has been shown to increase life satisfaction considerably (Helliwell and Putnam 2005; Björnskov 2003; OECD 2001; Powdthavee 2007).

that all human beings seek to optimize (physical well-being and social well-being) and five instrumental goals by which they are achieved (stimulation, comfort, status, behavioral confirmation, and affection). Other authors—among them Ryff (1989) and Lane (2000)—consider values such as responsibility, personal growth, purpose in life, mastery of one's environment, self-directedness, and loyalty to other people important. Some scholars argue that long-term happiness is on the same level as higher-order goods, such as health, entertainment, or nutrition (Kimball and Willis 2006). Liberal thinkers argue that personal freedom is even more important than happiness, and even that individuals should have the option of being unhappy. This may have the added benefit that people do not become too complacent and keep aspiring to achieve more. In this sense, unhappiness may even be productive.

Happiness is not a static goal that individuals are able to attain by aspiring to it. Rather, happiness is a by-product of a "good life" (*eudaimonia*, or civil happiness, as expounded by Aristotle) producing satisfaction over the long run. Those who try to achieve happiness by purposive action are unlikely to attain sustained happiness. Evolutionary theory tells us that humans did not evolve to be happy but to survive and reproduce (Camerer 2007; Camerer, Loewenstein, and Prelec 2004; Rayo and Becker 2007).

Despite these reservations, happiness is undoubtedly an overriding goal in most people's lives. This becomes clearer when the question is reversed: Who really wants to be unhappy in life? It is, in any case, crucial to inform people about the relationship between various actions and their well-being. But it should be left up to each individual how, and to what extent, he or she wants to make use of that knowledge.

Three concepts or levels of happiness can usefully be distinguished (Nettle 2005):

Momentary feelings of joy and pleasure, referred to in psychology as positive and negative affect. These feelings are often called "happiness."

Overall contentment with life, which is normally called "life satisfaction."

The quality of life achieved by developing and fulfilling one's potential, which has been called *eudaimonia* or "the good life."

Another issue is whether people's instantaneous level of happiness can be captured by self-reported measures of well-being. Is there a difference between people's hedonic experiences and their explicit reflective appraisals of experiences in reported subjective well-being (Schooler, Ariely, and Loewenstein 2003)? People sometimes are fully engaged in challenging activities and gain great pleasure from them. They are then subject to a "flow" experience (Csikszentmihalyi 1990). When people are in such a state, they do not assess and are unable to report their well-being. This means that there are limits to the measurement of instant utility. New insights will be available when we know more about correlations between reported subjective well-being and physiological measures of well-being. Correlations over time and across individuals would allow us to study people with different frames of reference. Time series for physiological measures would allow us to assess whether people change their reference standards in self-reported happiness over time. In view of the possible shortcomings of current happiness measures, it should be kept in mind that the required quality of happiness data depends on its intended use. When considering the measures of happiness, one should always take into account what they are to be used for. In many cases, even incomplete measures of happiness are useful. Moreover, the quality of the happiness data should be compared against alternative concepts of measuring people's level of well-being.

The success of happiness research for economics will be determined by the extent to which the findings can be integrated into established economic theory. There seem to be two main ways for research on happiness to contribute to the core of economics in the future. First, there is our understanding of utility; second, there is theory testing (discussed in the next subsection).

Econometric and experimental research methods, using proxy measures for well-being, can inform economics about a concept of utility with more psychological content. This understanding of experienced utility is closer to people's well-being than revealed behavior. There have already been a considerable number of contributions along this line. (For reviews, see Frey and Stutzer 1999; Kimball and Willis 2006.) The most important work has been done by Kahneman and co-researchers (1991, 1997, 2006), by the Leyden group around van Praag (1971, 1993, 1999), and by Easterlin (1995, 2001, 2003). A psychologically sounder notion of individual well-being challenges various basic assumptions of the economic approach incorporated in utility theory.

The following questions are relevant:

Do people consciously maximize their utility? This question is rarely asked; it is usually taken for granted that they do. Often the belief that the pursuit of happiness is the main source of human motivation is even viewed as a moral obligation in Western societies (i.e., as prescribed by their values). In particular, economics is based on conscious rational choice. However, such an approach has been criticized as unscientific. When modern economics was founded, William James (1890) and other psychologists argued that scientists should take all possible motives into account in their theories. People's behavior does not necessarily always aim at maximizing utility; it might be an impulsive act, or it might follow a sense of obligation. (For an overview of this debate, see Lewin 1996.) That people explicitly follow the goal of maximizing happiness should not just be assumed; it should be open for empirical research. (See, e.g., Kitayama and Markus 2000.)

Should people try to maximize their utility? This question is asked because people's attempts at assessing their own level of utility may be self-defeating. Hedonic introspection can reduce individuals' sensitivity to their own hedonic experience. It tends to undermine the utility that people want to achieve. Several empirical studies (e.g., Lyubomirsky and Lepper 1999) find that happy people are less introspective than unhappy people. The explicit pursuit of maximum happiness then hampers the ability to achieve it. A neat illustration is offered by Schooler, Ariely, and Loewenstein (2003), who studied the "costs of trying to have a good time" on New Year's Eve 1999. In a questionnaire sent by e-mail before the big event, Schooler et al. asked 475 people how large a celebration they were planning, how much they expected to enjoy it, and how much money and time they were expecting to spend on it. After the event, people were asked the same questions with regard to their actual experiences. They found that those people who expected a great party were more likely to be disappointed than those who expected only a small celebration or none at all. The difference between experienced and expected enjoyment was negatively correlated with people's anticipation and with the time they expected to spend on preparations. The active pursuit of happiness may also be self-defeating, because people have faulty theories about happiness. People who see the source of a good life more in terms of financial success consistently report lower self-esteem, vitality, and life satisfaction (Kasser and Ryan 1993; Diener and Oishi 2000; Kasser 2002).

Do people have preferences for processes apart from outcomes? In the assessment of institutions, it is important to understand whether processes themselves are a source of utility. Recommendations for institutional design may be quite different if people appreciate autonomy, participation, or self-determination independent of outcome. Data on subjective well-being allow direct empirical investigations of these aspects as a source of people's well-being. (This is discussed in chapter 10.)

Can people successfully predict their future utility?   Standard economic theory assumes that there are no systematic deviations between the utility predicted when choosing between alternative goods and the utility experienced when consuming the goods in the future. Scitovsky (1976, p. 4) criticized this view as "unscientific" because "it seemed to rule out—as a logical impossibility—any conflict between what man chooses to get and what will best satisfy him." In many carefully carried out experiments and surveys, psychologists studied how successful people are in forecasting the utility they are about to experience. (For a review, see Loewenstein and Schkade 1999.) They found that people often held incorrect intuitive theories about the determinants of happiness. Most importantly, people underestimate the speed with which they adapt to new experiences. As a result of these misguided predictions, there are systematic errors in decision making. When deciding between alternatives, extrinsic attributes are more salient than intrinsic attributes. People therefore underestimate the future utility produced by intrinsic attributes. As a result, they devote too little time to family members, friends, and hobbies. They overestimate extrinsic attributes and therefore put too much effort into acquiring income and gaining status, which makes them worse off overall. (See chapter 11.)

Testing Economic Theories and Predictions

With a proxy measure for utility at hand, it is possible to discriminate between competing theories that make the same predictions of behavior but differ in what they put forward as people's utility level. This kind of test may become a powerful tool in the process of falsifying theories. Some examples illustrate the potential use of happiness research for this purpose.

• Several theories try to account for labor supply and unemployment over the business cycle. In New Classical Macroeconomics, where a perfect labor market is assumed, individuals are assumed to adjust their labor supply over time in response to changes in wages and in interest rates. If they are unemployed, it is voluntary. According to this view, the loss of income due to unemployment is voluntarily chosen, and unemployed people suffer no utility loss. In contrast, New Keynesian Macroeconomics attributes involuntary unemployment to price and wage rigidities. Unemployed people would be willing to accept a job at the current wage rate, but cannot find one, and suffer a utility loss if they lose their job.

• From the behavior of unemployed people, it is difficult to assess how well these two models of the labor market perform. However, individual reports of subjective well-being provide information about the utility level of unemployed people. It can be studied whether unemployed people are better or worse off than people with the same income but less leisure time. It is one of the most robust findings in research on happiness in economics that unemployed people suffer large nonpecuniary costs. (See chapter 4.) This finding is at odds with the idea of voluntary unemployment.

• Social norms affect unemployed people's behavior (Stutzer and Lalive 2004). Stronger social work norms in a community significantly reduce the duration of unemployment of fellow residents who are looking for a job. This finding does not allow us to assess whether a stronger social work norm is effective as a result of social sanctions, or whether, in a community with a stronger social norm, unemployed people get social support and information that enable them to find a job more quickly. However, the two scenarios lead to different predictions about unemployed people's well-being. While they are expected to be better off if they get social support, they probably suffer even more when a stronger social norm to work primarily means social sanctions. The measured life satisfaction of unemployed people across Swiss communities is consistent with the latter view.

• Economic models can make systematically different predictions about the effect of excise taxes on people's utility, though they all predict that people reduce their consumption when a good is taxed. Normally, one assumes that people will be opposed to having a tax put on the goods they consume, because they suffer a utility loss. However, their utility rises when the tax helps them to overcome a bad habit. For consumption activities (smoking, drinking, eating chocolate), people may advocate "sin taxes" to overcome their weakness of will. Research on happiness can contribute to this debate. It allows us to directly study the effect of taxes on people's subjective well-being. In two longitudinal analyses across the United States and Canada, Gruber and Mullainathan (2005) performed such a test with data from the General Social Survey. They analyzed the effect of changes in state tobacco taxes on the reported happiness of people who were likely to be smokers. They found that a real cigarette tax of 50 cents rather than the current 31.6 cents significantly reduced the likelihood of unhappiness among predicted smokers. This result favors models of time-inconsistent smoking behavior in which people have problems with self-control.

• Many theories in regional, urban, and public economics assume that arbitrage across markets and across space are expected to equalize a person's utility level, *ceteris paribus*. For example, people are prepared to accept spending more time commuting only if they are either compensated by a higher salary or if they benefit from cheaper housing. Thus, there is a strong notion of equilibrium underlying economic models of location and federal competition. With data on subjective well-being, the prediction of equalized levels of utility can be tested directly. On the basis of seven waves of the German Socio-Economic Panel, a negative partial correlation between commuting time and life satisfaction was found (Stutzer and Frey 2007a). For standard economics, this result is a paradox.

Isolating the Consequences of Happiness

Persons who are satisfied with the life they lead can be expected to act differently than persons who are dissatisfied. Happy people are more optimistic, more sociable, and more enterprising, and they tend to be more successful in their private, economic, and social activities. As a consequence, they are happier in their marriages as well as in their jobs. Moreover, they can be expected to have a longer time horizon and to be willing to take more risk, which may make them more successful entrepreneurs (Bosman and van Winden 2006). So far, most of the research on the consequences of happiness for behavior has been done in the field of psychology, where there is a large experimental literature identifying a relationship between positive and negative affect (i.e., mood, emotions, feelings) and decision making (Hermalin and Isen 1999; Isen 2000; Lyubomirsky, King, and Diener 2005). In particular, even relatively small changes in happiness can markedly influence everyday thought processes. For example, positive affect tends to increase a person's willingness to help others. Happier people have been found to gain higher pleasure and/or lower psychic costs from aiding others (Isen and Levin 1972) and to be more creative (Isen, Daubman, and Nowicki 1987). Moreover, affective states serve important informational and motivational functions (Schwarz 1990).

Economic modeling of decision making has, so far, essentially ignored the role of affect. Economists have analyzed the adverse consequences of strong emotional states (arousal) and visceral influences on cognitive abilities (MacLeod 1996; Kaufman 1999; Loewenstein 1996, 2000). Other economists have focused on "rationalizing" emotions (Frank 1988; Romer 2000). Their goal is to explain why evolutionary forces have produced particular emotions.

Is Happiness a Cause, or an Effect?

The same factors may be determinants or consequences of happiness. Thus, being unemployed makes people unhappy, but unhappy people are less active and enterprising and are therefore less likely to find employment. Similarly, marriage may increase happiness, but happier persons are more likely to be married because they are more attractive partners. Identifying the direction of causality is important, as it is a precondition for trying to increase happiness by policy intervention. However, it is difficult to identify causal effects, and the economic approach to happiness is subject to the same econometric challenges faced by studies that examine the determinants of behavior, including the possibility of omitted variables and the possibility of endogeneity bias.

Helping to Make Sense of Paradoxical Observations

Standard economics finds it difficult to explain various empirical puzzles. A particularly important paradox needing explanation is that, in several countries, real income has risen drastically since World War II, but self-reported subjective well-being of the population has not increased, or has even fallen slightly. In the United States, for example, between 1946 and 1991, per-capita real income rose by a factor of 2.5 (from approximately $11,000 to $27,000 in 1996 dollars), but over the same period of time happiness, on average, remained constant. This well-established finding of happiness research has been called the "Easterlin Paradox"

(Easterlin 1974, 1995, 2001; Kenny 1999; Blanchflower and Oswald 2004b; Diener and Oishi 2000) and the "Happiness Paradox" (Pugno 2004a, 2007). Higher income is positively associated with people's happiness. Yet over the entire life cycle, happiness changes very little. The insights of happiness research that help us to understand these observations are put forward in chapter 3.

Another paradox is that, although work has been considered a burden since ancient times, empirical research on happiness strongly suggests that being unemployed, even when the loss in income is taken into account, depresses well-being markedly.

Improving Economic Policy

In most cases, it is impossible to make a Pareto-optimal policy proposal, because any social action entails costs for at least some individuals. Hence, an evaluation of the net effects, in terms of individual utilities, is needed. Economic policy must deal with tradeoffs, and macroeconomics deals particularly with tradeoffs between unemployment and inflation. Using data on reported life satisfaction for twelve European countries in the period 1975–1991, it has been calculated that a 1-percentage-point increase in the unemployment rate is marginally compensated for by a 1.7-percentage-point decrease in inflation (Di Tella, MacCulloch, and Oswald 2001). This result deviates significantly from the "Misery Index," which, for lack of information, has simply been defined as the sum of the percentages of unemployment and annual inflation. Another tradeoff that can be calculated from estimated happiness functions is the compensating variation for being unemployed versus holding a job. For the twelve European countries just referred to, a move from the lowest income quartile to the highest would not be enough to offset the adverse effect of unemployment, which suggests that unemployed people suffer high non-pecuniary costs.

Economic policy is concerned in part with how institutional conditions on happiness (for example, the quality of governance and the size of social capital) affect individual well-being. Research in 49 countries in the 1980s and the 1990s suggests that there are substantial well-being benefits from improved accountability, effectiveness, and stability of government, the rule of law, and the control of corruption. The data show that the effects flowing directly from the quality of institutions are often much larger than those flowing through productivity and economic growth (Helliwell 2003). Some findings of happiness research add more precise knowledge to what have become standard views in economics; other findings contradict them. One finding is the consistently large influence of non-economic variables on self-reported satisfaction. This does not mean that income, employment, and price stability are not important, but it does suggest that the recent interest in good governance and in social capital is well founded. The findings of happiness research also enrich our knowledge of the effects of discriminating with respect to gender, ethnicity, race, and age.

1.2   The Literature

For centuries, happiness has been a central theme of philosophy.[3] For a long time, the empirical study of happiness has been the province of psychology (Argyle 1987; Csikszentmihalyi 1990; Michalos 1991; Diener 1984; Myers 1993; Ryan and Deci 2001; Nettle 2005). There have also been important contributions by sociologists (Veenhoven 1993, 1999, 2000; Lindenberg 1986) and political scientists (Inglehart 1990; Lane 2000).[4] Only recently has psychological research been linked to economics. The early contribution of Richard Easterlin (1974) was noted by many economics scholars, but at the time it found few followers. The same may be said of Tibor Scitovsky's book *The Joyless Economy* (1976).[5] General interest among economists in the measurement and the determinants of reported subjective well-being was raised by a 1993 symposium in London, the proceedings of which were later published in the *Economic Journal* (Frank 1997; Ng 1997; Oswald 1997) and elsewhere (Clark and Oswald 1994, 1996). In the late 1990s, economists began to publish large-scale empirical analyses of the determinants of happiness in various countries and periods.

Happiness research excels in its interdisciplinary orientation. Scholars from various disciplines may emphasize one aspect more than another. Economists are particularly interested in the economic determinants of happiness and their consequences for economic policy, but their research

3. On how philosophers have dealt with the topic of happiness, see McMahon 2006; Bruni 2006. On the contributions of Aristotle, Bentham, Mill, and Kant, see also Bruni and Porta 2007; Sugden 2005; Nussbaum 2007; Nussbaum and Sen 1993.
4. Notable forerunners of sociological and political science research on happiness are Cantril (1965) and Brickman and Campbell (1971).
5. Even earlier, Bernard van Praag and his group in Leyden developed the concept of individual welfare functions based on reported subjective evaluations (van Praag 1968, 1971). However, their insights have seldom been taken up in interdisciplinary happiness research.

goes well beyond that. Conversely, psychologists focus on mental processes but have made major contributions to how economic factors (particularly income) affect subjective well-being. (See, e.g., Diener and Biswas-Diener 2002.) In current happiness research, in contrast with other areas of the social sciences, the integration among disciplines often goes so far that it is not possible to identify whether a particular contribution is due to an economist, a psychologist, a sociologist, or a political scientist. This is no small achievement, especially in view of the generally increasing differentiation of economics from the other social sciences.

In this book I do not intend to provide a general survey of happiness research. Lane (2000), Frey and Stutzer (2002a), and Nettle (2005) have already written books on the subject. Survey papers have been contributed by Ng (1978), by Diener, Suh, Lucas, and Smith (1999), by Easterlin (2004), by Frey and Stutzer (2002b, 2004b, 2005a,b), by Diener and Seligman (2004), and by Di Tella and MacCulloch (2006). There are useful collections of articles (e.g., Strack, Argyle, and Schwarz 1991; Kahneman, Diener, and Schwarz 1999; Easterlin 2002; Huppert, Kaverne, and Baylis 2004; Bruni and Porta 2005, 2007). There are important monographs focusing on various aspects of economic happiness research (e.g., Graham and Pettinato 2002a; van Praag and Ferrer-i-Carbonell 2004; Layard 2005; Bruni 2006). Research is being published in many different journals, and there is a specialized *Journal of Happiness Studies*.

2   The Relationship of Happiness to Utility

2.1   Objective and Subjective Utility

Standard economic theory employs an "objectivist" position, observing the choices made by individuals. Individual utility only depends on tangible goods and services and leisure. Utility is inferred from behavior (or revealed preferences), and is in turn used to explain the choices made. This "modern" view of utility has been influenced by the positivistic movement in philosophy. Subjectivist experience (e.g., captured by surveys) is rejected as being "unscientific," because it is not objectively observable. Most importantly, cardinality of utility and interpersonal comparability are not necessary for positive demand theory, which, in line with Occam's Razor, constitutes a great advantage (Robbins 1932; Hicks and Allen 1934). The axiomatic revealed preference approach holds that the choices made provide *all* the information required to infer the utility of outcomes. Accordingly, Kahneman et al. (1997) coined the term *decision utility*. Moreover, the axiomatic approach is applied not only to derive individual utility but also to measure social welfare. Comparisons of social welfare are based on the consumption behavior of households (Slesnick 1998; Ng 1997, 2001; Sen 1996).

The positivistic view still dominates in economics. "The popularity of this view in economics," Sen (1986, p. 18) observes, "may be due to a mixture of an obsessive concern with observables and a peculiar belief that choice . . . is the only human aspect that can be observed." Its dominance is reflected in the contents of microeconomic textbooks. However, not all contemporary economists subscribe to this view.

Numerous scholars have challenged the standard view of utility in economic theory from different angles. There are many examples of non-objectivist theoretical analyses in economics. Various analyses consider emotions (Elster 1998), self-signaling, goal completion, mastery, and meaning (Loewenstein 1999), intrinsic motivation (Frey 1997b; Osterloh and Frey 2000, 2004, 2006), altruism, reciprocity, and cooperation (Schwarze and Winkelmann 2005; Fehr and Gächter 1998, 2000; Fehr and Schmidt 2003; Gächter 2007), identity (Akerlof and Kranton 2005), status (Frank 1985a, 1999; de Botton 2000), and esteem and social recognition (Brennan and Pettit 2004, Frey 2006). In order to explain human behavior, interdependent utility functions are considered rather than interpersonally independent ones (Clark and Oswald 1998; Sobel 2005). This challenges established notions about welfare (Boskin and Sheshinski 1978; Holländer 2001; Layard 1980). In the vast literature on anomalies in decision making (e.g., Thaler 1992; Frey and Eichenberger 1994), it is questioned whether utility can generally be derived from observed choices.[1] Many studies (starting with Allais 1953, and including Ellsberg 1961) have demonstrated inconsistency in preferences. Human beings do not always know what they would like, are often subject to "projection bias" (Loewenstein, O'Donoghue, and Rabin 2003), and fail to maximize experienced utility (in contrast to decision utility).[2]

Consequentialism, of which utilitarianism is a special case, is not the only aspect important for behavior. Procedural utility should also be considered. (See chapter 10.) Thus, standard economic theory's exclusive reliance on an objectivist approach is open to doubt, both theoretically and empirically. In any case, the approach used by standard theory restricts the possibility of understanding and influencing human well-being.

The subjective approach to utility offers a fruitful complementary path to studying the world.

First, it allows us to measure human well-being directly. It follows an interpretation of utility in hedonistic terms in the broadest sense. This is emphasized by the term *experienced utility*, proposed by Kahneman et al. (1997). There are many research questions for which it is useful to take experienced utility, measured by reported subjective well-being, as a proxy for decision utility. It creates a basis for explicitly testing fundamental assumptions and propositions in economic theory, and for developing and testing new and broader theories of human behavior. If, however, the focus is on the economic consequences of mispredicting utility (see chapter 11), insights are derived from systematic divergences between the two concepts. Proposing a conceptual link between the two

---

1. Neuroeconomics offers a new approach to study motivation independent of behavior. See Fehr and Singer 2005; Fehr et al. 2005; Camerer 2007; Camerer et al. 2007.
2. See Kahneman and Thaler 2006 and chapter 11 below.

approaches, Kimball and Willis (2006) see happiness as consisting of two components: short-run happiness or elation (nurtured by recent news about lifetime utility) and long-run, sustained happiness.

Second, the empirical concept of reported subjective well-being can be applied to studies of remembered and predicted utility (Kahneman et al. 1997, 2004b; Kahneman and Riis 2005) as well as to studies of procedural utility.

Third, happiness is for many people an ultimate goal. That is not the case for other things we may want, such as job security, status, power, and especially money (income). We do not want them for their own sake, but rather to give us the possibility of making ourselves happier.

Happiness research thus constitutes an important part of the cross-disciplinary field of Economics and Psychology, sometimes misleadingly called Behavioral Economics.[3]

2.2 Measuring Individual Well-Being

A subjective view of utility recognizes that everyone has his or her own ideas about happiness and the good life, and that observed behavior is an incomplete indicator of individual well-being. If one accepts this view, individuals' happiness can nevertheless be captured and analyzed: a person can be *asked* how satisfied he is with his life. It is a sensible tradition in economics to rely on the judgment of the persons directly involved. People are reckoned to be the best judges of the overall quality of their lives, and it is a straightforward strategy to ask them about their well-being. There are different techniques for inquiring about people's well-being. They all provide indications of people's affective state or individuals' evaluation of their life satisfaction or happiness. Many surveys include questions on overall or "global" self-reports of satisfaction with life. Behind the score indicated by a person lies a cognitive assessment as to what extent that person's overall quality of life is judged in a favorable way (Veenhoven 1993). The umbrella term for these measures is *subjective well-being*. Different measures of subjective well-being capture to some extent its two basic notions of cognition and affect. *Affect* is the label attached to moods and emotions. Affect captures people's instant evaluation of the events that occur in their lives. The cognitive component refers to the rational or intellectual aspects of

---

3. On economics and psychology, see Frey and Stutzer 2007; Rabin 1998; Frey and Stutzer 2001; Camerer et al. 2003; Frey and Benz 2004.

subjective well-being. It is usually assessed with measures of satisfaction. It has been shown that pleasant affect, unpleasant affect, and life satisfaction are separable constructs (Lucas, Diener, and Suh 1996).

It is debatable to what extent these "traditional" measures of subjective well-being accurately capture the various notions of happiness and individual well-being put forward in the literature on the good life (Ryan and Deci 2001). A common concern refers to the emphasis on momentary positive affects in survey questions on individual well-being. Hedonic well-being is not necessarily the same as happiness. According to the eudaimonic view of happiness, people should live according to their true self (*daimon*). They then act according to their deeply held values. The underlying causes of well-being can be seen to be autonomy, competence, and relatedness. This is closely related to the value of intrinsic motivation (Deci 1971; Lindenberg 2001).[4] Ryan and Deci's (2001) Self-Determination Theory argues that the satisfaction of these basic psychological needs generally supports hedonic as well as eudaimonic well-being.

Individuals' well-being or life satisfaction can be measured in a variety of ways, some of which will now be discussed.

Asking People: Global Evaluations of Individual Life Satisfaction

This approach seeks to capture happiness by asking a representative sample of individuals about their overall satisfaction with their lives. A prominent example of a single-item question on a three-point scale is this, from the General Social Surveys (Davis, Smith, and Marsden 2001): "Taken all together, how would you say things are these days—would you say that you are very happy, pretty happy, or not too happy?" In the World Values Survey (Inglehart et al. 2000), life satisfaction is assessed on a scale from 1 (dissatisfied) to 10 (satisfied). People are asked "All things considered, how satisfied are you with your life as a whole these days?" The Euro-Barometer Surveys, covering all members of the European Union, asks a similar question: "On the whole, are you very satisfied, fairly satisfied, not very satisfied, or not at all satisfied with the life you lead?" Among the multiple-item approaches, the most prominent is the Satisfaction With Life Scale (Pavot and Diener 1993), composed of five questions rated on a scale from 1 to 7.[5]

---

4. For an economic analysis, see Frey 1997b.
5. For a survey of various measures of subjective well-being, see Andrews and Robinson 1991.

Because subjective survey data are based on individuals' judgments, they are prone to a multitude of biases. It therefore should be checked whether people are indeed able and willing to give meaningful answers to questions about their well-being. Moreover, reported subjective well-being may depend on the order of questions, the wording of questions, the scales applied, the actual mood, and the selection of information processed. The relevance of these errors, however, depends on the intended use of the data. Often, the main use of happiness measures is not to compare levels in an absolute sense but rather to seek to identify the determinants of happiness. For that purpose, it is not necessary to assume that reported subjective well-being is cardinally measurable or that it is interpersonally comparable. The subjective data can be treated ordinally in econometric analyses, so that higher reported subjective well-being reflects the higher well-being of an individual. Whether happiness measures meet this condition has been widely assessed in psychological evaluation studies.[6]

It has been shown that different measures of subjective well-being correlate well with one another (Fordyce 1988). Factor analyses of self-reports and non-self-reports of well-being have revealed a single unitary construct underlying the measures suggesting their validity (Sandvik, Diener, and Seidlitz 1993). Reliability studies have found that reported subjective well-being is moderately stable and sensitive to changing life circumstances (Ehrhardt, Saris, and Veenhoven 2000; Headey and Wearing 1991). Consistency tests reveal that happy people smile more often during social interactions (Fernández-Dols and Ruiz-Belda 1995), are rated as happy by friends and family members (Lepper 1998; Sandvik, Diener, and Seidlitz 1993) and by spouses (Costa and McCrae 1988), and are less likely to commit suicide. Helliwell (2006a) finds a strong negative correlation between national suicide rates and measures of life satisfaction, with other influences controlled for.[7] However, the high values of subjective well-being for Scandinavian countries are not matched by equally low suicide rates. This can be attributed to low rates of belief in God and high rates of divorce. Suicide is sometimes considered a more valid measure of happiness, because it refers to revealed behavior (ibid.). However, suicide captures only the tail end of the distribution of mental well-being. Though this is less of a problem in studying the determinants of low human well-being,

---

6. For comprehensive discussions of measurement problems, see Andrews and Robinson 1991; Michalos 1991; Veenhoven 1993; Larsen and Fredrickson 1999; Schwarz and Strack 1999; Di Tella and MacCulloch 2006.

7. See also Koivumaa et al. 2001; Stevenson and Wolfers 2006.

it inhibits meaningful statements about average well-being and thus welfare comparisons. Further validation comes from physiological measures: changes in brain electrical activity and heart rate account for substantial variance in reported negative affect (Davidson, Marshall, Tomarken, and Henriques 2000; Pugno 2004b). Accordingly, in an early survey, Diener concluded that "[the] measures seem to contain substantial amounts of valid variance" (1984, p. 551).

Nearly all of the empirical work so far undertaken in economic happiness research has been based on representative, large-scale sampling of individuals' global evaluations of their life satisfaction. This also applies to the econometric research presented in this book. The great advantages of this measurement approach lie in its good performance relative to its cost and in its availability for a large number of countries and periods. For example, the surveys on life satisfaction contained in the present-day World Values Survey cover 80 countries, representing over 80 percent of the world's population, over four waves.

Experience Sampling Method (ESM)

This approach collects information on individuals' experiences in real time in their natural environments (Csikszentmihalyi and Hunter 2003; Scollon, Kim-Prieto, and Diener 2003). It is designed to deal with some of the shortcomings of global satisfaction surveys.

A representative selection of individuals are supplied with a beeper or a hand-held computer and are asked at random times to give quick answers to a battery of questions with regard to positive and negative affects. Respondents are also asked to state the intensity of their feelings. This electronic diary seeks to practically apply Edgeworth's (1881) idea of measuring utility with a "hedonimeter" that captures immediate experience. Happiness can then be calculated by the aggregation of these instantaneous statements of affect.

This method, which so far has not been applied on a large scale, is more costly than representative surveys of global evaluations of life satisfaction.

Day Reconstruction Method (DRM)

This method collects data describing the experience a person has on a particular day through a systematic reconstruction undertaken the following day (Kahneman et al. 2004b). It relies on "time budgets" to capture how much time individuals spend in a particular activity. It is a reasonable approximation to experience sampling.

The same type of information can be collected by asking questions about feelings associated with particular episodes (the Event Recall Method). Respondents are asked to reconstruct the previous day by filling out a structured questionnaire. The respondents first recall the activities undertaken the previous day into working memory by producing a sequence of episodes. They then describe each episode in detail by identifying when, what, where, and with whom the episode took place. The respondents then rate these episodes in terms of positive affect (happy, warm/friendly, enjoying myself) or negative affect (frustrated/annoyed, depressed/blue, hassled/pushed around, angry/hostile, worried/anxious, criticized/put down). The respondents are also asked if they feel competent, impatient for the episode to end, or tired.

The Day Reconstruction Method has been applied to a sample of women from Texas. The activity with the highest positive affect is intimate sexual contact.[8] On average, however, sex takes up only about 10 minutes per day. Considerable pleasure is also derived from socializing and relaxing, which take up more than 2 hours per day. It may be typically Texan that prayer, worship, and meditation have a high positive affect and, on average, take up about 25 minutes per day. The Texan women watch TV more than 2 hours per day and quite enjoy it. For them, the least pleasurable activities during the day are housekeeping, work, and commuting. The high negative affect produced by their long commutes (they spend, on average, 100 minutes per day commuting) has also been found in Germany.

Capturing daily life experience by the Day Reconstruction Method allows more refined measures of happiness than is the case with representative surveys confined to one question. Carefully dividing the previous day into episodes induces the respondents to reflect carefully on how they felt during each time period. They are less prone to distortions of memory, which are known to be especially severe in the recall of affect (Robinson and Clore 2002).

DRM is new and has so far been empirically used only on an experimental basis. To what extent and for which specific issues happiness researchers will use it remain to be seen.

---

8. See also Blanchflower and Oswald 2004a.

The U-Index

In the measures discussed so far, there is no guarantee that the scales used map the corresponding feelings into numbers representing cardinal values that can be compared across individuals. The question is whether the answer "very satisfied" is really worth twice the value of "not satisfied." Kahneman and Krueger (2006) propose a "U-Index" (U standing for 'unpleasant') to avoid this cardinality concern. The U-Index is defined as the fraction of time per day that an individual spends in an unpleasant state. An episode is unpleasant if the most intense feeling the individual experiences in that episode is a negative one. The U-Index relies on the observation that the dominant emotional state of most people most of the time is positive. Hence, any episode during which a negative feeling occurs is a significant occurrence. It is thus assumed that a dominant negative emotion colors an entire episode. Obviously, this is a rather special assumption, focusing on a particular, unpleasant state of mind, while positive experiences are disregarded. This emphasis on the negative contrasts strongly with that part of happiness research associated with "positive psychology" (Diener and Seligman 2002), a movement that focuses on the pleasant part of the distribution of well-being (on the ground that psychology concentrated too much in the past on negative states, such as depression).

Brain Imaging

A quite different measuring approach to approximate utility in a quantitative way consists in scanning individuals' brain activities. It relies on functional magnetic resonance imaging (fMRI), which tracks blood flow in the brain using changes in magnetic properties due to blood oxygenation (Camerer, Loewenstein, and Prelec 2005; Zak 2004; Fehr, Fischbacher, and Kosfeld 2005). Happy individuals reveal a characteristic pattern of electro-cortical activity. They exhibit greater activity in the left prefrontal cortex than in the right (Davidson 2003; Pugno 2004b; Urry et al. 2004). This asymmetry in the prefrontal cortex between happier and less happy people correlates with self-reported measures of well-being, with behavioral activation (rather than inhibition), and even with antibody response to influenza vaccine (Kahneman 2004; Urry et al. 2004).

2.3 Evaluation

In addition to the five approaches discussed, there are several other measures. The Social Production Function approach, which distinguishes the universal goals of affection, behavioral confirmation, status, comfort, and stimulation as the relevant dimensions of subjective well-being, has been measured by structural equation modeling (Nieboer, Lindenberg, Boomsma, and Van Bruggen 2005). There are other measurement approaches under way. There is definitely no single ideal measure, but the various approaches must rather be judged on the grounds of what they seek to elucidate and for what purpose they are to be used.

Self-reported statements on life satisfaction, currently used by most economists engaged in happiness research, are far from an ideal measure of utility. In particular, cross-country comparisons have to be taken with a grain of salt. The reports of life satisfaction across seemingly similar countries sometimes differ markedly. For example, in the Euro-Barometer survey, 64 percent of the Danes studied said that they were "very satisfied with their life," but only 16 percent of the French. These national differences appear implausibly large to some scholars (Kahneman et al. 2004a; Kahneman and Riis 2005), but this has been disputed (Helliwell 2006b). Country-specific levels can sometimes be accounted for in happiness equations if repeated cross-sections for the same set of countries are studied. It is then possible to estimate country-specific constant terms while studying the correlation between aggregate variables and subjective well-being.

Another potential flaw of measuring subjective well-being is the possibility that what people mean by 'happiness' might shift over time. Measures of well-being (e.g., clinical depression, poor appetite, lack of sleep) that are less subjective than survey answers yield results similar to those obtained with happiness measures (Luttmer 2005).

For many tasks, self-reported measures of life satisfaction have proved to perform satisfactorily, especially for those issues economists are most interested in. They are, so far, the best available empirical approximation to the concept of individual welfare used in economic theory.

Subjective well-being can be modeled by a microeconometric *happiness function* ($W_{it} = \alpha + \beta X_{it} + \varepsilon_{it}$). This function has to be estimated by ordered probit or logit, because the dependent variable, life satisfaction, is discontinuous and restricted, owing to the use of different scales (1–10 in the World Values Survey, 1–4 in the Euro-Barometer, 1–3 in the

US General Social Survey). However, experience shows that, in many cases, ordinary least-squares regressions are a close approximation, and may be preferred because the estimated coefficients are easier to interpret (Ferrer-i-Carbonell and Frijters 2004).

True well-being serves as the latent variable. $X = x_1, x_2, \ldots, x_n$ are known variables, for instance socio-demographic and socio-economic characteristics, as well as institutional constraints on individual i at time t. The model allows us to analyze separately each factor that is correlated with reported subjective well-being. This approach has been successfully applied in numerous studies on the correlates of happiness. The findings of happiness regressions have now been replicated empirically in hundreds of studies. Advanced methods have been used recently to address non-random measurement errors.

Measurement errors, as well as unobserved characteristics, are captured in the error term ε. They are the source of potential biases. However, many mistakes in people's answers are random and thus do not bias the estimation results. This often holds true for the order of questions, for the wording of questions, and for actual mood.

Non-sampling errors are, however, not always uncorrelated with the variables of interest. A measurement-error perspective (Bertrand and Mullainathan 2001; Ravallion and Lokshin 2001) suggests that the inferences can be clouded by unobserved personality traits that influence individuals' socio-demographic and socio-economic characteristics and by how they respond to subjective well-being questions. For instance, people who do voluntary work report higher life satisfaction (Argyle 1999; Meier and Stutzer 2008; chapter 7 below). But volunteering does not necessarily make people happier. If extroverted people volunteer more often, and it is taken into consideration that extroverts tend to report higher satisfaction scores (DeNeve and Cooper 1998), then the observed correlation is biased. In addition to an unbiased estimation of partial correlations, the question of causality arises. Volunteering makes people happier. However, there is evidence that happier people are more willing to contribute to other people's well-being (Myers 1993). Therefore, the observed partial correlation could also mean that happier people do more voluntary work. The direction of causality cannot easily be identified even in a panel data analysis. Additional information from qualitative studies, or in the form of instrumental variables, is necessary. However, idiosyncratic effects that are time-invariant can be controlled for if the same individuals are re-surveyed over time. In a longitudinal or panel analysis, it is possible to consider a specific or "set point" well-being for each individual (Clark et al. 2006; Easterlin 2005). People tend to revert to their specific baseline level of happiness after a positive or a negative experience. In particular, they are, to some extent, able to cope with adverse experiences, such as harmful accidents, divorce, or the death of a loved one (Stroebe and Stroebe 1987; Pearlin and Schooler 1978).

A further reason for biases in microeconometric happiness functions may sometimes be relevant: the correlation of measurement errors with individual characteristics. For example, young people often report lower life satisfaction scores than old people. On the one hand, this could mean that young people in fact experience lower well-being. On the other hand, it is possible that age has an influence on how people react and respond to questions about their subjective well-being. An observed statistical relationship could then reflect only a spurious correlation. This kind of bias can hardly be overcome by econometric techniques. However, carefully developed psychological tests and a new generation of data help to mitigate these distortions.

In addition to the statistical preconditions required to study the determinants of happiness discussed so far, further conditions have to be met if welfare comparisons are to be undertaken on the basis of reported subjective well-being. These conditions are cardinality and interpersonal comparability of the individual statements of well-being. Economists are likely to be skeptical about both claims. But it should be noted that this skepticism coexists with well-established propositions in the literature on income inequality and poverty, taxation, and risk that accept implicit cardinal utility measurement and interpersonal comparability.

Evidence has been accumulated that both cardinality and interpersonal comparability may be less problematic on a practical level than on a theoretical level (Kahneman 1999). A method developed by Ng (1996) yields happiness measures that are comparable interpersonally, intertemporally, and internationally, using the concept of just perceivable increments. Ordinal and cardinal treatments of satisfaction scores generate quantitatively quite similar results in microeconometric happiness functions (Frey and Stutzer 2000). This is consistent with validation results of the income evaluation approach, which focuses on the translation of verbal evaluations into numerical figures in a context-free setting (van Praag 1991). It is shown that the meaning of a sequence of verbal labels is about the same for all the people in the sample, and that the verbal scale can be efficiently applied, as the underlying intervals are of about equal length.

The present state of research suggests that, for many purposes, measures of reported subjective well-being are of sufficient quality to allow us to study economic and institutional effects on happiness, and that they are a satisfactory empirical approximation to individual welfare for testing economic theories.

3   How Income Affects Happiness

In this chapter, three aspects of the relationship between income and happiness are discussed[1]:

Are persons with high income at a given point in time happier than those with low income (section 3.1)?

Does an increase in income over time increase happiness (section 3.2)?

Are persons in rich countries happier than those in poor countries (section 3.3)?

3.1   Happiness and Differences in Income between Persons

Higher Income Means Higher Happiness

Persons with higher income have more opportunities to achieve whatever they desire: in particular, they can buy more material goods and services. Moreover, they have a higher status in society. The idea of a relationship between income and happiness at a particular time and in a particular country has been the subject of a large empirical literature. As a robust and general result, it has been found that richer people, on average, report higher subjective well-being.[2] The relationship between income and happiness, both in simple regressions and when a large number of other factors are controlled for in multiple regressions, proves to be statistically (and normally highly) significant. In this sense, income does "buy happiness."

---

1. For surveys, see Easterlin 2001; Diener and Biswas-Diener 2002.
2. On the US, see Blanchflower and Oswald 2004b; Easterlin 1995, 2001; Di Tella and MacCulloch 2006. On the member countries of the EU, see Di Tella, MacCulloch, and Oswald 2001. On Switzerland, see Frey and Stutzer 2000.

Table 3.1, which is based on data from the general social survey, shows the relationship between equivalent income and mean happiness ratings in the United States in a pooled sample for the years 1994–1996. Equivalent income corrects for the size of the household by dividing household income by the square root of the number of household members. This table indicates that the mean happiness rating (the higher it is, the happier people are) rises with income. For the lowest decile of income, the mean happiness score is 1.94, for the fifth decile the score is 2.19; for the tenth and highest decile, it is 2.36. In the United States, people with higher income are happier.

Data for Europe from the Euro-Barometer Survey Series (1975–1991) show a similar relationship. For example, 88 percent of those persons located in the upper quartile of the income bracket rate themselves to be "fairly satisfied" or "very satisfied," whereas only 66 percent of those in the lowest income quartile do likewise (Di Tella, MacCulloch, and Oswald 2003). An analysis of the effect on happiness of the rapidly increasing real income in East Germany after reunification (Frijters, Haisken-DeNew, and Shields 2004) supports this result. Around 35–40 percent of the increase in life satisfaction experienced by the East Germans is attributable to the large increase in real household incomes. (Other important factors are increased personal freedom and improved public services.)

Table 3.1
Equivalence income and happiness in the United States, 1994–1996. Source: Frey and Stutzer 2002b; based on data from General Social Survey by National Opinion Research Center (variables 34, 157, and 1,028; "don't know" and "no" responses omitted).

	Mean happiness rating[a]	Mean equivalence income[b] (1996 US$)
Full sample	2.17	20,767
Income decile 1	1.94	2,586
Income decile 2	2.03	5,867
Income decile 3	2.07	8,634
Income decile 4	2.15	11,533
Income decile 5	2.19	14,763
Income decile 6	2.29	17,666
Income decile 7	2.20	21,128
Income decile 8	2.20	25,745
Income decile 9	2.30	34,688
Income decile 10	2.36	61,836

a. Based on scores of "not too happy" = 1, "pretty happy" = 2, and "very happy" = 3.
b. Total household income divided by square root of total number of household members.

However, additional income does not increase happiness ad infinitum. The relationship between income and happiness is not linear; there is diminishing marginal utility with absolute income. This finding corresponds to the utility function of income, as proposed in standard textbooks on economics. The data in table 3.1 also indicate that the same proportional increase in income yields a lower increase in happiness at higher income levels. Doubling income increases reported happiness, on average, by 0.05 score point for the bottom five deciles, but only by 0.03 score point for the top five deciles. Evidence for diminishing marginal utility is also provided by three successive waves of the World Values Survey, covering the periods 1980–1982, 1990–1991, and 1995–1997, and including between 18 and 30 countries (a total of 87,806 observations). It has been estimated that, for a person moving from the fourth to the fifth decile in the distribution of family income, subjective well-being increases by 0.11 (on a ten-point scale, with 1.0 indicating the lowest level of satisfaction and 10.0 the highest). In contrast, moving from the ninth to the tenth decile increases subjective well-being by only 0.02 (Helliwell 2003).

Most of the research on the relationship between individual income and happiness has been undertaken for advanced industrial countries. The results essentially carry over to both developing countries and to countries in transition (Graham and Pettinato 2002a,b; Hayo and Seifert 2003). The positive relationship between individual income and happiness within a society at a certain time is a robust phenomenon.

Differences in income, however, only account for a low proportion of the differences in happiness among persons. In the United States, for example, the simple correlation is 0.20 (Easterlin 2001, p. 468). Sometimes these findings are misleadingly interpreted as showing that income is not relevant to individual happiness. The relevance of income should be assessed with regard to the size of the coefficient in a multivariate analysis. A low correlation coefficient might indicate that other factors are also important in explaining why some people are happier than others. In particular, other economic factors (particularly unemployment) and non-economic factors (particularly health, but also personality) exert strong influences. One personality factor that might be relevant is that those individuals who prize material goods more highly than other values in life tend to be substantially less happy (Sirgy 1997). Similarly, people with intrinsic goals (i.e., those who define their values themselves) tend to be happier than those with extrinsic goals (i.e., those oriented toward some external reward, such as financial success or social approval) (Kasser and Ryan 2001; Kasser 2002).

Correlations do not establish causation. Higher income may make people happier, but happier people may also earn higher income (because they like to work harder and are more enterprising). The direction of causality can be tested by looking at a change in income not earned by the persons involved. In Britain, lottery winners and people receiving an inheritance report higher mental well-being in the following year. An unexpected gift of £50,000 is estimated to increase subjective well-being by between 0.1 and 0.3 standard deviation (Gardner and Oswald 2001).[3] This suggests that higher income indeed causes people to be happier.

There are many processes that may explain why higher income does not have more of an effect on happiness. The most important of these are that individuals adapt to their new standard of living and that they compare themselves to other individuals. It is not the absolute level of income that matters most, but rather one's position relative to the past and other individuals. This idea of relative income is part of the more general theory of aspiration levels.

Happiness Is Relative: The Role of Income Aspirations

Human beings are unable and unwilling to make absolute judgments. Rather, they constantly draw comparisons from their environment, from the past, or from their expectations of the future.[4] Thus, people notice and react to deviations from aspiration levels.[5]

Most economists would not deny that utility is inherently relative. Nevertheless, most economic models of human behavior assume invariant utility functions. Among the few exceptions, theories of preference change[6] have concentrated on habit formation (Marshall 1890; Modigliani 1949; Pollack 1970; Carroll, Overland, and Weil 2000). Concepts of interdependent preferences caused by comparisons with relevant others (Layard 2005; Frank 1985b; Pollak 1976; Clark and

---

3. See also Smith and Razzell 1975; Brickman, Coates, and Janoff-Bulman 1978.

4. Adaptation is a general phenomenon and goes beyond adaptation to changes in income. Clark et al. (2006), who use data from the German Socio-Economic Panel, spanning the period 1984–2003, find that there is complete adaptation to divorce, widowhood, and birth of the first child. Individuals return to their "set level" of well-being. In contrast, adaptation to marriage is found to be incomplete, and men (unlike women) do not adapt to unemployment.

5. For evidence from laboratory experiments, see Mellers 2000; Smith et al. 1989; Tversky and Griffin 1991.

6. For a survey, see Bowles 1998.

Oswald 1998; Sobel 2005) have remained rare. There is another class of interdependent utility models that focuses on fairness rather than on positional concerns (Becker 1974b; Fehr and Gächter 2000).

Income aspiration captures concerns for relative income, as well as adaptation to a previous income level. Higher income aspirations reduce the well-being people experience from a given income or consumption level (Stutzer 2004). The effect of income aspirations on people's subjective well-being is evident in empirically tested panel data for Germany, recounted below.[7]

Sources of People's Relative Evaluations of Utility

There are two main processes shaping individuals' aspirations and producing the relativity in people's utility evaluation.

Social comparisons   People are concerned about their position on the income ladder. It is not the absolute level of income that matters most, but rather one's position relative to other individuals. This idea of *relative income* is one part of the more general aspiration-level theory. Positional concerns are not a new aspect of human nature, but they are probably more pronounced today because of more extended possibilities for social comparison. In the past, many economists noted that individuals compared themselves to significant others with respect to income, consumption, status, or utility. Veblen (1899) coined the term "conspicuous consumption." The "relative income hypothesis" was formulated and econometrically tested by Duesenberry (1949), who posited an asymmetric structure of externalities. People look upward, not downward, when making comparisons. Aspirations thus tend to be higher than the level already reached. Wealthier people impose a negative external effect on poorer people, but not vice versa. As a result, rates of saving depend on the percentile position in the income distribution, and not solely on the income level, as in a traditional savings function. However, reference groups are not only partly exogenously given, but also to some extent actively chosen (Falk and Knell 2004). Even families in people's favorite soap operas may become the relevant others (Schor 1998). In a study of 5,000 British workers, the reference group consists of persons with the same labor-market characteristics (Clark and Oswald 1996). It has been shown that the higher the income of the reference group, the less satisfied people are with their jobs. Social comparisons

---

7. For a fuller account, see Stutzer and Frey 2004.

may also take place within the family (Neumark and Postlewaite 1998). Women decide to take up paid work, depending on whether their sisters and sisters-in-law are employed, and how much they earn. Individuals with a similar education level and age also form exogenous reference groups. (For Germany, see Ferrer-i-Carbonell 2005.) There is a negative effect of this group's comparison income on reported satisfaction with life. In a recent analysis with panel data for the United States, local average earnings in a region are associated with lower levels of subjective well-being, holding individual earnings constant (Luttmer 2005).

Getting used to new income or consumption levels   Additional material goods and services initially provide extra pleasure, but it is usually only transitory. Higher utility from material goods wears off. Satisfaction depends on change and disappears with continued consumption. The process or mechanism that reduces the hedonic effects of a constant or repeated stimulus is called *adaptation*.

Processes of hedonic adaptation supplement the socially comparative, or even competitive, processes in consumption. Together, they make people strive for ever higher aspirations. The concept of aspiration levels has a long history in psychology and sociology (Irwin 1944; Lewin et al. 1944; Stouffer et al. 1949), and adaptation-level theory is well grounded in psychology (Parducci 1995; Frederick and Loewenstein 1999). According to aspiration-level theory, individual well-being is determined by the gap between aspiration and achievement (Andrews and Withey 1976; Campbell et al. 1976; Michalos 1985). The extent and the mode of adaptation are likely to differ between persons and conditions (Frederick and Loewenstein 1999; Riis, Loewenstein, Baron, and Jepson 2005). The extent of adaptation is claimed to be more complete for income than for other life events, such as marriage or disability (Easterlin 2004) or leisure (Frank 1997).

Testing the Effect of Income Aspirations on Individual Utility
In order to study the role of income aspirations in individual well-being directly, an empirical measure for people's income aspirations is needed. Here, we take income evaluations as a proxy for aspirations. Income-evaluation questions have been developed within the individual welfare-function approach (van Praag 1971; van Praag and Frijters 1999). A cardinal relationship between income and expected welfare is established by asking individuals to add income ranges to a number of qualitatively characterized income levels. Individuals are asked

to respond to the following question: "Please try to indicate what you consider to be an appropriate amount for each of the following cases. In my/our situation, I would call a net household income per [month] of: about _____ very bad...about _____ very good." (van Praag 1993) When answering this "income-evaluation question," they should take their own situation with respect to family and job into account. People's answers provide information about income that is sufficient to meet their aspiration level (i.e., the income that is required to reach mean expected welfare).

Individual welfare functions have been estimated for several countries with good results, particularly for the Netherlands and Belgium (van Herwaarden, Kapteyn, and van Praag 1977). A particularly interesting aspect is the connection established between the parameter of what people consider "sufficient" income and their actual income, which measures the "preference drift" due to a change in income. A positive correlation suggests that the *ex post* evaluation of a higher income is smaller than its *ex ante* evaluation. Thus, what rich people consider "sufficient" income is higher than what poor people consider "sufficient" income.

In our test, we combine information about individuals' aspirations with data on subjective well-being for Germany, using data from the German Socio-Economic Panel Study (GSOEP). The two waves of 1992 and 1997 contain information about individuals' aspiration levels. They are captured by the question "Whether you feel an income is good or not so good depends on your personal life circumstances and expectations. In your case—the net household income of _____ Euros is just sufficient income." For the proxy of people's aspiration levels, on average, an amount of 1,950 Euros per month (at prices and purchasing power parities for 1999) is reported. Average household income in the sample is 2,450 Euros per month (at prices and purchasing power parities for 1999).

Reported subjective well-being is based on the question "How satisfied are you with your life, all things considered?" Responses range from 0 ("completely dissatisfied") to 10 ("completely satisfied").

A standard microeconometric happiness function is estimated. In order to make the interpretation of the results easier, least-squares estimations are presented. Individuals' reported satisfaction is regressed on income, on a number of socio-demographic and socio-economic characteristics, and on size of household. The first regression in table 3.2. shows that household income is positively correlated with reported satisfaction with life, *ceteris paribus*. The coefficient implies that doubling household income increases life satisfaction by 0.315 point on

Table 3.2
Effect of income aspirations on satisfaction with life, Germany, 1992 and 1997. Dependent variable: satisfaction with life [0–10]. Significance levels: (*) 0.1 > p > 0.05, * 0.05 > p > 0.01; ** p < 0.01. Data source: GSOEP.

	Pooled estimation		Pooled estimation		Individual fixed-effects estimation	
	Coefficient	t value	Coefficient	t value	Coefficient	t value
Household income, ln	0.454**	15.39	0.534**	16.54	0.327**	5.81
Income aspirations, ln			−0.259**	−6.06	−0.323**	−4.99
No. of household members$^{1/2}$	−0.363**	−5.83	−0.303*	−4.81	−0.321*	−2.50
Male	Reference group		Reference group		Reference group	
Female	0.055(*)	2.08	0.059(*)	2.23		
Age	−0.049**	−7.57	−0.046**	−7.06		
Age^2	0.48e−3**	6.93	0.45e−3**	6.45	0.09e−3	0.53
Years of education, ln	0.155(*)	2.22	0.213**	3.03	−1.963(*)	−2.26
No children	Reference group		Reference group		Reference group	
Children	0.072	1.73	0.062	1.49	0.047	0.70
Single, no partner	Reference group		Reference group		Reference group	
Single, with partner	0.137	1.82	0.165(*)	2.18	0.499**	3.07
Married	0.196**	3.06	0.227**	3.53	0.753**	4.25
Separated, with partner	−0.296	−1.25	−0.279	−1.18	0.458	1.17
Separated, no partner	−0.640**	−5.08	−0.620**	−4.93	0.041	0.18
Divorced, with partner	0.107	1.05	0.145	1.41	0.604**	2.74
Divorced, no partner	−0.337**	−4.05	−0.331**	−3.99	0.340	1.66

	Coefficient	t	Coefficient	t	Coefficient	t
Widowed, with partner	0.068	0.43	0.100	0.64	1.505**	3.72
Widowed, no partner	-0.065	-0.80	-0.051	-0.63	0.511*	2.37
Spouse abroad	-0.277	-1.12	-0.243	-0.99	0.616	1.27
Employed	Reference group		Reference group		Reference group	
Self-employed	-0.230**	-3.44	-0.242**	-3.62	-0.164	-1.36
Some work	-0.019	-0.23	-0.039	-0.49	-0.210	-1.83
Non-working	-0.135**	-3.30	-0.151**	-3.68	-0.188**	-2.67
Unemployed	-0.857*	-16.89	-0.871**	-17.16	-0.734**	-10.23
Maternity leave	0.165	1.79	0.152	1.65	0.023	0.17
Military service	0.684	1.34	0.658	1.29	-0.196	-0.24
In education	0.086	0.68	0.056	0.44	-0.309	-1.63
Retired	-0.052	-0.72	-0.069	-0.95	-0.139	-1.24
Western Germany	Reference group		Reference group		Reference group	
Eastern Germany	-0.837**	-29.29	-0.819**	-28.51	-1.009**	-4.53
Nationals	Reference group		Reference group			
EU foreigners	0.056	1.02	0.059	1.07		
Non-EU foreigners	-0.238*	-5.02	-0.237**	-5.01		
Year dummy 1997	-0.134**	-5.46	-0.141**	-5.74	-0.299**	-3.55
Constant	7.101**	103.98	8.071**	46.40	7.857**	25.02
Number of observations	19130		19130		19130	
Adjusted R^2	0.102		0.103			
Overall R^2					0.040	

the ten-point scale. The results for household size incorporate the fact that household income has to be shared among household members. However, household size also captures the fact that people live with others in what are probably close and supportive relationships. The result indicates that the two effects of household size on satisfaction with life have a negative net effect.

The first regression with German data in table 3.2 reveals the following additional results:

· Women are slightly more satisfied with life than men.

· The partial correlation between age and life satisfaction is U-shaped, with a minimum around age 50.

· People with more years of education report higher satisfaction scores than those with fewer years of education.

· People with a partner report, on average, higher satisfaction scores than those without a partner.

· Lower satisfaction scores are reported by self-employed people, non-working people, unemployed people, people living in Eastern Germany, and non-EU foreigners (compared to employees, people living in Western Germany, and German nationals).

In the two remaining regressions in table 3.2, the happiness function is extended to include the proxy measure for individuals' aspiration levels. It is thus tested whether, as proposed above, individuals' judgment of well-being is relative to their income aspirations. The results show, as theoretically expected, a negative effect on subjective well-being of the measure of individuals' income aspirations. This means that, when income level is taken into account, people experience lower well-being when they have higher income aspirations. A doubling of the aspiration level—measured by the income that is evaluated as "just sufficient"—reduces reported life satisfaction, on average, by 0.180 point. This result supports the basic underlying hypothesis that people's subjective well-being is negatively affected by their income aspiration, with the effects of income and other individual characteristics controlled for.

For the demographic control variables, the coefficients are similar in size to the first estimate. In contrast, the effect of household income on life satisfaction is larger (0.534) than in the first estimate. This indicates that, for a given aspiration level, higher income has a greater effect on well-being. The change in the size of the coefficient for household income provides indirect evidence that people adjust their aspiration levels according to their income level.

Another interpretation of the results in the second estimation suggests that the inference is clouded by unobserved personality traits that influence individuals' aspirations. The same holds for their response to questions of subjective well-being. For instance, competitive people who have high aims in life may report higher aspirations. They may also report lower satisfaction with life, because they want to leave room for improvement. As a result, the observed correlation would be biased. However, idiosyncratic effects that are time-invariant can be controlled for if the same individuals are re-surveyed over time. This is the case for our longitudinal data set, in which it is possible to consider a specific base-line well-being for each individual. The statistical relationship between income aspirations and reported subjective well-being is then identified by the change in aspirations between 1992 and 1997 for the same person.

The last two columns of table 3.2 report the result for an estimation with individual fixed effects that excludes spurious correlation due to time-invariant unobserved human characteristics. Partial correlations confirm the sizable negative effect of income aspirations on life satisfaction. A doubling of the aspiration level reduces reported life satisfaction, on average by 0.224 point. Thus, the results of the pooled estimation are supported. Again, the variables used as controls referring to gender, family structure, age, education, employment, location, and nationality reveal similar qualitative influences on happiness.

The evidence presented indicates that people's well-being is better understood when their income aspirations are taken into consideration. Income aspirations are one aspect of a concept of utility that makes it psychologically sounder. With this extension, various empirical observations can be explained (Easterlin 2004). For example, if average aspirations in society increase at the same rate as per-capita income, it can be better understood why people in industrialized societies did not become happier over the last decades, despite substantial growth in their economic wealth; this aspect will be more extensively discussed in section 3.2.

Another observation that can now be better understood is the low correlation between income and reported subjective well-being. If people evaluate their economic well-being relative to their aspirations, rather than in an absolute way, a fraction of people in an objectively bad economic situation may still be highly satisfied, and another fraction of people living under objectively good economic conditions may still report being highly dissatisfied.

Empirical Analysis of the Determinants of Aspiration Levels
The following two processes, which concern the formation of individual aspirations, have been studied empirically.

Social comparisons   Based on the same proxy measure for income aspirations as applied here, the effect of social comparisons has been studied across Swiss communities (Stutzer 2004). It is found that individuals' aspirations are systematically affected by the average incomes in the community in which people live. The richer one's fellow residents are, the higher the level of individual aspiration. This effect cannot be explained by a higher cost of living alone. It is shown that the aspiration levels of community members who interact within the community react far more to changes in average income than those of members who do not interact.

Adaptation   The relation between individual income and income aspirations was put to a quantitative test in the individual welfare functions of the Leyden group (van Herwaarden et al. 1977; van Praag and van der Sar 1988). As a robust result, it was found that aspirations increase with people's income level. The results indicate that a higher income is not fully translated into higher income aspirations. The "preference shift" through higher individual income is found to "destroy" 60–80 percent of the expected welfare effect of an increase in income. If interdependent preferences are taken into consideration in addition to habit formation, it cannot be rejected that the preference drift outbalances up to 100 percent of the welfare effect of income gains (van de Stadt, Kapteyn, and van de Geer 1985).

3.2   Income and Happiness over Time

The Easterlin or Happiness Paradox

Several scholars[8] have identified a striking and curious relationship: in the United States, the United Kingdom, Belgium, and Japan, per-capita income has risen sharply in recent decades, whereas average happiness has stayed "virtually constant" or has even declined. Graphically, the development of income and happiness diverges like open scissors.

---

8. Among them are Di Tella and MacCulloch (2006), Blanchflower and Oswald (2004b), Diener and Oishi (2000), Myers (2000), Kenny (1999), Lane (1998), and Easterlin (1974, 1995).

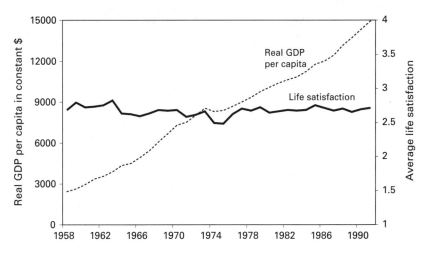

Figure 3.1
Satisfaction with life and per-capita income in Japan, 1958–1991. Source: Frey and Stutzer 2002b. Based on data from Penn World Tables and World Database of Happiness.

Consider Japan (figure 3.1). Between 1958 and 1991, per-capita income in Japan rose by a factor of 6. This is probably the most spectacular growth in income since World War II anywhere. The rise was reflected by the presence of an indoor toilet, a washing machine, a telephone, and a color television in almost all households, as well as a car (Easterlin 2000). Figure 3.1 also shows, however, that this tremendous rise in material well-being was *not* accompanied by an increase in average satisfaction with life. In 1958, average life satisfaction rated on a four-point scale was 2.7. In 1991, after more than 30 years of increasing affluence, average life satisfaction still scored 2.7 points.

Data from the general social survey reveal the same relationship in the United States. In the periods 1972–1974 and 1994–1996, overall mean equivalent real income in the sample has increased from US$17,434 to US$20,767 (19 percent). But the overall mean happiness rating has even decreased slightly, from 2.21 to 2.17. Income in all deciles (except the third) has increased, although mean happiness ratings have fallen or stayed constant in eight of the ten deciles.

Explanations

What can be inferred from the aforementioned cases? One possible position is to disregard the descriptive evidence on the following grounds:

• Denmark, Germany, and Italy experienced substantial growth in real per-capita income as well as a (small) increase in reported satisfaction with life in the 1970s and the 1980s (Diener and Oishi 2000).

• Whether a small increase or a small decrease in reported subjective well-being is measured depends on the observation period. Moreover, the relationships presented between income and happiness over time are not analyzed *ceteris paribus*. However, for the United States, a negative time trend is also found when individual characteristics are controlled for (Blanchflower and Oswald 2004b).

These arguments are, however, not very convincing. Rather, the observation that income and happiness do not necessarily increase *pari passu* can be taken as an indication that there is more to subjective well-being than income level alone. One of the most important processes people go through is that of adjusting to experiences. Human beings are unable and unwilling to make absolute judgments. Instead, they are constantly drawing comparisons from the past or from their expectations of the future. This explanation resorts again to aspiration-level theory. Additional material goods and services initially provide extra pleasure, but it is usually only transitory. Greater happiness wears off when it is generated by material things. Satisfaction depends on change and disappears with continued consumption. This process of hedonic adaptation induces people to aspire ever more.

Consequences

Three important lessons can be drawn from the aforementioned considerations:

• The upward adjustment of aspirations motivates human beings to accomplish more and more. They are never satisfied. Once they have achieved something, they want to achieve even more. The theory of "rising aspirations" holds not only for material goods and services but also for many immaterial achievements. A promotion, for example, leads to temporary happiness, but at the same time raises the expectation of, and the aspiration for, further promotions.

• Wants are insatiable. The more one acquires, the more one wants. The marginal utility of income is therefore no longer defined in this framework, because the utility function changes with income.

• Most people think that they felt less happy in the past and expect to be happier in the future (Easterlin 2001). This asymmetry can be explained by changing aspirations. When people look back, they judge their (or others') living standards based on current aspirations, and post-consumption bundles look relatively unattractive. However, as people predict their well-being in the future when experiencing a higher material living standard, they also mistakenly apply current aspirations for the evaluation and expect to be happier, not realizing that their aspirations will adjust over time.

3.3   Differences in Income and Happiness between Countries

Various studies provide evidence that, on average, people living in rich countries are happier than those living in poor countries (Diener, Diener, and Diener 1995; Inglehart 1990; Graham 2005). The differences in income between the countries are measured by using exchange rates at purchasing power parities to control for the international differences in the cost of living. Data on happiness are usually from the World Values Survey, the best source now available for international comparisons of life satisfaction (Inglehart et al. 2000).

Figure 3.2 illustrates the relationship between per-capita income and average life satisfaction in 63 countries, using data from the fourth

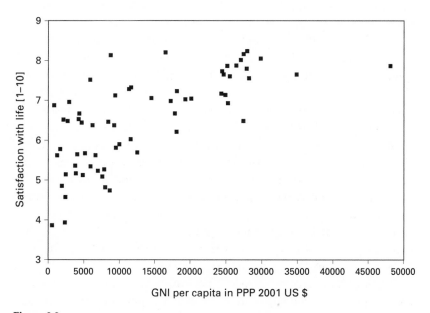

Figure 3.2
Life satisfaction and income levels across the world at the beginning of the twenty-first century. (GNI: gross national income. PPP: purchasing-power parity.) Sources: World Values Survey 1999–2004; World Development Report 2003.

wave of the World Values Survey in the early 2000s. The figure shows that reported subjective well-being tends to rise with income. Some of the authors identify a concave relationship: income provides happiness at low levels of development, but once a threshold of approximately $10,000 is reached the average income level in a country has little effect on average subjective well-being.

A visual inspection of the relationship between income and happiness across countries is, however, of limited value. The positive correlation may be produced by factors other than income alone. In particular, countries with higher per-capita incomes tend to have more stable democracies than poor countries. It may well be, then, that the apparent positive association between income and happiness is in reality due to more developed democratic conditions. Other conditions may also be correlated with income and may produce the observed positive correlation between income and happiness. And the higher the income, the better the average health of the population and the more secure its basic human rights. Thus, both health and basic human rights may possibly increase happiness along with income.

Moreover, the positive correlation may come as a surprise in the light of evidence presented for happiness over time, where no robust relationship between per-capita income and happiness is found. Two possible strategies further address the role of absolute income in happiness in and between countries. First, cross-sectional data for several periods can be combined to allow a control of time-invariant country-specific characteristics. These characteristics may include stable cultural differences, systematic distortions due to language differences, and so on. Such an approach is followed in the study by Helliwell (2003), which combines data for 49 countries from the first three waves of the World Values Survey. Instead of country-specific effects, separate base levels for six groups of countries are taken into consideration in the estimation equation: industrial countries, Scandinavian countries, countries formerly in the Soviet Union, other countries of Eastern Europe, Latin American countries, and other developing countries. It is found that national per-capita income (measured in percentage of the value for 1997 in the United States) has a very small effect on reported subjective well-being. A 10 percent increase in per-capita income in a country with half the per-capita income of the United States (and unchanged income distribution) increases average satisfaction with life by only 0.0003 point on a scale from 1 to 10, and the gain disappears even before the 1997 level of US real per-capita income is achieved (Helliwell 2003).

This evidence is more in line with the findings for income and happiness over time than with previous results from cross-section studies that neglected country- or region-specific determinants of reported subjective well-being. However, it may be argued that poor countries are not adequately represented in the data pool. Since the relationship between income and happiness seems relevant, especially from the perspective of national development, a second strategy could directly address subjective well-being in developing countries. However, few extended time series about reported subjective well-being in developing countries currently exist. Promising projects are a socio-economic panel in Russia (Ravallion and Lokshin 2001) and repeated surveys in 17 Latin American countries (Graham and Pettinato 2002a,b). The results suggest that the effects of individual income on life satisfaction are remarkably similar (and the same holds for age, education, marriage, health and unemployment; see Graham 2005) to those found in European countries. Evidence from Peru and Russia indicates that economic development is accompanied by extensive social mobility. For some people with fast-increasing aspiration levels, such mobility may depress overall gains in well-being from increased economic wealth. Although perceived past mobility and prospects of upward mobility have a positive effect on reported subjective well-being, a fraction of "frustrated achievers" report negative perceived mobility and low satisfaction with life, despite objective mobility (Graham and Pettinato 2002a,b).

Another aspect to consider is whether, when income and happiness between countries are compared, causality runs from income to well-being, as has been implicitly assumed so far. An inverse causation can well be imagined (Kenny 1999). It might, for instance, be argued that the more satisfied the population is with its life, the more it is inclined to work hard, and therefore the higher its per-capita income becomes. In other words, happy people may be more creative and enterprising, and being more creative and enterprising leads to higher income. This line of argument has not been well understood so far, but it should be considered seriously in the future.

The available evidence suggests that income and happiness are correlated across nations, but that the effects are small and diminishing. This indicates that other factors may be more important in explaining differences in reported subjective well-being between countries; on the other hand, it suggests that the notion that people in poor countries are happier because they live under more "natural" and less stressful conditions is a myth.

4   How Unemployment Affects Happiness

Full employment is an indisputable goal of economic policy, because employment is associated with prosperity. Unemployment causes costs, because valuable manpower is wasted and an economy's real output falls short of its potential output. Based on this view, some attempts have been undertaken to provide quantitative estimates of the welfare cost of unemployment. For example, Okun (1970) calculated that a 1-percentage-point reduction in the rate of unemployment is associated in the short run with an increase of roughly 3 percent in the ratio of actual output to potential. However, these attempts are very restrictive and do not take into account the opportunity cost of any business cycle and any structural policy, the alternative spending of time (i.e., the value of non-market activity), or the reasons for unemployment. Most importantly, approaches based on forgone income neglect any psychological effects of not having work. Taking data on subjective well-being into consideration, the welfare consequences of personal unemployment can be studied directly, as can the effects of general unemployment on employed and unemployed people.

4.1   Personal Unemployment

Voluntary or Involuntary Unemployment?

Viewed simply, the costs a person suffers when he becomes unemployed consist primarily in the loss of income. A countervailing effect on individual welfare is the additional amount of leisure enjoyed. Moreover, being officially unemployed opens up opportunity for work in the shadow economy for the duration of unemployment.

In a perfectly functioning labor market, there is no involuntary unemployment; there is only short-run search unemployment when employees switch jobs. The New Classical Macroeconomics entertains the view that individuals optimize their utility by comparing the loss of income due to unemployment against leisure gained and better job conditions in the future. People optimally choose to reduce or increase labor supply. They do not suffer a utility loss when becoming unemployed. Other theories, such as the New Keynesian Macroeconomics, do not share this optimistic view of a flexible labor market; they emphasize that most people suffer utility losses when they lose a job. This loss may be mitigated by unemployment benefits. Economic happiness research offers a complementary way to find out which of the two views better approximates reality.

The Findings of Happiness Research

Reports on subjective well-being help to identify the level of experienced utility of unemployed people in comparison with employed people. How particular people are affected when they become unemployed has been studied with individual data for many countries and many periods.[1] Employing Euro-Barometer data on satisfaction with life on a four-point scale for twelve European countries over the period 1975–1992, and controlling for a large number of other determinants of happiness (including income and education), Di Tella, MacCulloch, and Oswald (2003) find that the self-proclaimed happiness of unemployed people is *much* lower than that of employed people with otherwise similar characteristics. The loss of subjective well-being experienced by unemployed people amounts to 0.33 on a satisfaction scale ranging from 1 ("not at all satisfied") to 4 ("very satisfied").

Many other studies have also found, in many countries and many time periods, that personally experiencing unemployment makes people very unhappy.[2] In their ground-breaking study of Britain, Clark and Oswald (1994, p. 655) summarize their result as follows: " ... joblessness depressed well-being more than any other single characteristic, including important negative ones such as divorce and separation."

Some analyses offer additional results for *particular groups* of unemployed people. Many studies find that unemployment on average weighs more heavily on men than on women. Men do not adapt at all

---

1. See, e.g., Clark and Oswald 1994; Winkelmann and Winkelmann 1998; Clark 2003.
2. For a survey, see Darity and Goldsmith 1996. Björklund and Eriksson (1998) and Korpi (1997) provide evidence for Scandinavian countries, Blanchflower and Oswald (2004b) for the United Kingdom and the United States, Winkelmann and Winkelmann (1998) for Germany, and Ravallion and Lokshin (2001) for Russia.

well to unemployment (Clark et al. 2006). Younger and older employees suffer less when hit by unemployment than employees in the middle of their working years. For Germany, it has been found that unemployment does not reduce satisfaction with life in women over 50 (Gerlach and Stephan 1996). People with high education experience a larger decrease in their subjective well-being due to unemployment than employees with low education (Clark and Oswald 1994).

The aforementioned results all refer to the "pure" effect of being unemployed. Loss of income and other indirect effects that may accompany personal unemployment are controlled for. In this context, it is important to consider the effect of unemployment benefits (Di Tella and MacCulloch 2006). They must be expected to have a conflicting effect on individual well-being: on the one hand, larger unemployment benefits tend to lengthen unemployment spells; on the other hand, they help to reduce the material loss of being out of work. The high unemployment rate in European countries in recent decades has often been attributed to the tendency of high unemployment benefits to reduce work incentives. However, in Europe the happiness gap between employed and unemployed people did not narrow with increases in benefits during the period 1975–1992 (Di Tella, MacCulloch, and Oswald 2003). This suggests that the material support received from the government is unlikely to be responsible for the observed unemployment.

It may be argued that these findings could be interpreted quite differently. While the negative correlation between unemployment and happiness is well established, it may well be the case that the causation runs in the opposite direction implied so far. That is, it may be that unhappy people do not perform well, and therefore are more likely to be dismissed, whereas happy people are fitter for working life, which makes it less likely that they will lose their job.

The question of reverse causation due to a selection bias has been analyzed in many studies with longitudinal data gathered before and after particular workers lose their jobs because of (for example) a plant closure. There is evidence that unhappy people do indeed perform poorly on the labor market, but the main causation seems clearly to run from unemployment to unhappiness.[3] Studies in social psychology also identify effects of unemployment and re-employment on mental well-being.[4]

---

3. See, e.g., Winkelmann and Winkelmann 1998 for German panel data, or Marks and Fleming 1999 for Australian panel data, the latter considering in detail various effects on mental health.
4. For a survey, see Murphy and Athanasou 1999.

Since the lower subjective well-being of unemployed people can be explained neither by the lower income level nor by the self-selection of people who are less happy by nature, unemployment has to be related to non-pecuniary costs. The drop in happiness may, to a large extent, be attributed to psychological and social factors.[5]

Psychological Costs

Unemployment produces depression and anxiety and results in losses of self-esteem and of personal control. For those who are very involved in their work, being without a job is a particularly heavy burden. Numerous studies (e.g. Goldsmith, Veum, and Darity 1996) have established that unemployed people are in worse mental and physical health than employed people. As a result, they have a higher death rate and are more likely to commit suicide. A 1-percentage-point increase in State unemployment rates in the United States for 1972–1991 predicts an increase of suicides by 1.3 percent (Ruhm 2000). Moreover, unemployed people have a greater tendency to consume large quantities of alcohol. Their personal relationships are more strained. The psychic cost is considerably higher for those being dismissed for the first time. Individuals who have been unemployed before suffer less. To some extent, they become used to being unemployed. This finding may provide a partial explanation for persistent unemployment (Clark, Georgellis, and Sanfey 2001; Lucas, Clark, Georgellis, and Diener 2004).

Social Norms

The role of social norms in affecting unemployed people's subjective well-being has been analyzed by Stutzer and Lalive (2004). In line with the literature, a social norm is taken to be a behavioral regularity caused by a socially shared belief of desired behavior. It triggers informal social sanctions to enforce the prescribed behavior. Unemployed people feel internal pressure to comply with the norm to work and not be dependent on others. The social norm to work is seen to affect well-being in a simple way. Individuals differ in their beliefs as to whether it is right or wrong to live off public funds, such as unemployment benefits. One may distinguish two extremes: "weak-norm" communities, in which a large proportion of the inhabitants believe that it is right to live off public funds, and "strong-norm" communities, in which a large proportion of the inhabitants believe that it is wrong to live off public

---

5. For a survey, see Feather 1990.

funds. Unemployed people's efforts to find a job, and their willingness to accept a regular job, are higher in strong-norm communities than in weak-norm communities, *ceteris paribus*. Because of the social pressure imposed, unemployed people are less satisfied with their life in strong-norm communities than in weak-norm communities.

Citizens' work norms are to some extent reflected in actual political decision making when they have direct participation rights. This is the case in Switzerland, where in 1997 a referendum was held concerning the level of benefits to be paid out to unemployed people. Public discussion of the issues plays a large role in direct democratic decision making (Bohnet and Frey 1994; Frey 1994a). The share of voters in a community favoring a reduction of unemployment benefits is taken as a proxy for the strength of the social work norm. The referendum partially reflecting the influence of work norms was approved by a narrow margin of 50.8 percent. Social norms relating to work were indeed an important determinant of voting behavior, as figure 4.1 suggests. This figure compares the referendum results in the 26 Swiss cantons with survey answers on individual work values taken from Cotter et al. 1995. The horizontal axis shows the proportion of voters favoring a cut in unemployment benefits across cantons. The vertical axis shows the percentage of survey respondents in each canton who do not oppose the statement "An individual who does not live off his or her own income is useless." The correlation between the two measures of the strength of the social norm to work is 0.55. Clearly there is a strong positive correlation between these two measures of the strength of the social work norm across cantons.

Empirical results showing the effect of the social work norm on unemployed people's well-being are exhibited in table 4.1. The econometric analysis applies a weighted ordered probit model, because the dependent variable contains ranking information on subjective well-being. A positive coefficient indicates that the probability of stating higher life satisfaction increases. The marginal effect indicates the change in the percentage of persons belonging to a utility level of 9 or 10 when the independent variable increases by one standard deviation. When applied to the effect of being unemployed instead of employed, the probability of a person stating a level of subjective well-being of 9 or 10 is 34.9 percentage points lower.

The first coefficient in table 4.1 captures the effect of the social work norm in affecting life satisfaction for the employed. A small positive effect is estimated. Therefore, work seems to contribute more to satisfaction

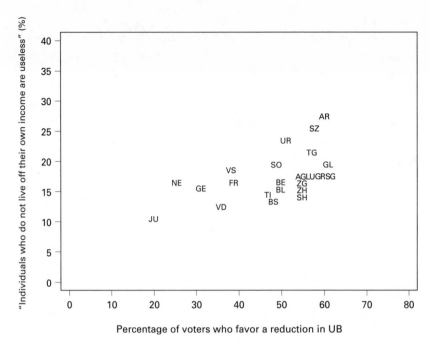

Figure 4.1
Correlation between the voting measure of the strength of the social norm and a survey measure of this norm. Horizontal axis: percentage of voters in a canton favoring a reduction in unemployment benefits (UB) in Swiss national referendum held in September 1997. Vertical axis: percentage of survey respondents in a canton not opposing the statement "Individuals who do not live off their own income are useless." This survey is documented in Cotter et al. 1995. For statistical reasons, the survey contains cantons only with more than 30 observations in the survey. Source: Stutzer and Lalive 2004. Based on Swiss Federal Statistical Office and Cotter et al. 1995. (Abbreviations stand for names of cantons.)

with life when people share a stronger social norm to work. The difference in well-being between employed and unemployed people, caused by a variation in the strength of the social work norm, is revealed by the interaction term for strength of norm and individual unemployment. The coefficient of this interaction variable is statistically significantly negative. Therefore, the higher the proportion of people in a community who are in favor of a cut in unemployment benefits, the lower the satisfaction with life of unemployed people living in the same community (compared with employed people). The reduction itself is massive. In estimating the marginal effect, an increase by one standard deviation in the proportion of voters in favor of lower benefits reduces the probability of an unemployed person's reporting a happiness score of 9 or 10

Table 4.1
Role of social-work norms in life satisfaction of employed and unemployed people, Switzerland, 1997. Dependent variable: satisfaction with life [1–10]. Weighted ordered probit estimation. White estimator for variance. Asymptotic z values (in parentheses) are based on robust standard errors that are adjusted to clustering on 125 communities. Marginal effects are for one standard deviation or change from 0 to 1 in case of dummy variables. Strength of social norm = percentage in favor of reducing unemployment benefits. Significance levels: (*) $0.1 > p > 0.05$, * $0.05 > p > 0.01$, ** $p < 0.01$. Sources: Stutzer and Lalive 2004, based on Leu, Burri, and Priester 1997, Swiss Association of Cities (various years), and data service of Swiss Federal Statistical Office.

	Weighted ordered probit	Marginal effect (score 9–10)
Strength of social work norm (%/10)	0.011(*)	4.75
	(1.96)	
Unemployed (U)	−1.214**	−34.91
	(−6.26)	
Strength of social work norm × U	−0.045**	−19.89
	(−3.03)	
Duration of unemployment (years)	−0.275**	−3.14
	(−2.90)	
Individual characteristics[a]	Yes	
Number of communities	125	
Number of subjects	1,397	
ln$L$	−2,358.83	

a. Control variables include indicators for age, sex, nationality, educational level, household situation, employment status, household equivalence income, frequency of social contacts, participation in club activities, year of interview, and region.

by approximately 19.9 percentage points. This result is consistent with the view that social norms play an important role in unemployed people's well-being.

Happiness research yields important insights into the strong negative consequences of unemployment on individual well-being. It stresses the shock and psychic cost of being out of work. But there is also some recovery: unemployed people to some extent adjust to their fate and become less unhappy over time. (See e.g. Clark and Oswald 1994.) Future research must inquire more deeply into the determinants of when, how, and to what extent unemployed people recover. Context effects also need further scrutiny: under what conditions, and to what extent, do unemployed people compare themselves to other unemployed and then feel better off? Knowing more about the form of recovery from the initial shock of becoming unemployed helps us to better understand *sustainable happiness* (Lyubomirsky, Sheldon, and Schkade 2005).

4.2   General Unemployment

People may be unhappy about unemployment even if they themselves are not unemployed. They may empathize with the unfortunate fate of the unemployed and they may worry about the possibility of their becoming unemployed themselves in the future. They may also fear negative consequences for the economy and society as a whole. They may dislike the increase in unemployment contributions and taxes that are likely to come in the future, they may fear increased crime and social tension, and they may even see the threat of violent protests and uprisings.

The study of twelve European countries over the period 1975–1991 by Di Tella, MacCulloch, and Oswald (2003) finds that—with all other influences kept constant—increasing the general rate of unemployment from 9 percent (the European mean) to 10 percent reduces stated life satisfaction by 0.028 unit on the four-point scale. This effect is considerable: the small rise in unemployment is equivalent to shifting more than 2 percent of the population down from one life-satisfaction category to another—for example, from "not very satisfied" to "not at all satisfied."

The overall effect of unemployment on social well-being can be calculated by adding the loss experienced by those made unemployed to the overall effect of unemployment. Consider again a 1-percentage-point increase in unemployment. In the preceding section, it was shown that unemployed people experience a fall of 0.33 in their happiness scale. This figure must be multiplied by the 1.0 percent of the population unfortunate enough to become unemployed: $0.33 \times 0.01 = 0.0033$. Added to the general effect of a 1-percentage-point unemployment increase of 0.028, it leads to a total decrease of 0.0313 (Di Tella, MacCulloch, and Oswald 2003). This calculation must be taken with a grain of salt. It is at best capable of gauging the effects of unemployment on happiness in an approximate way. One reason for caution is that various interactions may exist between personal and more general unemployment, which may in turn affect the evaluation of happiness.

An important interaction refers to reference groups. As is the case for income, individuals tend to evaluate their own situation relative to other individuals (Lalive 2005). For most people, unemployment lowers their happiness less if they are not alone with their particular fate. When unemployment is seen to hit many people one knows or hears of, both the psychological and the social effects are mitigated. Self-esteem is better preserved because it becomes obvious that being out of a job is due more to general developments in the economy than to one's own fault. Stigma and social disapproval are less prevalent if unemployment hits many other people at the same time.

In order to empirically test the effect of reference groups on reported well-being, happiness scores are regressed on three types of explanatory variables: personal unemployment, unemployment among a reference group, and an interaction variable combining personal and reference group unemployment.

Using as a reference group the employment state of one's partner or, alternatively, the region in which an individual lives, a happiness function of this type has been estimated for British data over the period 1991–1996, again with all other influences kept constant (Clark 2003). As in virtually all previous studies, unemployed people are much more dissatisfied than employed people, and the general level of unemployment lowers happiness. In contrast, unemployed people indeed suffer less when the partner and/or a large proportion of other people living in their region are also out of work. The same result is reached when general unemployment in the economy is taken as the point of reference.

Reference groups are of major importance for showing to what extent people are distressed by their own unemployment. However, what group one refers to is not exogenously determined, but can to some extent be chosen (Falk and Knell 2004). People out of work tend to associate with other people out of work, partly because they have time to do so, or partly because they retreat from normal community life. It is also known that marriages and partnerships have a high risk of breaking down when one of the partners is unemployed (Kraft 2001). In all these cases, the definition of the reference group adjusts to one's status in the labor market. Causation with respect to happiness, then, does not run unambiguously from the reference group to the evaluation of unemployment.

5

How Inflation and Inequality Affect Happiness

5.1 Inflation

Theoretical economics discusses the costs of an increase in the general price level—inflation—by looking at the distinction between anticipated and unanticipated inflation. When price increases are anticipated, individuals can adjust to them with little if any cost. But when price increases come as a "shock," no such adjustment is possible. Individuals' adjustment is more costly when increased inflation causes higher variability in aggregate inflation and in relative prices. People need to invest considerable effort in informing themselves about, and insulating themselves from, the expected price increases. They may make many different errors—for instance, underestimating the extent of future inflation, or how a particular price changes in comparison with other prices.

The welfare costs of rising prices can be captured by computing the area under the money demand curve, the basic idea being that economizing on the use of currency imposes costs by reducing well-being. Based on this method, the cost of a 10 percent yearly inflation has been calculated to be between 0.3 percent and 0.45 percent of national income (Fischer 1981; Lucas 1981). This is very little, and it suggests that an anti-inflationary policy is rarely worth the cost it causes by raising unemployment and producing real income losses.

Many economists would strongly disagree with the preceding conclusion. They point out that stable prices are an indispensable prerequisite for a sound economy, for only when prices are stable can actors behave rationally. Most economists take an intermediate position. The picture emerging from the existing empirical evidence on the costs of inflation is indeed far from clear.[1] The "common opinion" of academic

---

1. For a survey, see Drifill, Mizon, and Ulph 1990.

economists tends to be that rampant inflation is very dangerous for the economy, whereas constant (hence more predictable) but low inflation (e.g., 1–5 percent per year) is not seen as causing any major problems. The population seems to feel quite differently. An extensive survey of the United States, Germany, and Brazil (Shiller 1997) finds that people are concerned about issues connected with inflation that differ from those causing concern to economists. People seem to disregard the fact that inflation generally also increases their own nominal income. They concentrate on the possible harm, but not on the possible benefits, that inflation might bring to their standard of living. In addition, the survey identifies other concerns generally neglected by economists. One is that inflation allows opportunists to exploit others in an unfair and dishonest way; another is that inflation undermines the moral basis of society. Many fear that inflation produces political and economic chaos and a loss in national prestige due to the falling exchange rate.

Happiness research finds that inflation systematically and markedly lowers reported individual well-being. In combined time-series and cross-section studies, the development of inflation in several countries over the course of time can be analyzed. Of most interest is the study of twelve European countries over the period 1975–1991 by Di Tella, MacCulloch, and Oswald (2001). The mean rate of inflation was 7.5 percent per year. Average satisfaction is calculated from a cardinal interpretation of the four-point scale that gives "not at all satisfied" a value of 1, "not very satisfied" a value of 2, and so on. If individual socioeconomic characteristics and unemployment rate remain constant, an increase in the inflation rate by 1 percentage point—say, from the mean rate of 8 percent to 9 percent per year—is estimated to reduce average happiness by 0.01 unit of satisfaction (i.e., from an average level in the sample of 3.02 to 3.01). Hence, an increase in the inflation rate by 5 percentage points (a historically likely event) reduces subjective well-being by 0.05 unit. This effect is substantial, though not very large. It means that 5 percent of the population is shifted downward from one life-satisfaction category to the next lower one—e.g., from being "very satisfied" to "fairly satisfied."

In studying the tradeoff between inflation and unemployment, the results reported on the effect of unemployment on happiness can now be combined with the results concerning inflation just discussed (Di Tella, MacCulloch, and Oswald 2001; Wolfers 2003). The question is "By how much, on average, must a country reduce its inflation in order to tolerate a 1-percentage-point increase in unemployment?" Over the relevant range, happiness is assumed to depend linearly on the two economic factors, and the estimate controls for country fixed effects, year effects, and country-specific time trends. A 1-percentage-point increase in unemployment is calculated to compensate for a 1.7-percentage-point decrease in inflation. Thus, if unemployment rises by 5 percentage points (e.g., from 3 to 8 percent), inflation must decrease by 8.5 percentage points (e.g., from 10 to 1.5 percent per year) to keep the population equally satisfied. The "Misery Index," which simply adds the unemployment rate to the inflation rate, assigns the same weight to each variable. This presents a distorted picture of the tradeoff between unemployment and inflation by attributing too little weight to the effect of unemployment, relative to inflation.

5.2 Inequality

The market produces a distribution of income considered unacceptable by the citizens in most countries (Deaton 2005). Accordingly, there is a strong demand for redistribution by the government (Alesina and La Ferrara 2005). As a consequence, modern governments engage in large-scale redistribution. This tendency increased markedly in the twentieth century. At the end of the nineteenth century, the share of government transfers was less than 1 percent of GDP in both Europe and the United States. By the end of the twentieth century, this share had increased to 14 percent of GDP in the United States, and to 22 percent in Europe. This difference can be almost wholly attributed to the larger increase of government transfers in Europe than in the United States (Tanzi and Schuknecht 2000). Similarly, it has been found (Di Tella and MacCulloch 1996) that Europeans—with the exception of the Norwegians—prefer unemployment benefits higher than those available to Americans.

The effect of inequality in income on happiness differs markedly between Europe and the United States (Alesina, Di Tella, and MacCulloch 2004; Alesina and Glaeser 2004).[2] Income inequality is captured by the Gini coefficient and happiness by the Euro-Barometer Survey and the US General Social Survey. Europeans appear to have a strongly dislike for inequality in income, whereas in the United States there is no correlation between state-level inequality and happiness (with personal characteristics and state, county, and year effects controlled for). Alesina, Di Tella, and MacCulloch (2004) disaggregate this result within

2. For a survey, see Deaton 2005.

two dimensions: rich and poor and self-defined right- and left-wingers. Among Europeans, the poor suffer a loss of happiness from inequality, but the rich are not affected. In the United States, even the poor remain largely unconcerned about inequality. Those who consider themselves left-wingers exhibit a marked distaste for inequality, whereas those who consider themselves right-wingers are not affected by it. This effect is so strong in the United States that only rich left-wingers are negatively affected by inequality.

According to this study, only Europeans have their happiness negatively affected by inequality. No such effect in the United States can be explained by differences in the extent of upward social mobility. Most Americans believe in the possibility of moving up the social and income ladders, and so a large inequality in income indicates high opportunities in the future. In contrast, most Europeans believe that social mobility is low and that present income is a good indicator of future income. Therefore, individuals dislike an unequal income distribution. Sixty percent of Americans believe that the poor are lazy rather than just unlucky, whereas only 26 percent of Europeans think so (Alesina, Glaeser, and Sacerdote 2001). It is not clear whether the existing "folklore" that social mobility is greater in the United States than in Europe is in fact correct. Unclear data make it difficult to draw any firm conclusions (Atkinson, Bourguignon, and Morrison 1992).

Capturing the effect of income inequality on happiness is made more complicated by several effects transmitted by other variables. Inequality may affect individual happiness indirectly through health and income. Lower inequality improves health and increases income, which in turn increases happiness (Helliwell 2003).

II   Pushing Ahead

The second part of the book ventures into topics so far neglected or studied in greatly different ways. It seeks to demonstrate the range of issues that happiness research can address and the fascinating results and insights it can yield. This research goes well beyond the estimation of happiness functions and opens new avenues for economic research.

This part is based on research undertaken by the Zurich Group, a group of researchers associated with my chair in economics at the University of Zurich. Its members are therefore co-authors of this book, and I was actively involved as an author in all but one of the papers. The respective papers are not presented in full. Rather, their questions, their empirical approaches, and their results are outlined in support of a twofold aim.

The first four chapters in this part discuss substantive areas of inquiry. Chapter 6 demonstrates that good institutions increase life satisfaction. This is joint work with Alois Stutzer. Two such institutions are analyzed: direct democracy (i.e., individual participation rights via referenda) and federalism (i.e., decentralization of political decision making to lower jurisdictions).

Chapter 7 shows that autonomy and self-determination in work raises life satisfaction. This is joint work with Matthias Benz, Alois Stutzer, and Stephan Meier. The self-employed report higher job satisfaction than employees and people doing voluntary work and are more satisfied with their life than other people. Careful testing shows that a causal relation does indeed lead in that direction.

Chapter 8 studies a central question in the economics of marriage: Are happy people more likely to get married, or does marriage make people happy? This is joint work with Alois Stutzer. Our analysis, using panel data, concludes that both causal directions are relevant. Marriage increases happiness. Although happiness decreases over the duration of a marriage, it does not decrease to its pre-marital level.

Chapter 9 deals with the question of whether watching television makes people unhappy or whether unhappy people watch more television. This is joint work with Christine Benesch and Alois Stutzer. It is not clear if, on average, watching television makes people unhappy. But those with high opportunity costs of time suffer a considerable loss in their life satisfaction due to lack of self-control, whereas retired people and those not working do not suffer.

The next three chapters consider new interpretations and aspects of utility.

Chapter 10 deals with "procedural utility," a new feature of happiness. This is joint work with Matthias Benz and Alois Stutzer. We show the importance of this source of individual well-being in many areas of society, including different sectors of the economy.

Chapter 11 analyzes whether, to what extent, and where individuals commit systematic errors in their consumption decisions. This is joint work with Alois Stutzer. The issue of misprediction cannot be analyzed in standard theory, because it is assumed that individuals always maximize their utility and are well aware of what this utility is. A particularly important instance is the difficulty of predicting utility from future consumption. It is argued that people make choices that reduce their utility according to their own evaluation. This chapter also discusses why such errors of prediction are difficult to unlearn.

Chapter 12 addresses the valuation of public goods. This is joint work with Simon Luechinger and Alois Stutzer. The Life-Satisfaction Approach has substantial advantages over the standard methods of valuing public goods, such as the Contingent Valuation and Hedonic Market approaches. The life-satisfaction approach is illustrated by the cost imposed on individuals by terrorist activities. It is shown that individuals in areas more strongly affected by terrorist incidents in France are willing to give up substantial amounts of income for a reduction of terrorism to the lower levels of terrorism prevailing in other parts of the country.

6

The Public Sphere

6.1 Democracy

This chapter views democracy from a new perspective. Until now, democracy has normally been seen as a value in itself. From an instrumental point of view, democracy has been understood as the institution that results in political decisions closest to the preferences of the citizens. This discussion endeavors to show that democracy, understood as the constitutionally guaranteed participation rights of the citizens, systematically increases the population's subjective happiness and life satisfaction to a considerable extent. Happiness research allows us to identify two different reasons for this increase in happiness. Democracy increases outcome utility by providing the people with more desirable political decisions (outcome utility). The right to participate in the process of political decision making is, moreover, valued as such (procedural utility).

Effects of Representative Democracy on Happiness

Dorn et al. (2007) undertook an international comparison between 28 countries over the period 1988–1998 in order to identify whether individuals living in more democratic nations felt happier than individuals in countries with less extensive democratic institutions. The data set covers more than 25,000 people. Happiness is measured by the responses to the question "If you were to consider your life in general these days, how happy or unhappy would you say you are, on the whole?" The answer categories are "very happy," "fairly happy," "not very happy," and "not at all happy." Table 6.1 reports the percentage of respondents for the self-reported happiness in the 28 countries involved.

Table 6.1
Shares (percent) of self-reported happiness in 28 countries. Mean score is obtained by transforming the ordinal scale to a cardinal scale (score 4 for "very happy," score 3 for "fairly happy," score 2 for "not very happy," and score 1 for "not happy at all"). Source: Dorn et al. 2007; based on 1998 International Social Survey Program.

	Very happy	Fairly happy	Not very happy	Not at all happy	Mean score
Austria	22.6	67.8	8.6	0.9	3.12
Bulgaria	8.7	45.1	28.7	17.4	2.45
Canada	25.4	57.8	14.5	2.2	3.06
Chile	27.5	32.3	34.8	5.4	2.82
Cyprus	21.7	50.6	22.5	5.2	2.89
Czech Republic	8.9	71.3	17.9	1.8	2.87
Denmark	31.8	57.7	8.7	1.8	3.19
France	14.1	65.1	17.8	3.0	2.90
Germany, West	17.7	66.2	13.5	2.6	2.99
Germany, East	9.3	61.2	25.3	4.2	2.76
Hungary	4.7	45.1	39.6	10.6	2.44
Ireland	44.1	50.9	4.4	0.6	3.38
Italy	12.4	65.9	18.2	3.5	2.87
Japan	14.3	74.1	10.0	1.6	3.01
Latvia	4.6	43.9	45.0	6.5	2.47
New Zealand	33.0	59.9	6.4	0.6	3.25
Norway	22.1	66.6	10.4	0.9	3.10
Philippines	27.8	53.3	15.0	3.9	3.05
Poland	19.0	63.0	15.3	2.7	2.98
Portugal	19.5	37.5	34.9	8.0	2.69
Russian Republic	4.7	49.4	37.1	8.8	2.50
Slovakia	7.1	58.3	26.2	8.4	2.64
Slovenia	9.3	58.6	28.8	3.3	2.74
Spain	19.2	68.1	11.1	1.6	3.05
Sweden	24.4	61.2	12.8	1.6	3.08
Switzerland	28.4	62.1	8.5	0.9	3.18
United Kingdom	35.1	58.1	5.7	1.1	3.24
United States	36.7	52.4	8.9	2.0	3.24

Table 6.1 reveals (in the last column) that the happiest people were, on average, in Ireland, closely followed by Denmark, Switzerland, the United Kingdom, the United States, and New Zealand. High mean happiness scores were also recorded for Sweden, Spain, Austria, and Canada. In contrast, the least happy people were in the formerly communist countries Hungary, Russia, Latvia, Slovakia, and Slovenia.

Two different indicators were used to measure the extent of democracy: a narrower indicator collected by the Polity IV project (Marshall and Jaggers 2004, scaled from 1 to 10) and a broader indicator collected by the Freedom House (Karatnycky 2000, scaled from 1 to 7). The happiness function estimated includes a large number of socio-demographic, economic and cultural determinants. There is no need to discuss them here beyond noting that they are in line with the direction and size of the influences on happiness described in the previous chapters.

Table 6.2 provides a selection of those parameter estimates relating to the effect of democracy on happiness. Three results may be observed:

• The parameter estimate, showing the effect of having had more extensive democratic institutions in 1988 on subsequent self-reported happiness, is positive (+0.068). This suggests that individuals living in countries with more extensive democratic institutions are more satisfied with their lives, even if many other determinants of happiness (socio-democratic, economic, and cultural) are taken into account. The effect is statistically significant (z value 2.54), indicating that one can place a certain amount of trust in the estimate.

Table 6.2
Partial effect of democracy on happiness in 28 countries, 1988–1998. Dependent variable: happiness [1–4]. Ordered probit estimate. Numbers in parentheses are the absolute value of the z statistics of the estimated parameters. Significance levels: * $0.01 < p < 0.05$. Source: Dorn et al. 2007; based on 1998 International Social Survey Program and Polity IV Index.

Democracy in 1988[a]	0.068*
	(2.54)
Change in democracy[a] 1988–1998	0.051*
	(2.06)
Control variables[b]	Yes
Number of observations	25,937

a. Democracy measured by Polity IV Index.
b. Control variables include age, gender, education, household size, marital status, employment status, subsistence income, relative income, income above or below poverty line, culture (language), and religion.

• Democratic institutions increase people's well-being considerably. An increase in the extent of democracy by one mark on the ten-point Polity IV Index increases self-reported happiness to an extent similar to an increase of $4,500 per year in an individual's income.

• The second estimate reported in table 6.2 indicates that an improvement in the level of democracy over the period 1988–1998 is accompanied by a statistically significant increase in happiness.

Overall, these results suggest that individuals living in countries with more extensive democratic institutions feel happier with their lives according to their own evaluation than individuals in more authoritarian countries. These results are not prompted by directly asking whether individuals would be happier living in a democracy. Rather, the subjective, self-reported evaluation of well-being has been gathered, independent of the objective political conditions. Moreover, many other influences on happiness are controlled for, and a certain amount of trust can therefore be placed in the results.

The quality of government also has a strikingly large influence in explaining international differences in well-being (Helliwell and Huang 2007). The first dimension of government quality, relating to the honesty and efficiency of government, increases life satisfaction more in poorer countries. The second dimension, relating to effectiveness, regulatory efficiency, rule of law, and lack of corruption, increases life satisfaction more in rich countries. Trust (or mistrust) in political institutions, such as the European Union, the United Nations, the European Central Bank, and one's national government, also significantly increases (or lowers) happiness (Hudson 2006). Freedom has also been found to be an important determinant of well-being (Veenhoven 2000), but it is difficult to disentangle from other influences.

Effects of Direct Democracy on Happiness

The preceding section provided empirical evidence that living in democratic institutions increases people's happiness. This analysis can be taken a step further by considering the effect on happiness of citizens' direct-participation rights. These rights refer to popular initiatives where the citizens can put an issue, either optional or mandatory, on the agenda. Popular initiatives and referenda can vary to some extent by requiring more or fewer signatures to propel them, or by covering more or fewer areas of decision (e.g., including or excluding fiscal affairs).

Switzerland is the only country in the world that systematically uses referenda at the national level and the sub-federal level. Remarkably, its 26 cantons differ in the extent of rights to direct political participation. The index, constructed by Stutzer (1999), assigns a value between 1 and 6 to each canton.

Life satisfaction is captured for Switzerland in the years 1992–1994 by the responses to the question "How satisfied are you with your life as a whole these days?" The scale ranges from 1 to 10.

The relationship between self-reported life satisfaction and the extent of the right to direct political participation is estimated by the weighted order probit technique in a cross-section of more than 6,000 persons (Frey and Stutzer 2000; 2002a; Stutzer and Frey 2003). Life satisfaction is dependent on a number of demographic factors (including age, gender, nationality, education, and family status), on two economic variables (employment and income), on size and type of community, and on the institutional variable of direct democratic rights.

Table 6.3 reproduces the estimation results, focusing on the effect of direct democracy on life satisfaction. The following results are found:

• The more extensive the direct-participation possibilities of the citizens, the higher their self-reported life satisfaction.

• This effect is statistically highly significant and considerable. An improvement of one point on the six-point direct-democracy index increases life satisfaction to about the same extent as an increase in income from the lowest category (less than CHF 2,000 per month to the second lowest category (between CHF 2,000 and 3,000). Even more revealing is the following thought experiment: When a particular

Table 6.3
Direct democracy and satisfaction with life in Switzerland. Dependent variable: satisfaction with life [1–10]. Weighted ordered probit estimation. Standard errors adjusted to clustering in 26 cantons. Significance level: ** $p < 0.01$. Source: Frey and Stutzer 2000; based on data gathered by Leu, Burri, and Priester (1997).

	Marginal effect (score 10)
Direct democratic rights	0.028**
Control variables[a]	Yes
No. of observations	6,134
Prob > F	0.001

a. The regression includes a large number of socio-demographic and economic control variables, as well as controls for size and type of community.

person moves from Canton Geneva, where the right to direct participation is quite restricted (index 1.75), to Canton Basel-Landschaft, where the right to direct participation is extensive (index 5.69), this person has an 11 percent higher probability of belonging to the group of citizens indicating that they are "completely satisfied." It was also shown that it is in fact the right to participate, rather than the actual participation, that affects people's happiness.

The studies mentioned (Frey and Stutzer 2000, 2002a; Stutzer and Frey 2003) went one step further by differentiating between two types of utility that constitute the measured increase in life satisfaction accompanying more extensive direct democracy. The first type of utility refers to outcomes, reflecting the greater acknowledgement given to more extensive participation rights as leading to individual preferences. The second type of utility is of quite a different nature. "Procedural utility" refers to the well-being experienced by citizens as a direct result of having the *right* to participate in political decision making. This includes the value assigned to being able to express ideological positions, irrespective of whether the act of voting has any effect on political outcomes.[1]

To disentangle the effects of "outcome utility" and "procedural utility," the following approach is used: Citizens can enjoy both types of utility because they have the right to vote. In contrast, non-citizens can only enjoy outcome utility (assuming they are treated in the same way as citizens), but, because they have no right to vote, are prevented from enjoying the procedural utility produced by political participation rights.

Table 6.4 shows the respective estimate. The regression contains the same socio-demographic and economic determinants as the previous estimates. In addition, the table reports the effect of membership in associations. This contextual control variable captures an important aspect of social capital and tends to increase life satisfaction. With respect to the distinction between outcome utility and procedural utility, the interaction term "participation rights × foreigner" is crucial. It indicates that foreigners—who are prevented from voting—experience lower gains in well-being from living in a more direct-democratic canton than citizens do. While the positive marginal effect of participation rights is 3.3 percentage points for citizens, it is reduced for foreigners by 2.3 percentage points to a smaller positive effect of 1 percentage point. This effect is estimated by taking into account that foreigners are on average less

---

1. On "expressive voting," see Brennan 1993.

Table 6.4
Procedural utility and participation rights. Dependent variable: satisfaction with life [1–10]. Weighted ordered probit estimation. Standard errors adjusted for clustering on 26 cantons. White estimator for variance. Source: Stutzer and Frey 2003; based on data gathered by Leu, Burri, and Priester (1997).

	Marginal effect (score 10)
Participation rights	0.033
Participation rights × foreigner	−0.023
Foreigner	−0.014
Control variables[a]	Yes
Membership in associations	0.057
No. of observations	6,124

a. The regression includes a large number of socio-demographic and economic control variables, as well as an indicator for urbanization and whether respondents live in a German-, French-, or Italian-speaking canton.

happy than the Swiss. Democratic institutions thus contribute to happiness. This is due both to outcome utility and to procedural utility (i.e., having the right to participate in political decisions on various issues via popular initiatives and referenda).

Open Issues

More extensive democratic institutions increase self-reported subjective well-being, both with respect to democracy as such and with respect to direct democracy. Although these results are based on careful econometric estimates, and take into account many other determinants of happiness, statistical concerns exist (as always) and deserve serious consideration.

Four major issues are mentioned here in order to bring the analysis into perspective.

Measurement   As has already been pointed out, there are various ways of measuring happiness and democracy. None of these measures is uniquely superior, because both happiness and democracy are multi-dimensional concepts. The empirical research discussed here deals with this issue by considering various measures of each, and analyzing the differing results in the estimates. In particular, the estimates by Kirchgässner and associates (Dorn et al. 2005) consider two somewhat different measures of the extent of democracy: the Polity-IV and the Freedom House measures. It is demonstrated that the estimation results are quite robust with respect to these two different measures. This enables us to place more trust in the results.

Multitude of influences on happiness   It has been pointed out that happiness depends on a great many factors. The econometric estimates reported accordingly take into account a large number of variables assumed to influence happiness. The crucial question is whether some important influences are overlooked or inadequately captured, because in that case the estimates would be biased (i.e., the coefficients estimated would be too small or too large), so that the influence of many or even all of the determinants would be wrongly captured. A suitable way of dealing with this problem is again to undertake robustness exercises, as indeed were undertaken for the estimates reported above.

Restricted data   More fundamental than the measurement problem is that, for systematic reasons, some data do not exist. Most importantly, in dictatorships and authoritarian systems happiness data are rarely available, and if such data are available they are of reduced value because they are fundamentally distorted. With respect to analyzing various types of democracies, it has to be pointed out that the variant "direct democracy" exists to any real extent in only one country. Therefore, there is not a sufficiently good data base for any cross-section estimates between countries. This places a serious limit on research. However, that limit may sometimes be overcome by looking at differences between sub-units—for example, differences between cantons within Switzerland. This technique, though, reduces the extent to which the results can be generalized to other countries.

Causality   The construction of a happiness function assumes that democracy affects happiness. However, the reverse relationship may be in effect: happy people may *choose* to have democratic institutions. Two causalities are thus to be considered. In the study reported here, the problem was addressed by taking the democratic institutions existing at the beginning of the time period under consideration, which excludes the possibility that level of happiness affects democracy. In the case of the Swiss study, the constitutions of the 26 cantons show relatively stable patterns with respect to citizens' direct-participation rights, so that the problem of reverse causality is reduced.

6.2 Federalism

Political decentralization is another major political institution expected to affect people's well-being. Decentralization of decision making allows individuals to express their preferences by leaving jurisdictions with whose performance they are dissatisfied. They are attracted to those jurisdictions that care for their preferences at low cost. The possibility of voting with one's feet (Tiebout 1956; Buchanan 1965; Hirschman 1970) tends to undermine regional cartels by politicians. Here, evidence is presented for the sub-federal level in Switzerland. The previous analysis on direct democracy is extended, taking the federal structure of Swiss cantons into account.

The division of the competences between communities and the cantonal government reflects the federal structure of a canton or, from the municipalities' point of view, their autonomy.

The extent of local autonomy is measured by an index (Ladner 1994). The index over the 26 cantons is based on survey results. Chief local administrators in 1856 Swiss municipalities were asked to report how they perceive their local autonomy on a ten-point scale, with 1 indicating "no autonomy at all" and 10 indicating "very high" communal autonomy. The aggregate variable refers to the 26 cantons in Switzerland. The other variables are the same as used in the estimation for table 6.3 when studying the effect of direct democracy on happiness in Switzerland.

Table 6.5 shows the results of an econometric estimate in which the variable "local autonomy" is added to the socio-demographic and economic factors in the happiness equation. For simplicity, only the coefficients for variables referring to the political institutions are shown. They indicate the partial effects controlling for the socio-demographic and economic variables. Moreover, the coefficients of the latter variables are almost unaltered. The estimate reveals a statistically significant positive effect of federalism on subjective well-being. For local autonomy, the share of persons indicating very high happiness increases by 3.3 percentage points compared to a situation in which their commune is one index point less autonomous vis-à-vis their canton.

Local autonomy and direct democracy are not independent of each other, of course. On the one hand, direct democracy fosters federal structures at the national and state level because citizens—in contrast to politicians—are most interested in strong federalism (Blankart 1998). On the other hand, people who bear the costs and benefits of government action are better identifiable in a decentralized system. Under

Table 6.5
Local autonomy and satisfaction with life in Switzerland in 1992. Dependent variable: satisfaction with life [1–10]. Weighted ordered probit estimation. Standard errors adjusted to clustering in 26 cantons. Significance levels: * $0.05 > p > 0.01$, ** $p < 0.01$. Source: Frey and Stutzer 2000; based on data gathered by Ladner (1994) and by Leu, Burri and Priester (1997).

	Coeff.	t value	Marginal effect (score 10)	Coeff.	t value	Marginal effect (score 10)
Local autonomy	0.098**	2.913	0.033	0.036	1.005	0.012
Direct democratic rights				0.071*	2.317	0.024
Control variables[a]	Yes			Yes		
No. of observations	6,134			6,134		
Prob > F	0.003			0.001		

a. The regression includes a large number of socio-demographic and economic control variables, as well as controls for size and type of community.

these conditions, referenda and initiatives lead to better political decisions and thus direct democracy is preserved. As a result, the indices for direct democratic rights and local autonomy are highly correlated ($r = 0.605$). This makes it impossible to clearly separate the effects of the two variables in one model. The second equation in table 6.5 jointly includes two institutional factors: local autonomy and direct democratic rights. The coefficient for the variable measuring federalism is roughly one-third as large as when it is taken alone, and it loses its statistical significance. The index for direct democracy has only a slightly smaller marginal effect on life satisfaction than estimated in table 6.3: 0.024 instead of 0.028. Direct democracy and federalism in Switzerland thus seem to be complements rather than economic substitutes. Local autonomy is one of the several "transmission mechanisms" of direct democracy's beneficial effects.

Self-Employment and Voluntary Work

This chapter discusses two areas in which specific features of work systematically affect individual happiness.

Section 7.1 analyzes why the happiness of self-employed persons is higher than those employed by an organization. It also enquires whether the causation runs in the opposite direction, namely that happier people tend to choose self-employment.

Section 7.2 looks at the higher life satisfaction of persons engaged in voluntary work. It again considers the possibility of reverse causation by self-selection.

7.1 The Happy Self-Employed

The Benefits of Self-Employment

Economic research on happiness has identified the major determinants of self-reported subjective well-being or happiness. Among the many factors systematically influencing it, employment stands out. Persons who are unemployed are much less happy than other persons, even when other influences such as lower income are controlled for. Being employed is of value over and above the income it generates.

Another important aspect linking happiness and employment has so far been neglected. It is that individuals derive utility from being self-employed because it gives them a higher measure of self-determination and freedom. In contrast, persons in dependent employment have to obey orders given by their superiors. Indeed, self-employment reflects the difference between the two most important decision-making procedures in the economy: the market and hierarchy. The self-employed seem to derive utility from their position as independent actors on the market, and of not being subject to a hierarchy, mainly for procedural reasons. Because approximately 10 percent of all individuals gainfully employed in Western countries are self-employed, a substantial proportion of workers is affected.

In the three countries considered here (Germany, the United Kingdom, and Switzerland), self-employed workers show higher job satisfaction as a proxy measure for utility from work.[1] The raw difference, smallest in West Germany (0.21 index point on a job-satisfaction scale from 0 to 10), reaches similar magnitude in Britain (0.21 index point on a job-satisfaction scale from 1 to 7) and in Switzerland (0.42 index point on a job-satisfaction scale from 0 to 10). These differences, however, reflect many characteristics that distinguish self-employed individuals from employed workers. Accounting for outcome aspects of work is therefore essential in assessing whether the differences in satisfaction are due to procedural utility. For example, self-employed people may work in particular jobs and industries that make them more satisfied with their jobs. On the other hand, it is known that the self-employed tend to earn less and work more than similar employed people (Hamilton 2000). This would lead to an underestimation of the utility gained from being self-employed if outcome aspects of work are not controlled for.

Extensive theoretical research by psychologists suggests that individuals prefer independence to being subject to hierarchical decision making. Ryan and Deci (2000) attribute an intrinsic value to self-determination, which is strongly related to independence and generally restricted under hierarchy. Self-determination is seen to provide procedural goods that serve innate needs of competence, autonomy, and relatedness. Similar approaches attach an intrinsic value to the actualization of human potentials (Ryff and Singer 1998) or to personal control (Grob 2000; Peterson 1999; Seligman 1992). These approaches see the possibility of acting independently as a value in itself (i.e., individuals do not necessarily expect better instrumental outcomes from it).

Some research by economists indicates that self-employment provides a utility premium. Blanchflower and Oswald (1998), Blanchflower (2000), and Blanchflower, Oswald, and Stutzer (2001) present evidence that the self-employed are more satisfied with their jobs. Hamilton (2000) convincingly shows that self-employment does not pay (i.e., that the self-employed are willing to forgo income for independence. Although this is strong evidence that self-employment provides (non-monetary) benefits, these authors do not study further the

---

1. For a more extensive treatment, see Benz and Frey 2008a.

precise constituents of these benefits. Hundley (2001) addresses this in more detail and finds that the self-employed are happier with their jobs because of more autonomy, more flexibility, more skill utilization, and, to some extent, more job security. This evidence is consistent overall with my hypothesis. Here, the question of whether the utility premium from self-employment reflects procedural utility from independence vs. hierarchy is explored in more detail.

Self-employed and employed people are essentially engaged in the same labor markets and the same production activities. This makes the two groups comparable. Of course, self-employed people face some other external constraints, in particular those imposed directly by the market but also those imposed by government laws and regulations. With respect to work, however, the main difference between the two groups is that the self-employed work independently whereas employees are subject to a hierarchy. People who prefer not to be subject to a hierarchy should also prefer smaller hierarchies over larger ones if procedural utility has normal properties.[2]

Job Satisfaction

Utility from work is measured by using self-reported job satisfaction as a proxy variable. Economists have used job satisfaction increasingly as a meaningful concept to analyze the labor market (Hamermesh 1977; Clark and Oswald 1996; Blanchflower and Oswald 1999; Clark 2001; for a survey, see Warr 1999). Self-reported job satisfaction can serve as an indicator for the utility people derive from their work. Job satisfaction is one of the several domain-specific subjective indicators of well-being (van Praag, Frijters, and Ferrer-i-Carbonell 2003). The empirical analysis conducted here is based on three major data sets from European countries: the German Socio-Economic Panel Survey (GSOEP), the British Household Panel Survey (BHPS), and the Swiss Household Panel Survey (SHP). These three surveys are among the most comprehensive sources of information on work-related aspects, income, and other socio-economic variables in Europe. The data sets have several advantages:

• Compared to other data sets previously used to test the effects of self-employment on job satisfaction (see e.g. Blanchflower 2000), they contain much more detailed information on such important aspects of work as income, working hours, occupation, education, and industry,

---

2. On the relationship between firm size and job satisfaction, see Benz and Frey 2008a.

and also on other individual and firm characteristics. This makes it possible to hold the outcome aspects of work more precisely constant when assessing the procedural utility from independence vs. hierarchy.

• The European surveys include measures of job satisfaction, whereas comparable US surveys (e.g., the Panel Study of Income Dynamics and the Current Population Survey) do not. Job satisfaction, however, is needed as a proxy for utility from work.

• Two of the three surveys, the GSOEP and the BHPS, have a panel structure that can be exploited in the empirical analysis. Individuals can generally be observed over several waves.

• The use of surveys from three countries allows one to get a broader picture of the robustness of the estimated effects than when only one country is studied. Although the three surveys come from different sources, they are similar in structure.

In the German GSOEP, job satisfaction is assessed using the question "How satisfied are you today with...your job?" Individuals are asked to state their job satisfaction on a scale from 0 (totally unhappy) to 10 (totally happy). The question asked in the British BHPS is similar: "All things considered, how satisfied or dissatisfied are you with your present job overall?" Answers are coded here on a somewhat narrower scale, from 1 (not satisfied at all) to 7 (completely satisfied). In Switzerland, the related question is "On a scale from 0 'not at all satisfied' to 10 'completely satisfied,' can you indicate your degree of satisfaction with your job in general?"

In general, individuals in the countries considered seem to be quite satisfied with their jobs. In West Germany over the period 1984–2000, average job satisfaction of all individuals in the workforce was 7.25 (standard deviation 2.00) on a scale from 1 to 10. In Britain over the period 1991–1999, workers were, relatively, slightly more satisfied with their jobs, indicating an average value of 5.43 (standard deviation 1.36) on a scale from 1 to 7. Job satisfaction was highest in Switzerland in 1999, where the average worker stated a job-satisfaction score of 8.10 (standard deviation 1.72) on a scale from 1 to 10.

The analysis focuses on self-employed people, and the question is asked whether they reap utility from not being subject to a hierarchy. The dummy "self-employed" takes on the value 1 when individuals state that they are self-employed in a given year, and is 0 when people in the workforce are employed by an organization. In West Germany, on average 8.3 percent of the total workforce sampled in the GSOEP was self-employed in the period 1984–2000, and this ratio was relatively constant over the period (min. 7.5 percent, max. 9.9 percent). In Britain, 12.0 percent of the workforce was self-employed on average during the period 1991–1999 (min. 11.0 percent, max. 12.5 percent). In Switzerland, the ratio was 10.2 percent in 1999.

The three surveys contain detailed information on important control variables. Income and working hours are core outcome aspects of work and have to be controlled for when assessing non-outcome utility from work. In the empirical analysis, the total personal income of an individual is used to account for effects of income on job satisfaction. The influence of working hours is measured by using the total hours an individual works in an average week (including overtime hours). Apart from these core control variables, the surveys include information on tenure, age, gender, highest education attained, whether people work part-time or full-time, and which occupation and industry they work in. This creates a large and detailed set of control variables on the objective aspects of work.

For all three countries considered, the descriptive statistics show higher job satisfaction for self-employed workers. The difference is smallest in the case of West Germany (0.21 index point on a scale from 0 to 10) and reaches similar magnitude in Britain (0.21 index point on a scale from 1 to 7) and Switzerland (0.42 index point on a scale from 0 to 10). These differences, however, might reflect a multitude of characteristics that distinguish self-employed individuals from employed workers. Thus, whether higher job satisfaction among the self-employed can be attributed to procedural utility from being independent has to be investigated in more detail.

Econometric Analysis

As a first step, multivariate regressions are run that include the control variables just discussed. The basic regressions presented in table 7.1 are estimated using an ordered logit model, as job satisfaction is an ordinally scaled dependent variable. The weighting variables applied allow representative results on the subject level for the respective country. Moreover, in the case of the German and British panels, the estimated robust standard errors are corrected for repeated observations on the individual level over time.

The multivariate regressions confirm that self-employed individuals are more satisfied with their jobs than employees, even when outcome aspects of work are controlled for. For all three countries, substantial

Table 7.1

Job satisfaction and self-employment in West Germany (1984–2000), Great Britain (1991–1999), and Switzerland (1999). Dependent variable: job satisfaction [scales: West Germany 0–10, Great Britain 1–7, Switzerland 0–10]. Ordered logit regressions with robust standard errors (clustered for individuals). Standard errors in parentheses. Significance levels: ** $p < 0.01$. Source: Benz and Frey 2008a; based on German Socio-Economic Panel, British Household Panel, and Swiss Household Panel.

	West Germany	Great Britain	Switzerland
Self-Employed	0.196**	0.278**	0.418**
	(0.064)	(0.056)	(0.112)
Employed	Reference group	Reference group	Reference group
Control variables[a]	Yes	Yes	Yes
Year dummies	Yes	Yes	No
No. of observations	70,229	52,022	3,431
No. of individuals	11,700	13,380	3,431
F value	5.85**	13.84**	3.38**

a. Control variables include personal income (ln), working time, working time squared, age, age squared, tenure, tenure squared, part-time work, gender, education, occupation, and industry.

and highly significant effects are found. Their size is comparable to the raw differences. This corroborates and, at the same time, extends results previously reported in Blanchflower 2000, in Blanchflower, Oswald, and Stutzer 2001, and in Blanchflower and Oswald 1998. The results indicate that self-employed people do not reap that much more utility from their work because the outcomes are different. In the following sections, it is further investigated whether it is procedural utility from being independent vs. being subject to a hierarchy that explains this result.

For example, the regressions in table 7.1 do not consider the possibility that self-employed people may be a selection of people who have a natural tendency to be more satisfied with their jobs, or are in other respects different from employed workers. The estimated coefficients would not then reflect non-instrumental benefits from being self-employed, but merely personality differences between the two groups. This concern is addressed using two different methodologies.

Individual Fixed-Effects Regressions

These are run for West Germany and Britain, where the panel structure of the surveys allows one to observe the same persons moving into self-employment or out of it. The results from these linear fixed-effects regressions indicate that the job satisfaction effects of self-employment are a robust phenomenon. For Germany the estimated coefficient for being self-employed is 0.11 ($t = 1.87$); for Britain it amounts to 0.16 ($t = 5.42$). This is remarkable, for in both panels only about 20 percent of all observations on being self-employed come from persons who either move in or out of self-employment. The fixed-effects regressions only take into account these "changers" when estimating the coefficient for being self-employed, and disregard the other 80 percent of the observations (which go into individual fixed effects). While the results remain stable, it is nevertheless a shortcoming of this approach that observed moves in and out of self-employment are relatively low, and that, at the aggregate level, they fluctuate around a relatively stable overall ratio of self-employment of the work force. It would be interesting to study a situation where large inflows into self-employment take place, thereby also changing the aggregate ratio of self-employment in an economy to a considerable extent.

A "Natural Experiment" in East Germany
This approach takes advantage of a like situation that created a type of "natural experiment" on self-employment creation (Meyer 1995; Besley and Case 2000). After the Iron Curtain fell in 1989, East Germany experienced a fundamental and largely unexpected change in the structure of its economy. Notably with respect to self-employment, the situation changed dramatically: self-employment became a realistic option for East Germans for the first time. Self-employment had been severely restricted under the socialist regime in the German Democratic Republic, because it did not fit into a socialist economic system. Consequently, the ratio of self-employment in the workforce is estimated at a low 2.1 percent for the last year of the German Democratic Republic (Lechner and Pfeiffer 1993). East Germans were first sampled in the GSOEP in 1990 and every year thereafter. The GSOEP thus offers the unique possibility of observing the developments in self-employment and its consequences in the ex-GDR regions after 1989.

Table 7.2 summarizes the results from this natural experiment on self-employment creation. The sudden absence of restrictions on self-employment indeed created a steady and substantial rise in the ratio of self-employed people in the workforce. As early as 1990, the ratio had risen from 2.1 percent to 3.4 percent, and it grew to 7.3 percent in the years 1990–1992. Afterward, the ratio approached a stable 7.5 percent to 8.5 percent, converging to approximately the ratios of self-employment found in West Germany at this time. What were the effects on job

Table 7.2
Job satisfaction and self-employment in East Germany, 1990–2000. Dependent variable: job satisfaction [0–10]. Ordered logit regressions with robust standard errors (clustered for individuals), and OLS fixed-effects regression, respectively. Standard errors in parentheses. Significance levels: * $0.01 < p < 0.05$, ** $p < 0.01$. Source: Benz and Frey 2008a; based on German Socio-Economic Panel.

	1990 (ordered logit)	1991–2000 (ordered logit)	1990–2000 (fixed effects)
Self-employed	—	0.384** (0.118)	0.656** (0.116)
Self-employed before fall of Iron Curtain	0.708* (0.290)	—	—
Self-employed after fall of Iron Curtain	1.446** (0.432)	—	—
Employed	Reference group	Reference group	Reference group
Control variables[a]	Yes	Yes	Yes
Year dummies	No	Yes	Yes
Individual fixed effects	No	No	Yes
No. of observations	2,675	17,389	20,064
No. of individuals	2,675	3,754	4,254
χ^2/F value	310.4**	3.51**	4.14**

a. Control variables include personal income (ln), working time, working time squared, age, age squared, gender, education, occupation, industry, and life satisfaction 5 years ago (only for the year 1990).

satisfaction experienced by the people moving into self-employment? The results presented in table 7.2 indicate that they were substantial. The ordered logit regressions for the East German workforce presented contain the same variables as the one for West Germany in table 7.1 and are run separately for 1990 and the years afterward. For 1990, the group of self-employed is split into those already in self-employment before 1989, and those who became self-employed immediately after the fall of the Iron Curtain. In the following years, only the net effect for all self-employed people is presented. The effects of becoming self-employed can be illustrated most strikingly by those people who became self-employed in 1990. Their job satisfaction is considerably higher than that of employed East Germans at the time (the estimated coefficient of 1.340 amounts to approximately 1.5 index points on a job-satisfaction scale from 0 to 10). Note that this effect is not due to a generally low job satisfaction among the employed in East Germany working in still mainly socialist firms; in fact, the average job satisfaction in the East German workforce was as high in 1990 as in West Germany (7.20 vs. 7.25); it only dropped sharply afterward (probably because of the onset of privatizations and tougher economic conditions, such as rising unemployment). Moreover, it is not the case that people who were intrinsically more satisfied were more likely to become self-employed after the fall of the Iron Curtain. The 1990 regression includes a variable on the "life satisfaction five years ago"; it captures the answers of East Germans to the question of how they rated their general satisfaction with life in the former GDR in 1985. If only intrinsically satisfied (or dissatisfied) people had become self-employed after the fall of the Iron Curtain, the inclusion of this variable would lower the estimated coefficient on the "newly self-employed" to zero. Furthermore, table 7.2 indicates that, for the years 1991–2000, a positive and mostly significant coefficient of being self-employed is estimated; this shows that the large amount of people moving into self-employment indeed enjoyed higher subsequent job satisfaction than their counterparts who had remained employed over the period (irrespective of objective outcomes like income or working hours). The results also hold if a fixed-effects model for the whole period from 1990–2000 is estimated (which again only considers observed "changers" in the estimation of the self-employed coefficient).

In sum, the fixed-effects and natural-experiment approaches presented suggest that self-employed persons are indeed more satisfied with their jobs. Moreover, this can be attributed to procedural benefits from work, as the regressions control for important outcome aspects of work. Self-employment as a source of procedural utility is explored more fully in Benz and Frey 2008a and in Benz and Frey 2008b.

7.2   Voluntary Workers Are Happier

Sources of Individual Well-Being

The ancient philosophers debated whether helping other people increases happiness. While one viewpoint of the pursuit of happiness supports helping others as the way to higher well-being (Smith 1759), a second viewpoint argues that *Homo economicus* maximizes his or her utility by behaving selfishly. Those people are expected to be happier than people who are prepared to carry costs in order to help others. Ultimately, it is an empirical question whether sacrificing time and money to help others is rewarding and reflected in people's happiness.

To discriminate empirically between the two rival views on pro-social behavior and happiness, a measure of people's individual well-being is needed. As in other parts of this book, reported subjective well-being is used as a proxy measure.

Volunteering can positively affect individuals' well-being for various motivational reasons. The different channels can be roughly divided into two groups. Firstly, people's well-being increases because they enjoy helping others *per se*. The reward is internally due to an intrinsic motivation to care for others' welfare. For example, people care about recipients' utility and receive a "warm glow" from helping, or they benefit from intrinsic work enjoyment. Secondly, people volunteer purposely to receive a by-product of voluntary work. People do not enjoy volunteering per se but their utility increases because they receive an extrinsic reward from volunteering. For example, volunteering is undertaken as an investment either in human capital or in a social network.

This section (which is based on Meier and Stutzer 2008) reports empirical results on whether individuals who volunteer are more satisfied with their life than non-volunteers.[3] The empirical evidence on the relationship between volunteering and life satisfaction is based on the German Socio-Economic Panel (GSOEP) for the period 1985–1999. In addition to questions about their socio-economic situation, participants are asked about their life satisfaction and the extent of their voluntary work.

Even if the raw correlation confirmed that volunteers are more likely to report high subjective well-being than non-volunteers, causality is not established. Volunteering may not increase life satisfaction, but satisfied people are more likely to volunteer. Such causality problems are pervasive in the earlier literature.[4] The issue of causality is once more directly addressed by taking advantage of a natural experiment: the collapse of the GDR. Volunteering was still widespread in East Germany when the first wave of data of the GSOEP was collected (shortly after the fall of the Berlin Wall but before reunification). Because of the shock of reunification, a large portion of the infrastructure of volunteering (e.g., sports clubs associated with firms) collapsed and people randomly lost their opportunities for volunteering. Comparison of the change in subjective well-being of these people and of people from the control group who had no change in their volunteer status it possible to analyze whether volunteering is rewarding in terms of higher life satisfaction.

---

3. See also Meier 2006, 2007; Oberholzer-Gee 2007.
4. For an overview, see Wilson and Musick 1999.

Empirical Analysis

Volunteering is captured by the following question in the GSOEP: "Did you perform voluntary work?" Individuals can answer this question on a four-point scale (4 for "weekly," 3 for "monthly," 2 for "less frequently," 1 for "never"). In total, 23 percent of the German population volunteers in one form or another. These numbers on the extent of volunteering correspond to results from a study by Anheier and Salamon (1999). Fourteen percent of the population do voluntary work frequently ("weekly" or "monthly"); 86 percent do voluntary work less frequently or never ("less frequently" or "never"). Individuals' happiness or life satisfaction is measured with a single-item question: "How satisfied are you with your life, all things considered?" Responses range on a scale from 0 ("completely dissatisfied") to 10 ("completely satisfied").

Figure 7.1 presents the correlation between frequency of volunteering and life satisfaction for the pooled data set. The descriptive statistics show a sizable positive relationship between volunteering and life satisfaction. People who never volunteer report, on average, the lowest scores of life satisfaction. For each subsequent category, higher reported life satisfaction is measured. While people who never volunteer report an average life satisfaction of 6.93 points, people who volunteer weekly

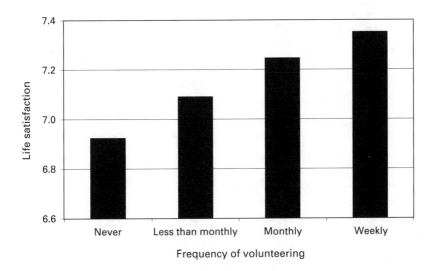

Figure 7.1
Volunteering and life satisfaction. Source: Meier and Stutzer 2008. Based on German Socio-Economic Panel, 1985–1999.

report an average life satisfaction of 7.35 points (i.e., 0.42 point higher ($p < 0.01$ in a t test). When people are divided into two groups, those who volunteer weekly or monthly report, on average, a life-satisfaction score of 7.30; those who volunteer less frequently or never, report, on average, a score of 6.95 ($p < 0.01$).

The raw correlation between volunteering and life-satisfaction scores does not take into account that a third factor—for example, the person's financial situation—may influence both the frequency of volunteering and the reported subjective well-being. To control for individual characteristics, a multivariate regression approach is used.

Table 7.3 presents the relationship between life-satisfaction scores (the dependent variable) and frequency of volunteering (the independent variable), controlling for a number of socio-economic and demographic variables. The four dummy variables from "never volunteering" to "weekly volunteering" capture the frequency of volunteering. Included in the reference group are individuals who never volunteer. The estimation of the first model is based on ordinary least squares, and the

Table 7.3
Life satisfaction and volunteering, Germany, 1985–1999. Dependent variable: satisfaction with life [0–10]. OLS regression with robust standard errors (clustered for individuals). t values in parentheses. Significance level: ** $p < 0.01$. Source: Meier and Stutzer 2008; based on German Socio-Economic Panel.

	Column 1	Column 2
Never volunteering	Reference group	Reference group
Less than monthly volunteering	0.079**	−0.014
	(4.00)	(−0.89)
Monthly volunteering	0.263**	0.026
	(9.75)	(1.19)
Weekly volunteering	0.295**	0.081**
	(10.02)	(3.48)
Control variables	Yes	Yes
Year dummies	Yes	Yes
Individual fixed effects	No	Yes
No. of observations	125,468	125,468
No. of individuals	22,016	22,016
F value	93.52**	79.26**

a. Control variables include net hourly wages (ln), wages not applicable, wages not available, working time, working time squared, working time not applicable, working time not available, household income (ln), household size square root, age, age squared, years of education (ln), marital status, dummy for children, employment status, dummy for Eastern Germany, and dummies for EU foreigners and non-EU foreigners.

estimated robust standard errors are corrected for repeated observations at the individual level over time. This model indicates that people who volunteer report higher life satisfaction. In particular, those who volunteer weekly or monthly report higher satisfaction scores. The differences are sizable and statistically highly significant. People who volunteer weekly report, on average, a subjective well-being score 0.30 point higher than somebody who never volunteers. People who volunteer monthly report, on average, a subjective well-being score 0.27 point higher than the reference group. This result is consistent with the hypothesis that volunteering increases utility. The regression of the first model, however, does not control for unobserved time-invariant individual differences. For example, more outgoing personalities are more likely to volunteer and to report high subjective well-being. The panel structure of the GSOEP allows for the control of such spurious correlations due to unobserved individual heterogeneity by using a model with individual fixed effects.

The second model reports the results of the ordinary-least-squares estimation with individual fixed effects. Although the effects become smaller, an individual who volunteers weekly still reports, on average, a subjective well-being score 0.08 point higher than an individual who never volunteers ($p < 0.01$). The effect remains robust if volunteering is measured using a dummy variable that equals 1 if an individual volunteers weekly or monthly, and 0 if an individual volunteers less often or never (not shown here). People who volunteer frequently report, on average, a life-satisfaction score 0.054 point higher ($p < 0.01$).

Dealing with Causality by Using a Natural Experiment

The question of causality is still open. The question of whether volunteers reporting higher life-satisfaction results from happiness through helping others or from happiness having led to volunteering cannot be answered based on the results of the fixed-effects estimations. As in the study on self-employment reported in section 7.1, the question of causality is addressed by analyzing a situation where, because of an exogenous shock, people randomly lose the possibility of volunteering. If they report, *ceteris paribus*, lower life satisfaction afterward, the effect is more likely to be causal. If there is no change in subjective well-being, previous findings reflect to a large extent third factors and reverse causality.

The German reunion constitutes an ideal natural experiment, which exogenously changed the situation for many volunteers in the former

GDR. After the breakdown of the GDR, a large proportion of the infra-structure for volunteering collapsed. In East Germany, where volun-teering was widespread, many opportunities were linked with the old structures, e.g. sports clubs connected with nationally owned companies. After reunification, these structures disappeared, and many volunteers were "forced" to stop volunteering. The proportion of respondents to the GSOEP in East Germany who indicated weekly or monthly voluntary work decreased by 8 percentage points. This can be seen as an exogenous and dramatic reduction in voluntary work. What has been the effect of this exogenous shock on the subjective well-being of volunteers?

After reunification, average life satisfaction decreased in East Germany (Frijters, Haisken-DeNew, and Shields 2003). If volunteering influences well-being positively, the decrease of life satisfaction is expected to be greater for people who lost their opportunity for volunteering because of the collapse of the volunteer infrastructure. Figure 7.2 compares the life satisfaction of the same East Germans in 1990 and in 1992, depend-ing on their volunteer status. For individuals who had to stop volun-teering ("stop volunteer"), life satisfaction decreases substantially. While the life satisfaction of people who did not change their volunteer status ("always volunteer" or "never volunteer") decreases by 0.53 point, the life satisfaction of people who had to stop volunteering decreases by 0.72

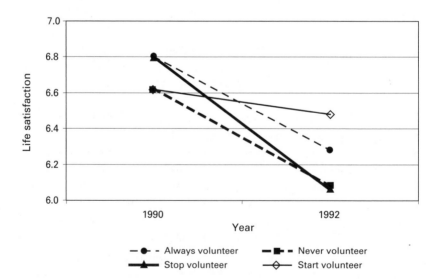

Figure 7.2
Loss of volunteer work and decrease in life satisfaction. Source: Meier and Stutzer 2008. Based on German Socio-Economic Panel, 1990–1992.

point. The difference of −0.19 point is statistically significant ($p < 0.10$). The life satisfaction of people who volunteered frequently in 1990 drops from the high level experienced by those who volunteer down to the level that is reported by non-volunteers. This result supports the causal interpretation that volunteering positively affects life satisfaction.

The simple difference-in-difference analysis nears causal inference. Nevertheless, there are at least two possible objections to the interpretation of the findings:

• Other factors might affect both voluntary work and life satisfaction. For example, people who become unemployed are less likely to volunteer, and at the same time report lower life satisfaction. The result, showing that people become less happy if randomly forced to stop volunteering is, however, supported in a multivariate regression which includes individual fixed effects and controls for a number of socioeconomic and demographic variables: people who lost their volunteer opportunities report a drop in life satisfaction greater by 0.23 point than do people who did not change their volunteer status ($p < 0.05$). This result supports the causal interpretation that life satisfaction is influenced positively by volunteering and so refutes the first objection.

• Another interpretation of the effect could speculate whether people who were engaged in voluntary work in the GDR were associated with the old political system. After the collapse of the GDR, they lost not only their voluntary work, but also, and primarily, their connection with the regime. It can be hypothesized that this would have resulted in a loss of status and future perspectives. The empirical validity of this interpretation is analyzed by taking into account the answer to a question in 1990 about satisfaction with the GDR. "The following questions deal with the situation in the GDR: All in all, how satisfied or dissatisfied are you with democracy as it exists in the GDR today?" People answered on a four-point scale (1 = very satisfied, 2 = satisfied, 3 = dissatisfied, 4 = very dissatisfied). The empirical analysis shows that the effect on life satisfaction of ceasing to volunteer is the same for people who are satisfied (i.e., who answered 1 or 2) with democracy in the GDR (−0.74 point) and for people who are dissatisfied (i.e., who answered 3 or 4) with the situation (−0.70 point). This result does not support the interpretation that people who were friendly to the regime lost the most when volunteering opportunities decreased at the time of reunion.

The breakdown of the GDR constitutes a unique natural experiment in analyzing the causal effect of volunteering on people's utility.

The results indicate that volunteering does increase happiness. The results are robust when controlling for other factors influencing life satisfaction, such as individual fixed effects, unemployment status, or other spare-time activities (Meier and Stutzer 2008).

In sum, volunteering is rewarding for volunteers in terms of higher life satisfaction. Relying on the collapse of the GDR as a natural experiment, this section summarizes results which show that, causally, volunteering makes people happy. Why, then, do not more people volunteer to increase their life satisfaction? Why do people seemingly fail to increase their utility by failing to engage in volunteering? People make mistakes in predicting utility from activities they experience in the future asymmetrically (i.e., they underestimate the benefits from intrinsic tasks, such as volunteering, and overestimate the benefit from extrinsic tasks, e.g. earning additional money from working overtime). Whether this leads to an underprovision of voluntary work—even from an individual standpoint—should be a subject of future research.

8   Marriage and Happiness

8.1   Theories of Marriage

Economic models of marriage focus on specialization and the division of labor. Becker's seminal work on the economics of marriage (1973, 1974a) is based on the gains married people acquire from household production and specialization of labor for different tasks.[1] The possibility of specialization with respect to the tasks in marriage is seen to offer substantial opportunities to increase the well-being of both partners. Sociological theories focus on spouses' joint consumption of household public goods, or on reciprocity and social equality in homogamous relationships. Homogamy describes the tendency for "like to marry like." People of similar age, race, religion, nationality, education, attitudes, and numerous other traits tend to a greater degree to marry one another than would be found by chance (Hughes et al. 1999). The tendency for "like to marry like" facilitates compatibility of spouses' basic values and beliefs. Becker's model predicts mating to be negatively assorted on (shadow) wages and, in the case of homogamous relationships, positively assorted on education. To study the validity of the assumption underlying these two sets of models, data on subjective well-being can be studied to provide systematic evidence on who benefits more and who benefits less from marriage. This chapter draws on research more fully described in Stutzer and Frey 2006.

In marriage, people engage in a long-term relationship with a strong commitment to a mutually rewarding exchange. The spouse expects some benefits from the partner's expressed love, gratitude and recognition, as well as from security and material rewards. This is summarized in the protection perspective of marriage. From this perspective of marriage's

---

1. For a survey, see Pollack 2002.

protective effects, economists have studied its financial benefits in particular. Marriage provides basic insurance against adverse life events and allows gains from economies of scale and specialization within the family (Becker 1981). With specialization, one of the spouses has advantageous conditions for human capital accumulation in tasks demanded on the labor market. It is reflected in married people's earning higher incomes than single people, *ceteris paribus* (Chun and Lee 2001).

Increased earnings are themselves surpassed by a wide range of benefits from marriage, as studied in psychology, sociology and epidemiology. When compared with single people, married people have better physical and psychic health (e.g., less substance abuse and less depression), and live considerably longer (Gardner and Oswald 2004). Sociology emphasizes the advantages of homogamous relationships.[2]

Recently there has been increasing interest in the effect of marriage on people's happiness. In a large number of studies covering different countries and time periods, it has been found that marriage goes hand in hand with higher levels of happiness (Diener et al. 2000; Stack and Eshleman 1998; Coombs 1991; Myers 1999). Married persons report greater subjective well-being than persons who have never been married or have been divorced, separated, or widowed. The possibility of reverse causation is discussed and empirically studied in Mastekaasa 1992 and in Stutzer and Frey 2006.

8.2   Empirical Analysis

Marriage Increases Happiness

The two claims about the major sources of increased well-being in marriage are directly tested with data on reported satisfaction with life. As in some of the previous chapters, we use data from the German Socio-Economic Panel. We restrict our analysis to people who married during the 17 years of the sampling period, and observe their well-being at the approximate time of marriage. Figure 8.1 shows average life satisfaction in the years before and after marriage, based on 21,809 observations for 1,991 people in Germany between 1984 and 2000. Average scores are calculated after taking into account respondents' sex, age, education level, parenthood,

---

2. For reviews of the evidence for the effects on health, see Burman and Margolin 1992; Ross et al. 1990. For additional survey evidence on income, mortality, children's achievements, and sexual satisfaction, see Waite and Gallagher 2000. For a survey that focuses on longitudinal evidence, see Wilson and Oswald 2005.

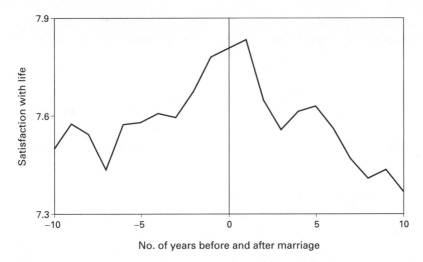

Figure 8.1
Life satisfaction in relation to marriage. Graph represents pattern of well-being after taking into account respondents' sex, age, education level, parenthood, household income, household size, relation to the head of the household, labor-market status, place of residence, and citizenship. Source: Stutzer and Frey 2006. Data from GSOEP.

household income, household size, relation to the head of the household, labor-market status, place of residence, and citizenship status.

Figure 8.1 shows a noticeable pattern: as the year of marriage approaches, people report higher satisfaction scores on average. In contrast, the average reported satisfaction with life decreases after marriage.

Several concepts may explain this pattern. Some psychologists suggest that marital transitions cause short-term changes in subjective well-being (Johnson and Wu 2002). Others take it as evidence of adaptation (Lucas et al. 2003). Adaptation in the marriage context means that people become accustomed to the pleasant (and unpleasant) stimuli they receive from living with a partner in a close relationship; after some time, they experience more or less their base-line level of subjective well-being. It is difficult to assess whether this adaptation is truly hedonic, or whether married people start using a different scale (satisfaction treadmill) for what they consider a satisfying life. There is also an explanation according to selection for the pattern. Many people might marry only if they expect to experience a rewarding relationship in the future. Their predictions of their future well-being as spouses are based on their current well-being. Therefore, the last year before marriage becomes the last year in which life satisfaction increases, because the couples experience a particularly happy time in their relationship at this time.

This chapter concentrates on the large changes in life satisfaction for the newly married. In the first year after marriage, the standard deviation of reported satisfaction with life is 1.60 and the mean is 7.64. In the second year, the standard deviation is 1.59 and the mean is 7.43 (on a scale from 0 for "completely dissatisfied" and 10 for "completely satisfied"). These numbers indicate large changes in how spouses feel in their lives as newly-wed couples. Studies look at the possibility of systematic differences for some sub-groups identified in theories of the marriage market.

The Potential for Specialization

One of the main predictions of Becker's theory of marriage is that the gain from marriage is positively related to couples' relative difference in wage rates (1974a, p. 11). The reason is that a large relative difference in wage rates makes specialization in running the household or participation in the labor market more beneficial.

The hypothesis is analyzed graphically in figure 8.2. The sample is divided into two groups of couples: one group, on average, with above-median relative difference and one group with below-median relative

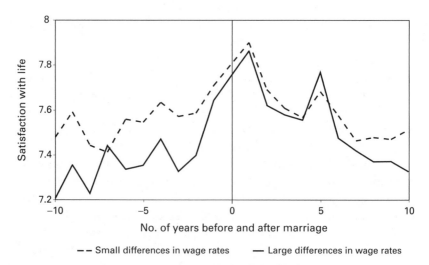

Figure 8.2
Differences in (shadow) wage rate between spouses and its effect on life satisfaction in relation to marriage. Graph represents pattern of well-being after taking into account respondents' sex, age, parenthood, household size, relation to the head of the household, labor-market status, place of residence, and citizenship. Source: Stutzer and Frey 2006. Data from GSOEP.

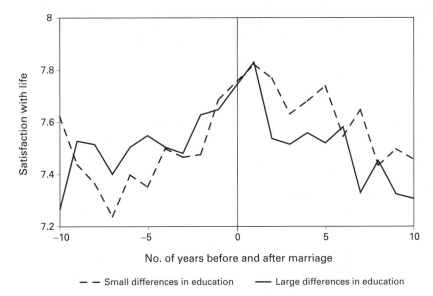

Figure 8.3   Differences in level of education between spouses and effect on life satisfaction in relation to marriage. Graph represents pattern of well-being after taking into account respondents' sex, age, education level, parenthood, household income, household size, relation to the head of the household, labor-market status, place of residence, and citizenship. Source: Stutzer and Frey 2006. Data from GSOEP

difference in wage rates. The averages presented are estimated *ceteris paribus*. However, not all the control variables mentioned for figure 8.1 are included. Since specialization is expected to provide benefits through increased household production, household income (as well as its close proxy education level) is not controlled for.

Figure 8.2 shows that there are no systematic differences in subjective well-being for the two groups in the years after marriage. Before marriage, however, individuals who will be in marriages with large differences in relative wage rates are less happy on average than those with small differences. This indicates that couples with large differences in relative wage rates benefit more from marriage. This is a finding that supports one of the main predictions in Becker's model based on the gains from specialization.

Benefits for Homogamous Couples

The differences between marriage partners in their level of education are considered, and measured by the number of years of schooling. It is hypothesized that couples with small differences in the level of education gain more from marriage than those with large differences.

Figure 8.3 presents the result of a graphical analysis, applying the same test strategy as the one previously used for specialization. Now the whole set of control variables, as in figure 8.1, is included. For the years before marriage, there are no systematic differences in the well-being of people who become partners in marriages with small and large differences in education. However, after marriage, couples with differences in education below the median report on average higher satisfaction with life. For the first seven years, the joint statistical significance of the differences is higher than 99 percent. This finding supports the hypothesis that couples with similar educational background benefit more from marriage.

Conclusions

Basic assumptions about the gains from marriage or protection can be directly studied using data on subjective well-being. The specialization hypothesis emphasized in economics is supported. When their life satisfaction before marriage is compared, couples with large relative wage differences (and consequently a high potential gain from specialization) benefit more from marrying than couples with small relative wage differences. However, the finding indicates that there are no systematic differences between the two groups after seven years of marriage. Our results are in line with theories emphasizing the importance of similarities between partners. Similar or homogamous partners are expected to share values and beliefs to facilitate a supportive relationship. Spouses with small differences in their level of education stand to gain on average more satisfaction from marriage than spouses with large differences.

What happens when a marriage is dissolved? The course of an individual's well-being pursues a similar course to that in marriage—with a negative sign (Gardner and Oswald 2006). Divorce is traumatic in the short run; the happiness of the former couple falls drastically, and it affects men and women equally. Nevertheless, two years after the marital breakdown, both are on average significantly better off than two years before the breakdown. In this sense, divorce is beneficial. Somewhat surprisingly, it does not seem to matter whether a person remarries quickly after divorce, and whether there are any dependent children.

Watching Television

Europeans spend, on average, 3 hours and 30 minutes per day watching television; Americans spend as much as 4 hours and 50 minutes per day (IP International Marketing Committee 2004). In many countries nowadays, watching television occupies almost as much time as working. Over their entire life (including youth and old age), many people spend more time in front of their TV than doing paid work. They must enjoy this entirely voluntary and freely chosen activity, or else they would not engage in it. According to the standard neoclassical economic theory of revealed preference, people are assumed to know best what provides them with utility and are free to choose the amount of television consumption they prefer. Because people watch so much television, it provides them with considerable utility.

However, recent developments (particularly in economics and psychology) cast doubt on this conclusion. The theory of revealed preference has been questioned, most prominently by Sen (1982, 1995). In general, it is not possible to infer the utility produced by observing behavior, because individuals do not always act in their own best interest. Many anomalies and biases in behavior have been identified (see e.g. Thaler 1992), and these undermine the direct link between observed behavior and utility gained. Individuals may, for example, systematically mispredict the utility derived from future consumption. (See chapter 11.) We argue here that people may also be subject to habits they do not fully control. They may often consume more of some goods, such as drugs, alcohol, or tobacco, than is beneficial for them. They have a self-control problem (Schelling 1984). As Gruber and Mullainathan (2005) show empirically, smokers consider themselves better off when smoking is restricted by a tax. This chapter puts forth the view that television viewing is another case where the consumption decisions made by individuals are systematically distorted according to their own evaluations. They have a self-control problem, which is induced mainly by television's offer of immediate benefits at very low immediate costs; many costs are only experienced in the future. Therefore, the extent of television viewing does not generally maximize utility, and on average people become less happy.[1]

Data on subjective well-being are used to study whether people make systematic mistakes in choosing how much time to devote to television viewing. If that is indeed the case, there will be a negative correlation between the extent of television viewing and life satisfaction, even after controlling for a large number of covariates of individual well-being. However, a negative correlation between television consumption and subjective well-being could well be a result of reverse causation: unhappy people may well watch more television than happy people. If television viewing serves as a substitute act (e.g., for human relationships or more active forms of leisure for the lonely and bored) and involves negative long-term consequences for well-being, the negative correlation might even be the result of a self-enforcing circle. These causality issues cannot be resolved with an extensive set of control variables in a multiple regression analysis or with panel data. Instead, it would be advisable to study large-scale, externally influenced changes in people's opportunities for watching television. To our knowledge, suitable data, such as a natural experiment, do not exist; instead, we look at the question of whether the utility costs of extensive television consumption depend on the opportunity cost of time. This offers indirect evidence of the direction of causality. Is it mainly people with significant opportunity costs of time who regret how much time they spend watching television? We argue that people with flexible working hours, who can freely transfer time between leisure and work, primarily suffer from their self-control problem. In contrast, people with low opportunity costs of time, such as retired or unemployed people or individuals with fixed working hours, are little burdened by their lack of will power. They experience no significant utility loss, therefore, even if they spend many hours watching television.

Section 9.1 develops the basic testable hypothesis of television overconsumption. Section 9.2 reviews the existing literature on the link between television viewing and subjective well-being. Section 9.3 presents the data and gives the results of the econometric estimates.

---

1. See Frey, Benesch, and Stutzer 2007; Benesch, Frey, and Stutzer 2006.

9.1   Overconsumption of Television

Television lends itself to overconsumption in the sense that individuals later regret that they devoted so much time to viewing. However, it seems difficult to overcome this weakness of will: although many people are dissatisfied with their own past behavior, they nevertheless repeatedly devote more time to watching television than is good for them according to their own evaluation. They have a self-control problem. This is the basic claim we want to address empirically.

That television lends itself to overconsumption is due mainly to the immediate benefits and the negligible immediate marginal cost of engaging in this activity. One merely pushes a button. In contrast with going to the cinema or the theater, or participating in any outdoor activity, there is no need to be appropriately dressed before leaving home, to buy a ticket, or to reserve a seat in advance. Television viewing does not require any special physical or cognitive abilities (Kubey and Csikszentmihalyi 1990). Unlike other leisure activities, television viewing need not be coordinated with other individuals. It is quite possible to sit alone in front of a television, whereas other leisure activities (such as tennis or golf) require a partner with similar time availability and similar preferences. In comparison with other leisure activities, television viewing consequently has an exceedingly low or nonexistent entry barrier. At the same time, it offers entertainment value and is considered to be one of the best ways of reducing stress. Many of the costs resulting from such consumption behavior are not experienced immediately. The negative effects of insufficient sleep, for example, only arise the next day, and the consequences of underinvestment in social contacts, education, or career take much longer to appear. These characteristics of the consumption good induce many individuals to fall prey to excessive television viewing.

There is some anecdotal evidence that individuals may have self-control problems with regard to their television viewing. Forty percent of US adults and 70 percent of US teenagers admit that they watch too much television (Kubey and Czikszentmihalyi 2002). They crave television and admit being addicted to it (McIlwraith 1998; Kubey and Czikszentmihalyi 2002). Another interesting observation is that short- and long-term evaluations of television consumption tend to diverge. Robinson and Godbey (1999: p. 299) put it this way: "We may not enjoy television in general, but the programs we saw last night were pretty good." Some individuals abstain completely from watching television, because they know that they would not be able to control it. They cancel their cable subscription, lock their TV away in a closet, or place an uncomfortable chair in front of it. Such self-control mechanisms are not necessary for time-consistent individuals. To lower the utility or raise the cost of an undesired alternative would be irrelevant and unnecessary.

In general, self-control problems and time-inconsistent preferences have been confirmed in many laboratory experiments,[2] and the theory[3] has been applied to many issues. Recently, empirical evidence from the field has been presented for saving decisions (Angeletos 2001), for food consumption (Cutler et al. 2003; Shapiro 2005), for job searches (DellaVigna and Paserman 2005), for labor supply (Fang and Silverman 2007), and for health-club visits (DellaVigna and Malmendier 2006).

9.2 Literature

In view of the huge amount of time devoted to watching television, there are surprisingly few studies in economics devoted to this issue. However, close to economics is the "uses-and-gratifications" approach (Rubin 2002), which studies how individuals deal with the media. Much research has been devoted to identifying the various functions television fulfils for actual and potential viewers. It is assumed that they compare the utility derived from the functions and maximize it subject to constraints. This approach, though, has so far led to few empirically testable propositions.

More standard media economics analyzes how preferences for specific media contents and time budgets determine demand. Some studies, especially in the European tradition (Heinrich 1994; Kiefer 2003), take the information provided by television as a "merit good" and discuss the legitimacy of government intervention in the media market. Schröder (1997) and Kiefer (2001) consider the harmful effects of television consumption and compare it to smoking. They propose regulations in the media market as a self-control mechanism at the social level.

The household production approach (Becker 1965) studies the demands for leisure and recreation. However, in contrast with the enormous importance of television viewing as a leisure activity, only a few studies seek to analyze the determinants of its demand and the utility derived. Two approaches can be distinguished.

---

2. For an overview, see Frederick et al. 2002.
3. See, e.g., Laibson 1997 and O'Donoghue and Rabin 1999.

Short-Run Aspects

"Activity enjoyment ratings" capture instant aspects of television viewing. In the context of time-use studies, individuals are asked to rate television viewing in comparison with other leisure activities. In the United States in 1985, television viewing proved to be valued somewhat higher than the average enjoyment of 7 derived from other activities, with its rating of 7.8 on a scale from 0 to 10. Nevertheless, it ranks lower than most other activities undertaken in leisure time (Robinson and Godbey 1999, p. 243). On the index of positive affect of 900 Texan women constructed by Kahneman and co-workers (2004b), television ranks at 4.2 (on a scale from 0 to 6), roughly in the middle of all activities. At 2.2 hours per week, it is one of the most time-consuming activities of these women.

With the "experience sampling method," participants using a beeper or a hand-held computer are randomly asked how they feel at a particular moment in time. On the affect scale, comprising cheerfulness, friendliness, happiness, and sociability, television viewing is located in the lower part of the scale and can hardly be distinguished from reading, working, hobbies, and idling. On the other hand, eating, social contacts, sports, and sex are clearly ranked more highly (Kubey and Csikszentmihalyi 1990). This short-run evaluation captures the momentary affect, but it is difficult to determine the utility individuals would have derived had they done something else.

General Satisfaction with Television

Long-run aspects of the utility derived from television consumption are captured in surveys on the general satisfaction with television viewing (not related to a specific moment or time period devoted to it). In a survey undertaken in the United States in 1975, television viewing was given an average rating of 5.9 points on an enjoyment scale ranging from 0 to 10. It ranked considerably behind most other leisure activities and below the average of 6.8 of all rated activities. In 1995, television viewing at 4.8 points ranked even lower when compared with all other leisure pursuits. Surprisingly, women rated it even below cleaning (Robinson and Godbey 1999, pp. 243 and 250). But such surveys are faced with the problem that television viewing is associated with a negative image ("couch potato"), and there is a general consensus that most programs are stupid. For that reason, the answers given may reflect what is taken to be socially desirable. It should be noted that surveys on *general* life satisfaction (as used in our study) are not affected by this bias.

Several studies relate television viewing with subjective well-being. In a 1979 study of roughly 3,000 Americans (Morgan 1984), people who watched a lot of television considered their life more "lousy" on an index comprising the aspects lonely, boring, depressing, unsatisfying, uneventful, and unhappy; they considered their life less "great" on an index comprising the aspects interesting, active, meaningful, fun, fulfilling, stimulating, and exciting, in comparison with people watching less television. In a random survey of 1,000 West Germans, there is also a negative correlation between the duration of television viewing and general life satisfaction, controlling for size of household, education, and age. Espe and Seiwert (1987) postulate a causal influence of dissatisfaction with life on television consumption but offer no corresponding evidence. In another study for Germany, based on the German Socio-Economic Panel, a curvilinear relationship is found between number of hours spent watching television and life satisfaction (Jegen and Frey 2004). Moderate television consumption is related to higher life satisfaction than if there were no consumption or extensive consumption. However, on the basis of panel information, short-term individual variation in television consumption is not correlated with overall life satisfaction in an economically relevant manner. Television viewing has also been found to have a negative effect on life satisfaction because of reduced time spent in relational activities (Bruni and Stanca 2007), increasing materialism (Sirgy et al. 1998), reduced subjectively perceived relative income, and increasing income aspirations (Layard 2005; Bruni and Stanca 2006).

9.3   Results

Data

To empirically address the hypothesis on television overconsumption, the first wave of the European Social Survey (ESS) is used. The ESS was carried out in 22 European countries in 2002 and 2003. In each country, approximately 1,200–3,000 people were interviewed, resulting in a usable sample of 42,021 observations.

In addition to life satisfaction and television viewing time, the ESS includes a large number of socio-demographic characteristics. Control variables to be used are household income (adjusted for comparative price level at current US prices), gender, age, marital status, employment status, education, working time, nationality, and type of location.

As the dependent variable we use the response to the question "All things considered, how satisfied are you with your life as a whole nowadays?" Answers are given on a scale ranging from 0 ("extremely dissatisfied") to 10 ("extremely satisfied"). The average life satisfaction amounts to 7.0 (standard deviation 2.7). This average varies considerably between countries, and ranges from 5.6 in Hungary to 8.4 in Denmark. To control for unobserved "cultural" differences, country fixed effects are included in the regression analysis.

Television consumption is captured by the single question "On an average weekday, how much time do you spend watching television?" Answers are given in eight categories that range from "no time at all" to "more than 3 hours." Approximately 3 percent of respondents don't watch any television at all, whereas over 20 percent spend more than 3 hours per day in front of their television (figure 9.1). This percentage varies considerably between countries. Whereas only about 10 percent of respondents in Switzerland watch more than 3 hours of television per day, more than 38 percent do so in Greece.

Happiness Function

On the basis of on the data described, a microeconomic happiness function is specified. An individual's life satisfaction depends on his or her television consumption and on personal characteristics, as well as on country-specific effects.

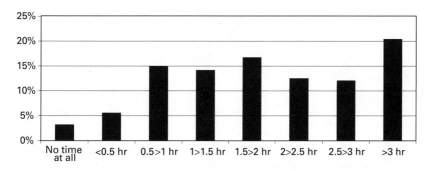

Figure 9.1
Reported television consumption in 22 European countries, 2002–2003. Source: Frey, Benesch, and Stutzer 2007. Based on European Social Survey.

Because the extent of television consumption is captured in a categorical variable with an open-ended category for those who spend much time on television viewing, television consumption cannot be included as a continuous variable. Instead, we include dummy variables in the regression equation. Those who watch television less than half an hour per day form the reference group, because those who don't watch television at all probably represent a special selection of individuals. The six categories of people who watch more than half an hour of television a day are combined into three categories.

Effects of Television on Happiness

Table 9.1 reports the partial correlation between television consumption and reported life satisfaction. To avoid overloading the table, the regression coefficients for the control variables are not explicitly shown. An ordinary least-squares estimator is applied. In view of the categorical nature of the dependent variable, an ordered probit is appropriate. The similarities in the relative size of the coefficients indicate that the least-squares estimator delivers a satisfactory approximation of the partial correlation. Therefore, the least-squares results are discussed.

Table 9.1
Television consumption and life satisfaction. Dependent variable: life satisfaction [0–10]. Ordinary least-squares estimates. Significance levels: * $0.05 > p > 0.01$, ** $p < 0.01$. Source: Frey, Benesch, and Stutzer 2007; based on European Social Survey (Wave1) and World Development Indicators.

	OLS coefficient	t value
No TV at all	−0.110	−1.56
< 0.5 hr TV	Reference group	
0.5–1.5 hr TV	−0.101*	−2.18
> 1.5–2.5 hr TV	−0.101*	−2.14
> 2.5 hr TV	−0.183**	−3.84
Control variables[a]	Yes	
Country fixed effects	Yes	
Observations	42,021	
R^2	0.18	

a. Control variables include indicators for working hours, household income, age, gender, citizenship, marital status, children, education, employment status, type of community, and household size.

People who view television for less than half an hour per day are more satisfied with their lives, *ceteris paribus*, than people who choose any other level of television consumption. Those who view television for anything between half an hour and 2.5 hours have average reported life satisfaction at approximately 0.10 point lower than those in the reference group of people who view it for less than half an hour. The estimated effect is even larger for people who view it for more than 2.5 hours a day. On average, they report life satisfaction 0.18 point lower than people in the reference group. All the differences are statistically significantly different from zero, at least at the 95 percent level. The general finding is thus consistent with the basic hypothesis that extensive television viewing makes people worse off, because it indicates overconsumption due to a self-control problem.

The partial correlation cannot easily be explained as spurious and simply reflecting some specific individual characteristics of people who spend a lot of time in front of the television. A large set of sociodemographic characteristics is taken into consideration which is systematically related to reported life satisfaction, and may also be related to television consumption. These characteristics include, for example, respondents' age, sex, nationality, marital status, household income, level of education, and employment status.

So far, the negative partial correlation between television consumption and subjective well-being has been interpreted in terms of overconsumption leading to a lower utility level. However, the partial correlation could well be the result of reverse causation. It is quite plausible that unhappy people watch more television than happy ones. The problem can be attenuated to a certain extent by controlling for as many situational factors as possible in the regression equation. However, it can neither be resolved with an extensive set of control variables in a multiple regression analysis nor with panel data. Ideally, one would need information about exogenous changes in the opportunities for television consumption, e.g. due to satellite television's being shut down or due to television's being introduced in a new place because of technical innovation. We are not aware of any such event that could be connected to survey data on reported subjective well-being.

For further analysis of the effect of television consumption on subjective well-being and for shedding light on the issue of causality, an additional hypothesis is formulated that exploits the heterogeneity in the expected effect of television overconsumption for different groups of people.

Opportunity Costs of Time and Watching Television

So far, it has been assumed that self-control problems in television consumption affect everybody alike. It is now proposed that individuals with high opportunity costs of time can in particular use time more profitably than by viewing television. This includes, for instance, the self-employed (e.g., craftsmen, lawyers, architects, or artists) or individuals in high positions (e.g., managers, top bureaucrats, or politicians), who can freely transfer time from leisure to work. For this group of individuals, the self-control problem of watching too much television generates considerable costs. Their utility is lower because of their inability to fully control themselves. In contrast, individuals with low opportunity costs of time suffer little, if any, disutility when they fail to view the amount of television they would consider optimal for themselves. Accordingly, it is hypothesized that television consumption significantly lowers the life satisfaction of individuals with high opportunity costs of time, whereas it has no discernible effect on the life satisfaction of individuals with low opportunity costs of time.

Identifying the Opportunity Costs

Opportunity costs of time cannot be measured directly in our data. Therefore, we use different indicators to distinguish between individuals with high and low opportunity costs of time:

• People who can freely transfer time between work and leisure tend to have higher (monetary) opportunity costs of time in comparison with people who work fixed hours. Hence, respondents are assigned to the two groups according to the flexibility of their working hours. Answers to "Please say how much the management at your work allows you to be flexible in your working hours" are given on a scale ranging from 0 ("I have no influence") to 10 ("I have complete control"). Respondents who indicate a value between 0 and 5 form the group with low opportunity costs of time, and those who give an answer between 6 and 10 form the other group. Only individuals who are employed (at least part-time) are included in these sub-samples.

• As a second indicator, employment status and profession are used. Retirees and unemployed people tend to have lots of free time and therefore form the group with low opportunity costs of time. Working people, especially those who are self-employed and those in high positions and professions (legislators, senior officials, managers, and professionals according to ISCO-88 classification) are assigned to the group with high opportunity costs of time.

Results

Table 9.2 reports the results of linear regression estimates for the different groups according to the different criteria. Columns 1 and 2 show the estimation results for sub-samples with high and low opportunity costs of time (according to flexibility of working hours). Individuals in the group with high opportunity costs of time who watch more television than the reference group report lower life satisfaction, *ceteris paribus*. The effects are considerable. The subjective well-being of viewers who watch television for half an hour or more per day is between 0.33 and 0.38 point lower than that of light viewers who spend less than half an hour per day watching television. The effects are statistically significant at the 99 percent level. In contrast, for people with low opportunity costs of time, the coefficients of all television-viewing categories are smaller (between 0.04 and 0.14) and not statistically significant.

A similar picture emerges when comparing the self-employed, managers, senior officials, legislators, and professionals against retirees and unemployed persons (columns 3 and 4 in table 9.2). Coefficients in the high opportunity costs of time sub-sample are considerable in size. The average life satisfaction of people who view television for more than 1.5 hour per day is between 0.23 and 0.39 point lower than that of people who view it for less than half an hour per day. These effects are statistically significant at the 95–99 percent level. In contrast, for the group with low opportunity costs of time, no correlation is visible between television consumption and reported life satisfaction. The coefficients are very small and not statistically significant. The coefficient for watching television for 0.5–1.5 hour is not statistically significant in either group.

Of course, the questions still arise as to whether the negative correlation for people with high opportunity costs of time is a causal relationship and, if so, in which direction the causality goes. However, it is difficult to understand why dissatisfied people with high opportunity costs of time resort to television viewing, while dissatisfied people with low opportunity costs of time do not.

Table 9.2
Television consumption and life satisfaction: opportunity costs of time. Dependent variable: Life satisfaction [0–10]. Ordinary least-squares estimations, t values in brackets. Group 1 (column 2) contains employed respondents with flexibility of working hours of 6 and higher on a scale from 0 to 10 and group 2 (column 3) of 5 and lower. Group 3 (column 4) contains the self-employed, as well as managers, senior officials, legislators, professionals (according to ISCO-88 classification), and group 4 (column 5) contains retirees and the unemployed. Significance levels: * $0.05 > p > 0.01$, ** $p < 0.01$. Source: Frey, Benesch, and Stutzer 2007; based on European Social Survey (Wave 1) and World Development Indicators.

	Flexibility of working hours as distinction criteria		Employment status / profession as distinction criteria	
	Group with high opportunity costs of time	Group with low opportunity costs of time	Group with high opportunity costs of time	Group with low opportunity costs of time
No TV at all	−0.355*	0.056	−0.238	−0.251
	(−2.33)	(0.33)	(−1.58)	(−1.24)
< 0.5 hr TV	Reference group	Reference group	Reference group	Reference group
0.5–1.5 hr TV	−0.328**	−0.072	−0.074	−0.105
	(−3.59)	(−0.69)	(−0.80)	(−0.70)
> 1.5–2.5 hr TV	−0.339**	−0.041	−0.229*	0.052
	(−3.62)	(−0.38)	(−2.38)	(0.35)
> 2.5 hr TV	−0.377**	−0.140	−0.389**	−0.012
	(−3.78)	(−1.28)	(−3.76)	(−0.08)
Control variables[a]	Yes	Yes	Yes	Yes
Country fixed effects	Yes	Yes	Yes	Yes
Constant	6.203**	5.410**	6.203**	6.919**
	(12.39)	(10.45)	(10.94)	(11.93)
Observations	6,460	7,062	5,950	8,974
R^2	0.14	0.15	0.16	0.22

a. Control variables include indicators for working hours, household income, age, gender, citizenship, marital status, children, education, employment status, type of community, and household size.

Conclusions

This chapter discusses the question of whether long hours of television viewing indicate imperfect self-control, which reduces well-being. On average, *ceteris paribus*, people who spend a lot of time watching television do indeed report lower life satisfaction. This negative effect is much larger for people with high opportunity costs of time than for those with low opportunity costs of time.

The observed correlations are strong and do not disappear when a large set of individual characteristics are controlled for. Overall, the empirical results show that individuals have systematically imperfect foresight and control over their own behavior in a major present-day human activity. The utility gained is lower than what could be achieved. Rational choice explains a large fraction of what people do. Television consumption might, however, pose a challenge, perhaps even a particularly relevant one, because watching TV is one of the most time-consuming activities of people today. Hardly anyone would deny that watching TV provides pleasure, at least some of the time, and that it is an important source of information. Yet, as our research suggests, some people are not able to optimally trade off the benefits and the (future) costs associated with it.

10   Procedural Utility

10.1   The Concept

Procedural utility means that people also value the conditions and processes that lead to outcomes, rather than only the outcomes (Frey, Benz, and Stutzer 2004; Benz 2005, 2007). Procedural utility represents a completely different approach to human well-being from the standard approach applied in economics. The economic concept of utility as generally applied today is outcome-oriented: individual utility is seen as a result of benefits and costs associated with instrumental outcomes. In contrast, procedural utility refers to the non-instrumental pleasures and displeasures of processes. The procedural view is also important for another reason: happiness is difficult, if not wholly impossible, to attain directly. Happiness is more a side product of a "good life," which means that the process matters and not the outcome.

Procedural utility is an important determinant of human well-being that should be incorporated more widely and usefully into economic theory and empirical research. So far, this approach has been largely neglected, although concepts similar to procedural utility have a long history in other social sciences.

This chapter outlines three building blocks of a concept of procedural utility and offers thoughts on how procedural utility can be fruitfully integrated into the existing economic approach. It also reviews evidence from a broad range of social sciences and other areas to show that procedural utility is a relevant concept for economics. Finally, it argues that procedural utility is of great relevance to policy.

Outcome Utility in Standard Economics

Economic analysis has focused on instrumental outcomes ever since the positivist movement in economics in the 1930s. Without doubt, this focus was of paramount importance for the success of the economic approach to behavior in the social sciences. Obviously, individuals care greatly about instrumental outcomes, as reflected in the costs and benefits of available alternatives; economics has derived a powerful model of human behavior from this insight.

Paradoxically, the positivist movement in economics did not imply such a focus on instrumental outcomes. In fact, economics has been deliberately vague about the content of human preferences. In the 1930s, economists abandoned the idea that utility could be observed directly and adopted the view that the only way to infer utility was from revealed behavior. Individuals could place value on anything. Economics, therefore, is also potentially open to the idea that individuals enjoy procedural utility.

Procedural utility poses a challenge, however, to the concept of utility as it is *practically* used in much of economics. The existing theoretical cornerstones of economics in the form of expected utility theory and game theory generally define preferences over monetary payoffs. As a result, economic models as they are applied today often adopt a narrow view of human utility by focusing on instrumental outcomes. The notion that instrumental outcomes are not the only source of utility and not the only driving force behind behavior is now almost completely absent from economic analysis. Nevertheless, this stance has also been criticized. Sen (1995, 1997) is the most prominent economist to argue repeatedly that models of economic choice should combine preferences for outcome with those for processes. Procedural utility means that there is something beyond instrumental outputs as they are captured in a traditional economic utility function. People may have preferences about *how* instrumental outcomes are generated, and preferences about processes generate procedural utility.

The Building Blocks

The concept of procedural utility goes beyond instrumental outcomes and contributes to a broader understanding of non-instrumental concerns. It rests on three building blocks that deviate in important respects from the concept of utility usually applied in economics:

• Procedural utility emphasizes utility as *well-being*. Utility is understood in a broad sense as pleasure and pain, as positive and negative affect, or as life satisfaction. This reinstates the original economic idea that utility consists of everything that an individual values. The research on reported subjective well-being or happiness in economics introduces well-being as a direct measure of human utility.

• Closely connected with the first point is that procedural utility focuses on *non-instrumental* determinants of utility. It is not exclusively concerned with instrumental outcomes brought about by different decision-making procedures. Instead, the processes and institutions under which people live and act are seen as independent sources of utility.

• The concept of procedural utility emerges because people have a *sense of self*, and so it incorporates a central tenet of social psychology into economics: that people care about how they perceive themselves and about how others perceive them.[1] Procedural utility exists because procedures provide important feedback information to the self. Specifically, they address innate psychological needs of self-determination differently. Psychologists have identified three such psychological needs as essential: autonomy, relatedness, and competence. The desire for autonomy encompasses the experience of organizing one's own actions or the experience of being causal. The need for relatedness refers to the desire to feel connected to others in love and care, and to be treated as a respected member of social groups. Lastly, the need for competence refers to one's predisposition to control the environment and to experience oneself as capable and effective. Different procedures can be expected to provide different procedural goods serving these needs; in this respect, they contribute to individual well-being regardless of the instrumental outcomes traditionally studied by economists. The concept of procedural utility thus draws heavily on insights into the understanding and the motives of the self contributed by psychologists, particularly Deci and Ryan (2000).

Procedural utility can therefore be defined as the well-being gained from living and acting under institutionalized processes that also contribute to a positive sense of self and address the innate needs for autonomy, relatedness, and competence.

Example

The general concept of procedural utility is illustrated by one of the most prominent studies in the field of procedural fairness, which may be the best-investigated aspect of procedural utility (Lind and Tyler

---

1. For a survey, see Baumeister 1998.

1988). Lind et al. (1993) investigate a situation in which litigants are involved in an arbitration process. At the end of arbitration, the court orders an award, and the parties can decide whether they want to accept this award or reject it and go to trial. Economists would typically study such a situation by considering the costs and benefits of accepting an award. Indeed, the predictions that they are likely to make are borne out: award acceptance depends on instrumental outcomes such as the ratio between the actual award and the amount originally demanded, or the litigants' evaluation of whether the outcome was favorable or unfavorable (which can be seen as a good proxy for the expected net benefit of going to trial). Overall, however, the fairness of the arbitration procedure is found to be much more important as a basis for acceptance than instrumental outcomes. Litigants who judge the arbitration process as fair are much more likely to accept a court-ordered award, irrespective of instrumental outcomes. This result emerges because procedures convey important feedback information to the self, thereby affecting individuals' well-being. Procedures seen as fair are those, for example, that give individuals "voice." To be given a say in one's own concerns generates procedural utility because it addresses innate needs of self-determination such as autonomy and competence; it also affects innate needs of relatedness, because it is an important signal about one's standing in a group.

Possible Objections

Two objections with respect to procedural utility should be considered.

Difference from Outcome Utility
It may be argued that procedural utility cannot be distinguished from what in standard economics is called an "outcome." Procedural utility as proposed here has the sense of an "outcome" in that procedures are supposed to affect human well-being in important ways. However, procedural utility clearly differs from what economists consider relevant outcomes in practice and in their models. In general, "outcomes" in economics are understood to be "instrumental"; they are often defined in monetary terms, and in particular by income.

Integration into Standard Economic Theory
It may be argued that procedural utility is not sufficiently different to merit a new category. But procedural utility allows one to better orga-

nize the determinants of human well-being, thereby leading to a better understanding of what is valued by individuals. When studying the potential value of the concept of procedural utility, consider the example of the economic analysis of institutions as undertaken in the New Institutional Economics. This analysis studies institutions as decision-making mechanisms that lead to different instrumental outcomes for the parties involved. In contrast, the category of procedural utility allows one to highlight aspects disregarded by this kind of analysis—for example, that institutions also directly contribute to people's well-being when they serve innate needs of autonomy, relatedness, and competence. This, in turn, has potentially important implications for the design of institutions. If individuals' overall evaluation of a situation (in the sense of overall satisfaction or utility) depends on utility from instrumental outcomes as well as on utility from the procedure used, one cannot simply focus on instrumental outcomes alone. An unfavorable instrumental outcome is more likely to be accepted if the procedure applied was "good," and a favorable outcome might provide little overall satisfaction if the procedure that brought it about was "bad." The concept of procedural utility therefore sheds new light on the study of institutions.

10.2   The Sources of Procedural Utility

Categories

The sources of procedural utility can be classified into two broad categories:

Institutions
People have preferences for the ways in which allocative and redistributive decisions are made. At the level of society, the most important formal systems for reaching decisions are the price system (i.e., the market), democracy, hierarchy, and bargaining (Dahl and Lindblom 1953). People may gain procedural utility from these institutions because they express judgments about the people involved. For example, a constitution that secures civil liberties such as freedom of speech may greatly contribute to people's self-worth. In contrast, a constitution that denies offenders their political rights may be deeply disturbing to individuals' sense of self, irrespective of instrumental outcomes. Institutions have a direct effect on individuals' well-being by addressing innate needs of autonomy, relatedness, and competence.

Interactions between People

People evaluate actions taken toward them not only by their consequences, but also by how they feel treated by other people. Such treatment is importantly shaped by institutions, which provide people in
exchange relationships with incentives for positive treatment of each
other in everyday interactions. For instance, labor law and company statutes shape the interaction between managers and employees. Another
example is the organization of the health-care system as it guides the
relationship between medical suppliers and patients. Institutions, then,
also have an indirect effect on individuals' well-being by motivating and
restricting how people are treated, thereby affecting their sense of self.

There is often a smooth transition between the two categories. On the
one hand, institutions select people according to their treatment of fellow workers, citizens, and consumers, and motivate them on the same
basis. On the other hand, people who evaluate institutions, processes,
or authorities usually base their judgment on the treatment experienced
by the specific people involved with the institutions.

Emergence

Procedural utility may emerge at levels that are different and sometimes hard to distinguish. Nevertheless, the multitude of sources does
not mean that the concept can be applied arbitrarily. Whether procedural utility emerges from institutions such as the market, democratic
decision making, or hierarchy, or whether it stems from procedural
differences on a smaller scale (e.g., procedural differences within an
organization, a political system, or a legal framework), there is common
ground to all these channels of impact: individuals judge processes positively to the extent that they address innate needs of self-determination. Theoretical hypotheses can therefore be derived. With respect to
procedural differences on a smaller scale, there is a clear understanding
from the large literature on "procedural fairness" or "procedural justice" about what constitutes a good procedure (Lind and Tyler 1988).
Since procedures on this level often involve the way in which authority
is exercised in organizations, public administrations, or legal contexts,
innate needs are mainly affected by relational information that procedures convey, such as assessments of impartiality, the trustworthiness
of superiors and authorities (Bohnet 2007), the extent to which individuals feel they are treated with dignity, and the extent to which individuals are given voice. (See also Tyler et al. 1997.) When institutions of

a larger scale are considered, such as democracy or hierarchy, one can derive similar hypotheses. For example, democracy can be expected to have positive procedural utility effects because it enhances individuals' perception of self-determination. In contrast, hierarchy is likely to produce procedural disutility because it interferes with individuals' self-determination. Arguments and results along these lines will be discussed in detail in section 10.3.

In the end, whether procedural utility is a fruitful category rests on its empirical relevance. Since procedural utility has been shown to matter in a broad range of areas (the economy, the polity and society, organizations, law), empirical evidence from these areas will now be reviewed.

10.3   Economy

There are many areas in which individuals derive procedural utility in their capacity as economic subjects. To demonstrate the quantitative importance of the utility gained depending on the process used, two areas are discussed here. The first relates to instances where individuals act as consumers, and the second to situations where people act as income earners.

Consumption

Consumption is probably the area where procedural utility would be least expected: it generally takes place in well-functioning markets where transactions are focused on instrumental outcomes. Nevertheless, procedural utility has also been found to play a role in consumers' decisions. The first evidence of this was presented by Kahneman et al. (1986), who investigated customers' reactions to a situation where the price of a good (snow shovels) was increased in a well-defined situation of excess demand (the morning after a large snowstorm). Eighty-two percent of the individuals surveyed considered the price increase unfair and so rated a normal functioning of the market mechanism as unacceptable. The reaction can be interpreted in terms of procedural utility: people are negatively affected emotionally when they perceive behavior toward them as exploitation, because it undermines their status as consumers (who are presumed to be on an equal standing with the suppliers). Similar reactions to price increases have been noted in the United States (Konow 2001), in Switzerland and Germany (Frey and Pommerehne 1993), and in Russia (Shiller et al. 1991). All these studies place individuals in a situation of excess demand, and find that a consistently high percentage of consumers see a price increase as an unfair means of overcoming the shortage. Under these particular circumstances, the general population in many countries does not appear to consider the price mechanism a fair procedure of allocation. Applying a similar questionnaire methodology, Anand (2001) documents the effects of procedural fairness in different situations of economic choice. If consumers have procedural concerns, this can impose a constraint on profit maximization by suppliers, which will affect market equilibrium.

Concerns with the market mechanism, however, should not be studied in isolation. Instead, different institutions of allocation should be compared. Frey and Pommerehne (1993) contrast the utility that individuals attribute to the price system with alternative mechanisms of allocation and find that a somewhat lower percentage of the respondents (73 percent) consider a similar price increase unfair. Nevertheless, the market still fares worse than other mechanisms of decision making. For example, an allocation by "tradition" (first come, first served) is considered by far fewer people to be unfair (24 percent), and similarly an allocation by administrative procedures (by the local authorities) was considered unfair by 57 percent. Only a random allocation, which assigns the goods with equal probability to everybody and has therefore been suggested as a particularly rational allocation mechanism (Intriligator 1973; Mueller 1978), fares worse than the price system; only 14 percent of the respondents consider it fair. Institutions do indeed seem to play an important role in consumers' decisions. People care about their perceived treatment as customers beyond instrumental outcome considerations.

Of course, studies such as these, which are undertaken to evaluate the utility individuals attach to processes, can only be a first step. They do not test actual behavior. It cannot be excluded that people react differently when confronted with the same situation, or a similar one, in real life. Laboratory experiments present an intermediate case. They study behavior, but not in real life, and so the problem of external validity remains. Nevertheless, economic experiments are beginning to provide important evidence on these issues. For example, Tyran and Engelmann (2005) study consumer boycotts in reaction to price increases in an experimental market. They show that boycotts are mainly called and executed for expressive reasons, and that boycotts serve to punish sellers for apparently unfair price increases. They find that boycotts do not primarily serve an instrumental goal. For example, boycotts are undertaken although they often fail to hold down prices and are not profitable for consumers, and are undertaken irrespective of fact that successful boycotts are a public good.

Little evidence currently exists to indicate which allocation procedures are seen as acceptable under certain circumstances. Nevertheless, the studies make it clear that consumers' overall evaluations of allocations are not merely dependent on instrumental outcomes. Instead, the allocation procedures by which instrumental outcomes are brought about appear to play an independent role.

Income Earners

When individuals act on the labor market, they are often confronted with the institution of hierarchy. Hierarchy means that production and employment are integrated into an organization, and decisions are characterized by some degree of authority. Hierarchy can be considered to be the most fundamental institution by which decisions are taken in society with respect to work organization and production, and is therefore an essential and widespread feature of the economy.

Does hierarchy involve procedural utility aspects? The theoretical arguments discussed above lead to a clear proposition: individuals prefer independence to subjection to hierarchical decision making. Hierarchy constitutes a procedural disutility because it interferes with innate needs of self-determination: autonomy and the experience of competence are generally restricted under hierarchy, and strongly associated with independence. A respective empirical test is discussed in chapter 7.

Procedural aspects within hierarchies have also been studied in other contexts. It is well known, for example, that workers often resist nominal pay cuts. The resulting downward wage rigidity has macroeconomic consequences, because it can cause excess unemployment in recessions (Bewley 1999; Fehr and Götte 2005). In workers' resistance to pay cuts, the apparently crucial issues are not only outcome or distributional fairness, but also process. It has been shown, for example, that employee' reactions to pay cuts are less adverse if they occur through fair processes—e.g., when management thoroughly and sensitively explains the basis for the pay cuts (Greenberg 1990a).

10.4 Polity and Society

In their capacity as citizens, people are subject to different political and societal procedures that generate procedural utility. This section discusses democratic institutions, procedures for allocating public goods, taxation, redistribution, and inequality.

Democratic Participation

A large literature in the social sciences, especially in psychology, political science, and sociology, attributes a positive value to participation, because it enhances individuals' perception of self-determination.[2] The rights to participate in political decisions are essential to any democratic institution. Those rights include voting in elections, launching and voting on referenda, and running for a seat in the legislature. Citizens may gain procedural utility from such participation rights over and above the outcome generated in the political process, because they provide a feeling of being involved and having political influence, as well as feelings of inclusion, identity, and self-determination. By being able to participate, citizens may feel that the political sphere takes their wishes seriously into account in a fair political process; if participation is restricted, they may feel alienation and apathy toward the political institutions.

It may even be hypothesized that the right to participate in political decision making accords the citizens more encompassing self-determination than actual participation, because political participation rights are a comprehensive characteristic of political institutions and affect people's well-being, and not only during a restricted period of political activation. With the rights to participate, the decision of whether to participate is left up to the individual. People may value the right to participate even if they rarely or never exercise it themselves.

Can it be empirically shown that citizens derive procedural utility from political participation rights? Chapter 6 presents results employing an empirical identification strategy based on the idea that the status of being a national differs fundamentally from that of being a foreigner.[3] Nationals have the right to vote and to participate in political decision making, whereas foreigners do not have these rights. Nationals should consequently derive more utility from political participation rights than foreigners if they enjoy procedural utility. This hypothesis is tested econometrically by using a survey based on more than 6,000 interviews with residents of Switzerland, where there is a unique variation in the

---

2. For an extensive survey, see chapter 13 of Lane 2000.
3. For a fuller treatment, see Frey and Stutzer 2005c.

political participation rights among citizens. In addition to elections, Swiss citizens have access to direct democratic instruments (initiatives, referenda) which differ substantially from canton to canton. As a proxy measure for utility, an index of reported subjective well-being is used as the dependent variable. As reflected in reported life satisfaction, the estimated overall utility effect from more extended political participation rights is sizable in itself. Citizens and foreigners living in jurisdictions with more developed political participation rights enjoy higher levels of subjective well-being. However, the positive effect on reported satisfaction with life is smaller for foreigners, reflecting their exclusion from procedural utility. The positive effect of participation rights is about three times larger for the citizens than for the foreigners—i.e., a major part of the welfare gain from favorable political procedures seems to be due to procedural utility. The results hold when a large number of determinants or correlates of subjective well-being (in particular, sociodemographic characteristics, employment status, household income, and proxies for political outcomes) are controlled for.

The procedural utility of political participation rights may also be reflected in revealed behavior. In an experimental study conducted before the elections to the German *Bundestag* in 1994, Güth and Weck-Hannemann (1997) investigated the amount of money that would have to be paid to individuals to persuade them to destroy their voting card, thereby giving up the right to vote in the election. Despite the fact that a single vote almost never changes the outcome of an election, most individuals were not willing to sell their voting right even for large amounts of money. Sixty-three percent of voters refused to destroy their voting card even for the highest sum offered (DM200, approximately US$100 at the time), and only 5 percent agreed to give up their voting right for less than DM10 (about US$5). These findings show that individuals place a high value on their voting right that goes beyond any outcome utility they may receive from altering the election result. Political participation rights seem to be a source of procedural utility, because they enhance individuals' possibilities of self-determination and co-determination.

Allocation of Public Goods

One of the most pressing problems of government policy is to find ways and means to overcome "NIMBY" (Not In My Back Yard) resistance by individuals to public undertakings that are generally considered important and desirable, such as hospitals, airports, and nuclear waste dumps.

Traditional economic theory offers a straightforward solution to this problem. As in the aggregate, the benefits are larger than the costs, the prospective gainers must be taxed, and the revenue must be redistributed to the prospective losers. The most elegant and efficient procedure is to undertake an appropriate auction (Kunreuther and Kleindorfer 1986; O'Sullivan 1993). However, as it turns out, the use of the price system in such cases meets with much resistance; indeed, the procedure based on the price system works rarely if ever. The individuals expecting to lose from the siting of a particular project tend to consider the monetary compensation offered to them a bribe, something to which they fundamentally object. Bribing disregards people's sense of self as decent citizens and so generates negative procedural utility.[4] Indeed, it has been empirically demonstrated (Frey and Oberholzer-Gee 1997) that offering monetary compensation to the inhabitants of a nearby village to persuade them to accept a site leads to a counterproductive reaction: support for the site falls. But if the compensation is offered in a way that addresses the concerns of the individuals affected, the proposed project has a better chance of being accepted. For example, if people fear that the location of a nuclear waste dump produces health risks, they should be offered improved medical facilities; if they fear the noise generated by an airport, they should be helped with insulating their homes. Such material compensation within a predetermined dimension is inefficient, according to traditional welfare theory. Individuals appear to be prepared to accept a worse instrumental outcome if they feel that the process does justice to their concerns.

Institutional differences also play a role. Oberholzer-Gee et al. (1995) investigated the acceptability of various decision-making procedures for siting a noxious facility. The 900 persons interviewed ranked procedures in the following order: 79 percent saw negotiations (bargaining) as an acceptable procedure for siting, 39 percent found referenda (democracy) acceptable, 32 percent found a decision by lottery acceptable, and only a few saw the price system as an acceptable procedure (20 percent in the form of willingness to accept, 4 percent in the form of willingness to pay).

Treatment of Taxpayers

Individuals may value procedural differences in their role as taxpayers. This is an aspect that has been completely neglected by economic

---

4. See the crowding theory developed in Frey 1997b.

research on taxpayer behavior. Public economics or neoclassical public finance uses a model of taxpayer behavior (Allingham and Sandmo
1972) that is based only on outcome considerations: the extent of tax
evasion depends negatively on the probability of being caught and the
size of the punishment if caught.[5] From an empirical point of view, this
model faces two major problems. Firstly, it is difficult, if not impossible,
to account for the level of tax evasion. In view of the low deterrence
applied in most countries, taxpayers would be expected to evade more
often than they do (i.e., compliance is too high). For the United States,
Alm et al. (1992, p. 22) argue, "a purely economic analysis of the evasion
gamble implies that most individuals would evade if they are "rational," because it is unlikely that cheaters will be caught and penalized."
Secondly, the econometric parameter estimates are unsatisfactory.
Often they do not turn out to be statistically significant, and sometimes
their signs are inconsistent with the theory (Pommerehne and Weck-
Hannemann 1996; Torgler 2005, 2007). Therefore, new insights into tax
compliance and tax evasion may be gained by taking issues of procedural fairness into account. For example, taxpayers may respond systematically to their treatment by the tax authority: when the tax officials
treat them with respect and dignity, their willingness to pay taxes may
be supported or even raised. In contrast, when the tax officials consider
taxpayers merely as "subjects" who have to be forced to pay their dues,
the taxpayers may respond by actively trying to avoid taxation.

Using a sample of Swiss cantons in the years 1970–1995, Feld and
Frey (2002) and Frey and Feld (2002) find econometric evidence that
taxpayers indeed act according to these predictions. Individuals seem
to experience higher utility when treated more respectfully in the taxation process, and therefore seem to be more willing to pay their taxes.
Moreover, tax authorities in Switzerland behave as if they are aware of
taxpayers' reaction to being treated respectfully or not. Deterrence is
only one of the motivational forces used by the authorities; often they
rely on respectful procedures of tax collection.

Redistribution and Inequality

Social inequality is a concern for many individuals and governments.
Unhappiness with inequality often depends on the extent to which the
income distribution in a society is unequal, and also on the individual's

---

5. For overviews, see Andreoni et al. 1998; Slemrod and Yitzhaki 2002.

position in this distribution. However, this may not be the whole picture. A particular social inequality can also be judged with respect to the social processes that brought it about. For example, if social processes provide everyone with a fair chance to become successful and rich, inequality might be seen as less of a problem than when social processes are biased and unfair. Social inequality may be not only a problem of outcome distribution, but also a problem of fair social procedures.

People's attitudes toward redistribution depend on their perception of the causes for the primary distribution (Fong 2001, 2006). Survey evidence indicates that people prefer more redistribution if they believe that poverty is caused by circumstances beyond individual control. As was discussed in chapter 5, income inequality has a large negative effect on happiness in Europe, but not in the United States. Support for redistributive policies is strongly influenced by the extent of social mobility. Higher social mobility lowers people's support for redistribution. This can, of course, be interpreted in terms of outcome: if the probability of one's becoming rich is high, one will be less likely to support redistributive policies, because one might become a net payer. But social mobility can also be interpreted in procedural terms: if people see that society offers equal opportunities, on average and in an objective sense of actual income mobility, they may be less concerned with inequality, because they see social processes as fair. Alesina, Di Tella, and MacCulloch (2004) report evidence that lends support to the second interpretation. Although on average the extent of social mobility lowers support for redistribution, its effect depends substantially on individuals' perceptions of fairness in the mobility process. Those who feel that equal opportunities really exist are less concerned with inequality when mobility is higher; they judge the "objective condition" of higher mobility as indeed offering everybody a chance, and so they withdraw their support for redistribution. In contrast, those who see social mobility generally as a biased process do not lower their redistributive support in the light of higher mobility—probably because they feel that higher mobility, even when viewed objectively, generates opportunities for some individuals, but not all.

Organizations

It is in the area of organizations that procedural utility has been studied most intensively. In hierarchies, many decisions are made in an authoritarian way. Under such circumstances, individuals' concerns with procedures must be expected to be high. The literature on procedural fairness or justice in organizations is so large that meta-analyses exist (Cohen-Charash and Spector 2001). The studies consistently find that concerns for procedural fairness are highly relevant and widespread in the employment relationship. Procedural fairness has been shown to matter for employees' behavior and satisfaction, as well as for attitudes toward change (mergers and acquisitions, layoffs, restructuring, strategic planning) and for human resources (personnel selection, performance evaluation, and compensation[6]). Procedural aspects that researchers have identified as important include organizational policies and rules (e.g. providing advance notice for decisions and opportunities to give voice; see Greenberg 1990b; Lind and Tyler 1988), but they also encompass the interpersonal treatment of people (Bies and Moag 1986). Individuals have been found to generally value fair procedures beyond organizational outcomes. Procedural fairness effects prevail when individual outcomes as well as aspects of distributional fairness are controlled for in the analysis. Without doubt, then, procedural utility is a relevant part of what is valued by individuals when they work in organizations.

Law

In law, as in organizations, procedural aspects are expected to be important, because people are often subject to decisions by authorities. Law is therefore an area in which procedural fairness has been thoroughly analyzed. Many studies find that people react adversely to unfair legal procedures, irrespective of the objective judgment made by a court. Unfair procedures lead individuals to rate the legitimacy of authorities and their satisfaction with a trial less highly; they also affect subsequent compliance.[7]

One study has already been summarized as an example in section 10.1, because it investigates real-life behavior and so will be of most interest to economists. Lind et al. (1993) studied the acceptance of awards from court-ordered arbitration by real-life litigants, including corporate and individual litigants in federal courts. The authors find that litigants who judge the arbitration process as fair are much more likely to accept a court-ordered award (irrespective of the objective outcome).

---

6. For an overview, see Konovsky 2000.
7. For an overview, see Tyler 1997.

The decision to proceed to a formal trial was most strongly influenced by procedural fairness considerations. This is remarkable, for the studied disputes involved sums of up to US$800,000. The objective size of the award and other instrumental factors also predicted acceptance, although to a much lesser extent. Therefore, the study shows that utility from procedures is important in lawsuits beyond outcome utility.

10.5 Relationships between Procedural Utility and Outcome Utility

If procedural utility exists, how can it be fruitfully integrated into the existing economic approach? This section explores theoretical relationships between procedural utility and standard outcome utility.

Independence of Procedures and Outcomes?

If processes generate utility, a first question to ask is how this changes our understanding of the relationship between processes and outcomes. This is of particular importance for the study of procedures that are employed at the level of society (decision-making mechanisms such as the market, democracy, or hierarchy) and the evaluation of the outcomes they produce. The question touches on fundamental issues of social choice, such as how a society can sensibly arrive at aggregate social welfare judgments. The following thoughts draw mainly on the work of Amartya Sen (1995), who brilliantly summarized the issues in his presidential address to the American Economic Association.[8]

Most of the economic approaches to social welfare (and most of the political science approaches) are purely outcome-oriented. The most extreme form is probably embodied in the "New Welfare Economics." Its criterion for social decision making is the Pareto principle: a social improvement is achieved (e.g., by a public project, regulation, or deregulation) if at least one person's utility is increased while no other person's utility is reduced. Procedures do not play any genuine role in this approach, and certainly it attaches no intrinsic value to procedural aspects (e.g., whether a given outcome is achieved by preserving fundamental rights or freedoms of individuals). The same criticism can be made of the Public Choice approach or of Institutional Economics more generally. Although these approaches are concerned with the study of

8. See also Sugden 1981, 1986.

procedures, this is mainly because of their interest in the outcomes they produce. For example, if different democratic decision-making procedures are studied, or if production in hierarchies is compared with markets, institutions are evaluated according to the outcomes they produce. These approaches disregard a potentially large source of human well-being by not taking into account pleasures and displeasures experienced through processes. As Sen (1995, p. 12) puts it, "it is hard to be convinced that we can plausibly judge any given utility distribution ignoring altogether the process that led to that distribution (attaching, for example, no intrinsic importance whatever to whether a particular utility distribution is caused by charity, or taxation, or torture)." Consequently, judgments on social welfare outcomes should not be made independently of the procedures by which a society arrives at these outcomes; instead, the procedural utility stemming from different socio-economic decision mechanisms should be taken into account. This view is already implicitly present in some parts of economic analysis. Economists often seem to favor markets as allocation mechanisms not only because markets produce better outcomes, but also because markets institutionalize a favored treatment of trading partners in interaction. However, the empirical questions are still whether and under what conditions individuals gain procedural utility from market mechanisms, or whether (as other economists would argue) they attach an intrinsic value to more egalitarian decision mechanisms, such as democracy.

Can procedures be reasonably evaluated while ignoring the outcomes they produce? Libertarians, including Nozick (1974), take an extreme affirmative position. In Nozick's treatment of "right rules," personal liberties as well as rights of property are given high intrinsic value almost irrespective of the outcomes produced by a system based on these rights and liberties. Nevertheless, even a purely procedural approach has to consider the possibility that the consequences of such a liberal society might be catastrophic. "Indeed," Sen (1995, p. 12) writes, "it can be shown that even gigantic famines can actually take place in an economy that fulfills all the libertarian rights and entitlements specified in the Nozick system."

In summary, there are good reasons for taking procedural and outcome concerns simultaneously into consideration when analyzing socio-economic decision mechanisms. It follows that the relative importance of "right procedures" and "good outcomes" is most effectively studied within the same empirical framework of individual well-being.

Tradeoff between Process and Outcome?

The evidence discussed shows which institutional arrangements satisfy process concerns and outcome concerns simultaneously. For example, in the case of democratic participation rights, the procedure seems to produce positive procedural utility as well as better outcome. This can be seen as a fortunate instance of a socio-economic decision mechanism, which is rated positively by individuals as being a desirable process as well as having good outcomes. A more general analysis, however, obviously has to take into account the frequent tradeoff between procedural and outcome concerns. This subsection explores this aspect on a more individual level, moving the analysis away from considerations of social choice.

In a simple microeconomic analysis, procedural utility enters the utility function in addition to any instrumental arguments of utility, and it is possible to trade off procedural utility against the other arguments. This can be practiced in the equilibrium approach of compensating variation. For example, if workers intrinsically value a specific organizational procedure, they should be willing to accept a lower wage (a worse instrumental outcome) to work in an organization that is applying it. However, there is no simple tradeoff, because outcome and process utility are not perfectly separable.

Psychological research on procedural utility emphasizes the subtle cross-effects between outcome and process evaluations (and almost completely neglects equilibrium considerations). In general, the quality of procedures is seen as more important when outcomes are bad and less relevant when outcomes are good. Lawsuits are one area where such tradeoffs have been thoroughly studied.[9] Many studies find that people react adversely to unfair judicial procedures, especially when the result of the lawsuit is bad for them; when the outcome is good, individuals care less about procedural qualities, although they still care to some extent.

However, unfair procedures are sometimes self-protecting. Consider the organizational procedure of pay determination. If you were paid less in a year because your performance was weak, but the procedure of pay determination was extremely fair, would you be more satisfied with your pay? Yes, in part, because you would still favor a fair procedure over an unfair one. But there is a countervailing effect. If a

---

9. See chapter 4 of Lind and Tyler 1988.

procedure is fair, an unfavorable outcome has to be attributed to one-self; if it is unfair, one can blame the authority for the bad outcome (Brockner and Wiesenfeld 1996; Schroth and Shah 2000; van den Bos et al. 1999). This attribution effect predicts a complementary relationship between processes and outcomes: fair procedures are more valued when outcomes are good. The net relationship between procedural and outcome utility then depends on the relative strength of the substitutive and complementary effects. The two effects have been studied in a representative sample of British workers to determine procedural utility from pay-determination procedures (Benz and Stutzer 2003). Workers report higher pay satisfaction when they are involved in compensation questions and the gains in pay satisfaction are as equal in magnitude for high-wage workers as they are for low-wage workers.

Conclusions

Empirical evidence supports the existence and the relevance of procedural utility in many areas of the economy and society. Integrating procedural utility into economics enriches it and allows phenomena to be taken into account that are otherwise difficult or impossible to explain. To some extent, procedural fairness has been acknowledged in economic psychology or behavioral economics, although most attention has been paid to integrating outcome fairness into individual utility functions (Bolton and Ockenfels 2000; Fehr and Schmidt 1999; Konow 2003).

Institutions can be looked at not only as producing particular outcomes, but also as framing decision-making procedures. Under well-known conditions, the market leads to efficient outcomes, and moreover produces procedural utilities and disutilities. The use of market prices to equilibrate supply and demand sometimes meets with vigorous opposition from the people concerned. In particular, consumers perceive the raising of prices to ration demand as an unfair and disrespectful treatment, and prefer that other decision-making mechanisms should fulfill this task. Though such reactions have often been observed, economists solely concerned with the narrowly instrumental aspects of the price system are ill-equipped to deal with this empirical phenomenon. Still, it is important to see that every decision-making mechanism has advantages and disadvantages with respect to the procedural utility produced. When economists suggest policy actions and are concerned with their acceptability, they must also pay attention to the procedural utilities attached to the various decision-making systems.

Another aspect enriching economic theory relates to the procedural utility produced by individuals' possibilities of participating in social and economic decision making. The rights to participate in political and economic decisions are important characteristics of modern societies. In politics, participation rights range from voting in elections or referenda to running for a seat in a legislative body. In the economy, participation rights may range from exerting influence in one's work place and work organization to full-scale co-determination in the management of the firm or even complete self-determination in the form of self-employment. The evidence discussed in this chapter shows that individuals gain procedural utility from such participation possibilities over and above the outcome generated, because they provide a sense of being involved and having influence as well as a sense of inclusion, identity, and self-determination. Formal institutions of worker participation have been enshrined in the constitutions of some countries (the primary example being Germany, with its extensive co-determination rights), but economists have mainly analyzed its instrumental effects on outcomes, and on productivity and wages in particular. But the purely procedural aspects also must be taken into account.

Although the evidence discussed above inspires economic analysis and reasoning about economic policy in areas such as consumption and work behavior, people's willingness to accept public undertakings or to pay taxes, and issues of social inequality or corporate strategy, there is surely room for further promising research in several still-unexplored directions. For example, in the relationship between public administration and citizens, procedures can be expected to matter for people's evaluation of public services. The same is likely to prevail in the health-care system. For issues of redistribution, it might matter whether transfers are in cash or in kind, or whether they are publicly or privately funded. In the organization of economic activity, non-profit firms can be expected, for reasons of procedural utility, to apply procedures that are systematically different from those of for-profit firms (Benz 2005). The notion that hierarchy involves procedural disutility might add to our understanding of the boundaries of the firm. Fair procedures are likely to shape conflict resolution in bargaining between unions and firms. Finally, in government policy, further research might be devoted to the relations between procedural discontent and citizens' resistance to public policies and their compliance with the law.

Standard economic theory relies on revealed behavior, which takes as granted that all observed behavior is utility-maximizing from the point of view of the person acting. Individuals are perfectly informed about the utility they derive from alternative consumption bundles and are perfectly able to maximize utility. These assumptions imply that people do not make any systematic mistakes when they make decisions. Happiness theory departs from these far-reaching assumptions and separates the act of decision from the utility therewith experienced. Because it is possible to measure experienced utility independently by indicators of subjective well-being, possible systematic errors in individual decisions can be identified. This chapter considers the particularly important consumption decisions and tradeoffs that relate to the balance between work and life. People sometimes make systematic errors when predicting utility and therefore do not always reach the maximum utility according to their own evaluation. In particular, they mispredict both the satisfaction derived from higher income and the dissatisfaction produced by the additional effort needed to gain a higher income.

11.1 Sources and Consequences of Mispredicting Utility

The basic claim about people's misprediction of utility can be summarized as follows: Individuals systematically underestimate the utility of consumption aspects that care for intrinsic needs (time spent with family and friends and on hobbies; see e.g. Gui and Sugden 2005). In contrast, the characteristics relating to consumption aspects that care for extrinsic desires (income and status) are overvalued. Consequently, individuals tend to underconsume goods and activities with strong intrinsic attributes, in comparison with those with strong extrinsic attributes. According to their own subjective evaluation, individuals make distorted decisions when they choose between different options, and they obtain a lower utility level than they might otherwise have obtained. Individuals find it difficult and sometimes impossible to learn, because they have to compare attributes whose salience shifts over time.

The argument can be decomposed into four aspects:

• Goods and activities are characterized by "intrinsic" and "extrinsic" attributes.

• The future utility derived from intrinsic attributes of choice options is underestimated when making a decision, in comparison with the utility derived from the extrinsic attributes.

• Goods and activities characterized by strong intrinsic attributes are therefore underconsumed when compared with those that have strong extrinsic attributes.

• According to the individuals' own evaluation, the distorted decisions lower their utility.

These four aspects will now be discussed briefly. (For fuller treatments, see Frey and Stutzer 2004a, Stutzer and Frey 2007b, and, with an application to the political process, Frey and Stutzer 2006b.)

Intrinsic and Extrinsic Attributes

Standard economic theory assumes that individuals are able to compare the future utilities provided by the goods and activities consumed. They maximize their own utility in a rational consumption decision. It has sometimes proved useful to distinguish between the various characteristics of goods and activities (Lancaster 1966; Becker 1965) or the attributes of options (Keeney and Raiffa 1976), but such differentiations do not affect individuals' capacity to evaluate future utility. The standard economic model of consumer decisions is appropriate for most goods and activities, and for most situations. The theory's predictions are also unaffected when individuals make only random prediction errors, or when the extent of misprediction is the same for all goods and all activities.

In this chapter, we depart from these assumptions and argue that there are systematic differences in the degree of misprediction of utility that are derived from two types of attributes characterizing different options. The first attribute of goods and activities relates to "intrinsic needs." The psychological theory of self-determination put forth by Deci and Ryan (2000) provides a comprehensive view of three main aspects of these intrinsic needs:

• The need for *relatedness*. Individuals desire to feel connected to others by love and affection, in particular by having a family and friends and by being in a social setting.

• The need for *competence*. Individuals want to control the environment and want to experience themselves as capable and effective.

• The desire for *autonomy*. Individuals value the experience of being in charge of their actions or of being causal.

Attributes of intrinsic need are characterized by providing "flow experience" (Csikszentmihalyi 1990), which occurs when one is completely immersed in an activity, often a hobby.

The second attribute of goods and activities refers to "extrinsic desires," which induce people to acquire material possessions and to achieve fame, status, or prestige. Income is a crucial aspect of options in the choice set. A high income is in most cases a precondition for a high standard of material living.

Each option, each activity and even each good is multi-dimensional; in general, a particular choice alternative has both intrinsic and extrinsic need attributes—in brief, intrinsic and extrinsic attributes. Some goods and some activities have a stronger component of an intrinsic nature (e.g., time spent with friends); others are of an extrinsic nature, such as consumer articles that go beyond basic material needs (e.g., designer clothes). This analysis concentrates on need satisfaction from time and income that are available for discretionary use and does not consider the satisfaction of physiological needs.

The main proposition is that when one is making a decision the extrinsic attributes are more salient than the intrinsic attributes of different options. Individuals when making a consumption choice therefore tend to undervalue the intrinsic attributes relative to the extrinsic ones. This distortion leads to a systematic inconsistency between predicted and experienced utility. The latter can be understood as a hedonic experience (Kahneman, Wakker, and Sarin 1997). Both utility measures—predicted and experienced utility—diverge from traditional decision utility, which conflates the two, by looking only at the utility derived from individual behavior.

Intrinsic Attributes Are Undervalued When Predicting Utility

For the underestimation of future utility from intrinsic attributes in comparison with extrinsic attributes of goods and activities, the following major sources may be distinguished.

Adaptation Is Underestimated

Individuals are not good at foreseeing how much utility they will derive from their future consumption.[1] Research on affective forecasting shows, for instance, that people underestimate their ability to cope with negative events.[2] Usually, therefore, people have biased expectations about the intensity and duration of emotions. People fail to foresee that they will adapt more in the future than they predict at present.

Adaptation is more strongly underestimated for extrinsic aspects than it is for intrinsic aspects. People adapt less to goods and activities with strong intrinsic components because the (positive) experience tends to be renewed with every new act of consumption. Getting together with a good friend is always rewarding, and one does not get used to it in the sense of valuing this experience less and less. Instead, the opposite is true. Each interaction with the friend may widen the perspective and provide fresh pleasure and enjoyment. Similarly, many scholars have a flow experience when they immerse themselves in writing a paper or a book they have always wanted to write. The corresponding utility does not wear off. Many senior scholars who have written numerous papers and books experience an equal or even higher flow when writing a new work than when they wrote the first one.

The differential adaptation effect on the intrinsic and extrinsic attributes of goods and activities is consistent with much recent empirical evidence.[3] Individuals do not adapt their utility evaluation in the case of undesirable experiences that inhibit intrinsic need satisfaction. In particular, severe health problems, such as a chronic illness or an illness that gets progressively worse, reduces autonomy and lead to lasting reductions in reported subjective well-being (Easterlin 2003). Having a job is related to many experiences that provide flow and satisfy intrinsic needs, such as being in the company of workmates and experiencing expertise and autonomy. Accordingly, being unemployed is repeatedly found to

---

1. For empirical evidence, see Loewenstein and Adler 1995. For an extensive survey, see Wilson and Gilbert 2003.
2. See the discussion of adaptation in section 3.1.
3. For a survey, see Frederick and Loewenstein 1999.

have high negative non-pecuniary effects on subjective well-being, with little habituation (Clark et al. 2006). In contrast, having a job with high autonomy, as in the case of self-employed people, is related to high job satisfaction. As was shown in chapter 7, self-employed people derive more utility from their work than people employed in a hierarchical organization, irrespective of income earned or hours worked. The same holds for volunteers who, on average, are more satisfied with their life.

In contrast, there is empirical evidence that individuals exhibit strong adaptation in the case of goods and activities in which extrinsic aspects dominate. This has been demonstrated for income (van Praag 1993; Easterlin 2001; Stutzer 2004). When individuals experience a rise in income, their utility level rises at first, but most of this beneficial effect has evaporated after about a year. It has been estimated that about 60 percent of the utility increase due to an enduring higher position in the income distribution disappears over time (van Herwaarden et al. 1977).

The evidence of little or no adaptation for goods and activities characterized by intrinsic aspects and the evidence of strong adaptation for those characterized by extrinsic aspects suggest that individuals who underestimate adaptation or even disregard adaptation altogether make a bigger mistake when predicting future utility from extrinsic attributes than when predicting future utility from intrinsic attributes.

Memory of Experiences Is Distorted
When individuals make decisions about future consumption, they have to resort to their respective experiences. People reflect on specific moments from the past or access generalizations about emotions that are apt to occur in a particular type of situation (Robinson and Clore 2002). If specific information is available, it has priority in people's judgment. The more memorable moments of an experience thereby disproportionately affect retrospective assessments of feelings (Kahneman 1999). The most intense moment (peak) and the most recent moment (end) of an emotional event tend to count as "more memorable." This peak-end rule, or duration neglect, has been established in many experimental tests (Kahneman 2003).

Intrinsic attributes may be seen to relate to long-term experiences of moderate but enduring positive feelings. One needs time to experience the renewed enjoyment of the type of interactions mentioned above. The same holds for the ability to immerse oneself in a flow experience. In contrast, extrinsic attributes are related to short-run experiences, particularly peak emotions. Consequently, the intrinsic aspects of goods and activities related to duration (compared with the extrinsic aspects related to peaks) are underestimated when people predict utility based on retrospection.

Extrinsic Aspects Are Easier to Rationalize

Individuals have a strong urge to justify their decisions to themselves and to others.[4] It is not only predicted consumption utility that affects (e.g., the decision to buy something), but also whether people think that they are getting a bargain (Thaler 1999). There is a general tendency to resist affective influences and to take rationalistic attributes into account when making decisions. Hsee et al. (2003) call this "reason-based choice lay rationalism." In experiments, Hsee et al. find that people focus their decisions on absolute economic payoffs and play down non-economic concerns. When asked to give reasons during the phase of decision making, people heavily weight aspects of events that are easy to articulate, and neglect aspects that are important for experience (Wilson and Schooler 1991). Similarly, people tend to base their choices on rules and principles, and to bypass predictions on the experiential consequences of their choices (Prelec and Herrnstein 1991). People do not optimally consider, therefore, various attributes of options that would maximize predicted utility.

For extrinsic and intrinsic attributes, there is a similar inconsistency in decision making. It is much easier to provide rational justifications for extrinsic than for intrinsic characteristics. Consider a job offer providing more income but less leisure time. Most people find it very easy to justify acceptance of the job offer to themselves and to others, because the extrinsic monetary dimension is salient. In contrast, it is quite difficult to justify why the intrinsic characteristics provided by more leisure time are important enough that one would refuse a large increase in income. As a result, goods and activities characterized by strong intrinsic attributes tend to be given too little weight in decision making relative to extrinsic components.

Wrong Intuitive Theories about Sources of Future Utility

People have very diverse intuitive theories about what makes them happy (Loewenstein and Schkade 1999). These beliefs directly influence people in predicting future utility and can cause people to err. Their role is to guide the reconstruction of past emotions and make them consistent with

---

4. On pre-decision justification, see Shafir et al. 1993.

current self-conceptions or beliefs (Ross 1989). Intuitive theories interact, therefore, with the three previously discussed sources of misprediction.

One important belief refers to acquisition and possession (i.e., materialism) as central goals on the path to happiness.[5] People with material or extrinsic life goals report lower self-esteem and life satisfaction than people with intrinsic life goals (Kasser and Ryan 1996; Sirgy 1997). This correlation may indicate that people who believe intuitively in extrinsic attributes are prone to mispredict utility. In contrast, people with intrinsic life goals focusing on personal growth, relationships, and community spirit apply intuitive theories that emphasize intrinsic attributes; this leads to few mispredictions in future utility. Heterogeneity among individuals may lead to additional testable predictions when combined with previous reasons for misprediction.

Institutional Conditions
The differential effect of misprediction between intrinsic and extrinsic attributes also depends on the extent to which decisions involve market interactions. The monetarization of a good or an activity has the effect that individuals focus on extrinsic attributes more than they normally would. This applies to both work and consumption. An example is the introduction of pay for performance. This incentive tends to lead employees to regard as dominant the aspects of performance that are relevant to the compensation they receive. In contrast, aspects of performance that are not relevant to payment are crowded out (Frey 1997b; Frey and Osterloh 2005; Osterloh and Frey 2006.[6] In the area of consumption, advertising is often directed to extrinsic aspects of the goods to be sold. In comparison, lobbies for intrinsic values tend to be weak and often do not exist at all. To the extent to which "commercialization" occurs (Kuttner 1997; Lane 1991), individuals are influenced to make mispredictions about the future utility of goods. They are led to believe that the extrinsic characteristics, in comparison with the intrinsic ones, will make them happier than is actually the case.

Related Approaches and Evidence

The theory proposed here relates to various strands of literature in which similar phenomena have been identified and empirically studied:

5. See, e.g., Tatzel 2002.
6. For a survey of empirical evidence, see Frey and Jegen 2001.

• The aspect of underestimated adaptation to new situations has been neatly introduced in theoretical models of intertemporal decision making (Loewenstein et al. 2003). Based on the model of projection bias, various phenomena can be modeled, such as, for example, the misguided purchase of durable goods or consumption profiles with too much consumption early in life. Misprediction of utility thus provides an alternative to seemingly irrational saving behavior that is usually addressed in a framework of individuals with self-control problems. However, Loewenstein et al. (ibid.) do not explicitly model differences in adaptation across goods, across attributes of different options, or across people. As a result, the possible consequences of decision inconsistency for behavior and well-being are limited in their model.

• It has been argued that the "work-life" balance of individuals today is distorted. People are persuaded to work too much and to disregard other aspects of life. This proposition has been forcefully put forward for the United States, where individuals have been identified as "overworked" (Schor 1991). This is consistent with our hypothesis that individuals tend to focus too much on options characterized by strong extrinsic attributes, and especially on income, instead of on intrinsic attributes.

• Competing for status produces negative externalities, and therefore too much effort is spent on gaining status and acquiring "positional goods" (Frank 1985a, 1999; Layard 2005). "Positional goods" are characterized by very strong extrinsic attributes. Misprediction of utility therefore tends to magnify the distortions of status competition in consumption.

• Procedural utility (i.e., the satisfaction derived from the process, rather than from its outcome) relates to innate needs. The utility derived from a particular process contributes to competence, relatedness, and autonomy, and is therefore closely related to the intrinsic attributes of goods and activities. (See chapter 10 and Frey, Benz, and Stutzer 2004.) Sources of procedural utility tend to be underestimated in people's decisions. Consistent with this idea, it has been empirically shown (Tyler et al. 1999) that, when making decisions, individuals tend to prefer institutions promising favorable outcomes. But *ex post* they state that they would have preferred an institution more geared toward just procedures.

• A long tradition in economics argues that individuals focus too much on material goods and disregard goods providing non-material benefits (Lebergott 1993; Lane 1991). Most importantly, Scitovsky (1976) claimed that "comfort goods" are overconsumed in comparison with goods providing "stimulation." Comfort goods are described as defensive activities providing protection from negative affect. They comprise the consumer goods achieved through rapid productivity growth, and have a strong extrinsic component. In contrast, stimulation comes from creative activities providing novelty, surprise, variety, and complexity. These aspects emphasize the renewal of pleasures, which is also emphasized for intrinsic attributes.

In an empirical test of mispredictions of utility, Stutzer and Frey (2007a) analyzed people's decisions to commute for a longer or a shorter time. The commuting decision involves the tradeoff between the salary or the quality of housing on the one hand and commuting time on the other hand. Rational utility maximizers commute only when they are compensated. However, when people overestimate utility from goods serving extrinsic wants, they are expected to opt for too much commuting and to suffer lower utility. In a large panel data set for Germany, it is found that commuting is not fully compensated, and that, on average, people who commute 22 minutes each way (sample mean) would need an additional 35 percent of their monthly labor income to be as satisfied with their life as people who do not commute.

11.2   Why Is There Little or No Learning?

Systematically mispredicting utilities would be of little consequence for economics if individuals learned quickly when making repetitive choices. If this were the case, mispredicting would be a disequilibrium phenomenon that would not basically affect the notion of rational decision makers maximizing individual utility. However, a large literature suggests that learning is a complex process. People learn only if multidimensional goods and activities are boiled down to essentially one dimension expressed in monetary terms. In that case, individuals can rectify their mistakes to a greater degree within a short period of time. Standard economic models then apply fully.

In the situations pertaining to choice discussed here, where the importance of various attributes differs between the time when people decide and the time when they consume, learning is much more difficult. Learning about the application of decision making to future consumption must often be based on reconstructions of previously experienced feelings. This process is therefore subject to the same misperceptions as remembering the utility of past experiences.

Learning is particularly hampered when episodic memories become too few and people rely largely on their intuitive theories (Robinson and Clore 2002). Consequently, remembered utility and predicted utility become similar. They are quite independent of utility that has been experienced. Mitchell et al. (1997) document this phenomenon in three survey studies about enjoyment predicted before, experienced during, and recollected after a trip to Europe, a Thanksgiving vacation, and a bicycle trip in California. Although participants in fact enjoy the trip less than predicted, they report enjoyment levels similar to the ones predicted for after the trip when they recall the experience.

In general, an elaborate learning process is required about the utility produced by future consumption. Individuals must step back from their own decision-making activity, in which the extrinsic characteristics dominate the intrinsic characteristics. They must attempt to make an overall evaluation, including undertaking some critical self-examination, or they must resort to "double-loop learning" (Argyris and Schön 1978). Because elaborate learning is more costly, and is in itself subject to errors, individuals are not able to fully correct their mispredictions within a reasonably short time. In many cases, they are incapable of correcting them at all, resulting in the persistent misprediction of future utilities over time.

Limited learning can coexist well with people's partial awareness of their own or others' misprediction of utility. Many people talk, for example, about their difficulties and mistakes in balancing work and life. Nevertheless, they still make decisions that underestimate intrinsic attributes relative to extrinsic attributes.

A more fundamental reason for individuals' limited learning might lie in some functionality of utility misprediction in the evolutionary process. Rayo and Becker (2007) model how humans' utility functions formed to maximize success in genetic replication. Their model rationalizes people's neglect of adaptation (described as self-inflicted externality). In today's world, however, this utility function with an inbuilt misprediction is no longer helpful in guaranteeing an optimal mix between experienced utility and motivation for success in society.

11.3 Implications

Individuals systematically mispredict the future utility of goods consumed and activities undertaken. Goods and activities characterized by stronger intrinsic attributes (such as spending time with family and friends and pursuing hobbies) are undervalued relative to those characterized by stronger extrinsic attributes (such as most consumer goods). Because comparison across various attributes is both complex and necessary, learning is slow and imperfect, and so many distorted decisions are preserved over time. Consequently, individuals obtain a lower utility than they would if they were not subject to this systematic bias of misprediction.

In an empirical application, individuals' commuting decisions were analyzed with data on subjective well-being. People who spend more time commuting report lower life satisfaction (i.e., they are not fully compensated for the burden of commuting by a higher salary, a better living environment, or a lower rent). This is consistent with people's overestimation of future utility from extrinsic attributes of job offers and housing options, and their neglect of intrinsic attributes such as the physical burden of commuting and reduced time for spending with friends and family. A refined analysis addresses the basic hypothesis by exploiting the variation in people's intuitive theories of happiness. The possible tendency of people with extrinsically oriented life goals to mispredict utility is studied. Individuals who strongly emphasize extrinsic life goals are compensated the least and are therefore negatively affected by commuting.

That individuals are worse off according to their own best interests is the finding that distinguishes our analysis from the more traditional "consumption critique." According to the latter, individuals are not able to choose what is best for them, what is "best" is evaluated according to outside preferences.

Our analysis should not be a pretext for jumping to the conclusion that government intervention is necessary or even advisable. (See part III.) It is unlikely that politicians and public officials have the insight or the incentive to be able to overcome this misprediction of future utilities. Moreover, some individuals may at least be able to resort to double-loop learning and establish for themselves self-binding rules that help them redress the balance in favor of goods and activities with strong intrinsic attributes over those with strong extrinsic attributes.

12 The Value of Public Goods

12.1 Measurement Approaches

Standard Methods

The benefits from public goods are inherently difficult to measure because they are not exchanged on markets. Therefore, prices paid cannot serve as indicators of the value attributed to them by individuals. A wide variety of approaches to the measurement of preferences have been developed. (See e.g. Freeman 2003.) Two main avenues have been pursued:

Stated Preference Methods   The most prevalent method is Contingent Valuation. Individuals are directly asked to value the public good in question. However, the hypothetical nature of Contingent Valuation Surveys may entail unreliable and superficial answers and may induce strategic answering behavior.

Revealed Preference Methods   The behavior of individuals and the complementary and substitutive relationships between public goods and various marketed goods are used to infer the value attributed to public goods from market transactions in private goods. The most prominent examples are the Hedonic Method, the Travel Cost Approach, and the Averting Behavior Method. Revealed Preference Methods are based on stringent assumptions, crucial elements are inherently difficult to measure, and non-use values cannot be captured.

The Life Satisfaction Approach

With reported subjective well-being as a proxy measure for utility, public goods can be directly evaluated in utility terms. Basically, the

marginal utility of public goods or the disutility of public bads is estimated by correlating the degree of public goods or public bads with
individuals' reported subjective well-being. This approach avoids
some of the major difficulties inherent in both the Stated Preference
Methods and the Revealed Preference Methods. By measuring the
marginal utility of a public good or the marginal disutility of a public bad, as well as the marginal utility of income, the tradeoff ratio
between income and the public good can be calculated. This is called
the *Life Satisfaction Approach*.

The Life Satisfaction Approach can be used to value a wide range
of public goods and bads, and negative and positive externalities.
Hitherto, the approach was used only to value externalities in the environmental realm. Van Praag and Baarsma (2004) were the first authors
to use life-satisfaction data explicitly for the evaluation of environmental externalities. Using individual data, they analyze the effect of
noise nuisance in the area of the Amsterdam Airport. Subjective well-
being is influenced by perceived rather than objectively measured
noise levels; well-being and the noise level are largely independent
of each other. Moreover, the noise level depends on a number of intervening variables, including size of family and presence of a balcony or
a garden. Consequently, the estimated compensations vary considerably for different groups of people. Other authors have undertaken
cross-country analyses. For example, Welsch (2002) identifies a negative effect of urban air pollution (captured by nitrogen dioxide) on
average life satisfaction that translates into considerable monetary
values of improved air quality.

Here we will apply the Life Satisfaction Approach to a topic that
gained notoriety in recent years and is likely to be high on the political agenda for many years to come: terrorism, or security defined as
absence of terrorism.[1] The utility losses caused by terrorist activities are
estimated for France in the years 1973-1998.

12.2 Comparing Alternative Approaches

The Life Satisfaction Approach has several advantages over the standard Stated Preference and Revealed Preference Methods.

---

1. For a more extensive discussion of the data and empirical strategy, and for additional
and updated results, see Frey, Luechinger, and Stutzer 2007b.

Stated Preference Methods

The most prominent Stated Preference Method is *Contingent Valuation*, in which respondents are asked to value a specific public good under well-specified conditions. (See e.g. Carson et al. 2003.) This is often an unfamiliar situation, and often it gives rise to problems of strategic responses. Therefore, the credibility, the validity, and the reliability of results based on Contingent Valuation are subjects of heated controversy in economics. A number of guidelines have been developed to ensure credibility, validity, and reliability. The most important are the presentation of adequate information, the choice of a credible (hypothetical) payment mechanism, and the use of the referendum format (the only elicitation format that is incentive-compatible) (Arrow et al. 1993; Portney 1994).

Nevertheless, the basic problem of the Contingent Valuation Method remains. Because of the hypothetical nature of the questions asked and the unfamiliarity of the task, one cannot exclude the failure of respondents to consider the effect of their budget constraints and substitutes. Symbolic valuation in the form of attitude expression and superficial answers is likely to result (Kahneman and Knetsch 1992). Similarly, the problem of strategic behavior can be addressed only to a limited extent. The Life Satisfaction Approach is not affected by either of these troubles. It does not rely on respondents' ability to consider all relevant consequences of a change in the provision of a public good. It suffices if respondents state their own life satisfaction with some degree of precision. Moreover, there is no reason to expect strategic behavior.

Revealed Preference Methods

This other group of non-market-valuation techniques is based on the idea that, when choosing between different bundles of public and private goods, individuals make a tradeoff, revealing something about the value they place on these goods. Under specific circumstances, this allows inferences to be made about individuals' willingness to pay for the public good from market transactions in private goods.

The most elegant and frequently used Revealed Preference Method is the Hedonic Method. (See e.g. Blomquist, Berger, and Hoehn 1988; Chay and Greenstone 2005.) The public good is a qualitative characteristic of the differentiated market goods of housing and jobs; the housing and labor markets thus reflect the value of the public good. Wage and rent differentials serve as implicit prices and correspond in equilibrium to the individuals' marginal willingness to pay for the public good (Rosen 1974). Here lies a fundamental problem of the Hedonic Method: the method is based on the assumption that the housing market and the labor market are in full equilibrium. This assumption is justified only when households have a very high degree of information, when there is a sufficiently wide variety of houses and jobs, when prices adjust rapidly, when transaction and moving costs are low, and when there are no market restrictions (Freeman 2003, p. 366). In contrast, the Life Satisfaction Approach explicitly captures utility losses in the absence of market equilibria. Compensating variation in other markets, however, has to be accounted for in cross-section analyses. If this is not done, the Life Satisfaction Approach captures only the residual externality. In this case, the Life Satisfaction Approach and the Hedonic Method complement each other. Another drawback of the Hedonic Method is the need to account for adjustments people are apt to make in response to changes in the level of an externality, and for reactions of the supply side of the hedonic market.

A challenge common to all methods based on revealed preference is that consumption and relocation decisions are based on perceived rather than objective (dis-)amenity levels; should people's perceptions and objective measures correspond insufficiently, the estimates may be severely biased. The same caveat applies to some extent to the Life Satisfaction Approach. However, in contrast to Revealed Preference Methods, the Life Satisfaction Approach captures indirect effects of externalities on individuals' utility through effects on health and other channels, even if there are no direct effects. For example, whereas noise nuisance affects utility directly and results in corresponding defense expenditures or relocation decisions, exposure to nuclear radiation can damage health through an unnoticed process that nevertheless lowers life satisfaction. In this case, utility losses cannot be measured by Revealed Preference Methods, since there is no behavioral trace. For the same reason, Revealed Preference Methods cannot assess non-use values such as the existence value. In this regard, the Life Satisfaction Approach is superior, although it is not able to capture pure existence values (or pure public goods more generally). In addition, behavioral research has shown that a distinction exists between two notions of utility: experienced utility and decision utility. The experienced utility of an outcome encompasses the hedonic experience of that outcome, whereas the decision utility is the weight an individual assigns to that outcome in a decision (Kahneman 1994). If experienced utility and decision utility differ systematically, decisions in markets for private goods do not accurately reveal people's hedonic experiences from the consumption of public goods.

As the preceding discussion suggests, there are a number of ingenious approaches to valuing public goods. They are plagued, however, by a number of troubles that hamper or prevent their application to specific goods of interest. The Life Satisfaction Approach avoids several of these troubles, and its application instead of, or complementing, the traditional approaches seems promising.

12.3   Effects of Terrorism on Life Satisfaction

Citizens' well-being is systematically influenced by the political process, which includes terrorism (Frey and Luechinger 2003; Frey 2004). It is reasonable to expect that people living in a country rife with terrorism would be less happy than those living under more orderly political conditions. A good example is the Dominican Republic in 1962, when the political situation was very unsettled after President Trujillo's murder and political chaos was a real threat. The level of life satisfaction measured in that country was the lowest ever recorded: 1.6 on the normal 0 to 10 scale. In contrast, in politically stable democracies such as Switzerland, Norway, and Denmark, the population expresses high life satisfaction. The life-satisfaction values in the 1990s were 8.16 for Denmark, 8.02 for Switzerland, and 7.66 for Norway. Thus, happiness and political stability seem to be closely related.

However, the causation may again run in both directions: although it seems obvious that political unrest is dissatisfying, it is also reasonable to expect that dissatisfied people would resort to demonstrations, strikes, and terrorist actions, thereby creating political instability. But it would be a romantic view (Tullock 1987) to assume that revolutions are normally caused by unhappiness with existing political conditions. Most coups d'état, and even revolutions, are undertaken by competing political clans, parties or the military. An exchange of rulers occurs within the political class, and is only partially fuelled by the people's unhappiness with their rulers. The people's dissatisfaction is often taken as merely an excuse to seize power.

Data and Empirical Strategy

Using life-satisfaction data, several avenues can be pursued in evaluating the utility losses caused by terrorist activity. One possibility is to follow the lead taken by macro-happiness functions based on international cross-section and time-series analyses—for instance, trying to identify the effect of environmental conditions (Welsch 2002). Alternatively, the life satisfaction of the population in particular regions and cities affected by terrorism may be compared with the remainder of a country. This novel approach, illustrated here in the case of France, has also been applied to other countries (Frey, Luechinger, and Stutzer 2007b).

Life-satisfaction data are taken from the Euro-Barometer Survey Series (1970–1999). The variable is the categorical response to the question "On the whole, are you very satisfied [4], fairly satisfied [3], not very satisfied [2], or not at all satisfied [1] with the life you lead?" The number of terrorist incidents is used as an indicator for the salience and intensity of terrorist activity; this indicator is constructed on the basis of the RAND-St. Andrews Chronology of International Terrorism and the Terror Attack Database of the International Institute for Counter-Terrorism. The two regions of Ile-de-France (including Paris) and Provences-Alpes-Côte-d'Azur (which includes Corsica in the Euro-Barometer Surveys Series) are compared with the rest of France for the years 1973–1998. Figure 12.1 depicts the number of terrorist incidences across these three regions over time. A microeconometric happiness function is specified on the basis of these data sets. The life satisfaction of an individual living in a particular region at a particular time is explained by differences in the level of terrorism across regions and over time, by the individual's household income, by other personal and socio-demographic characteristics, and by regional and time-fixed effects. A robust estimator of variance is used to account for random disturbances which are potentially correlated within groups or clusters; here, the estimator is cross-sectional units for a specific year.

Results

The estimation results suggest that the number of terrorist attacks has a statistically significant negative effect on reported life satisfaction. For 15 terrorist attacks (approximately the average number of attacks in Paris during the period studied), an average reduction in satisfaction with life by 0.04 unit on the four-point scale of life satisfaction is estimated.

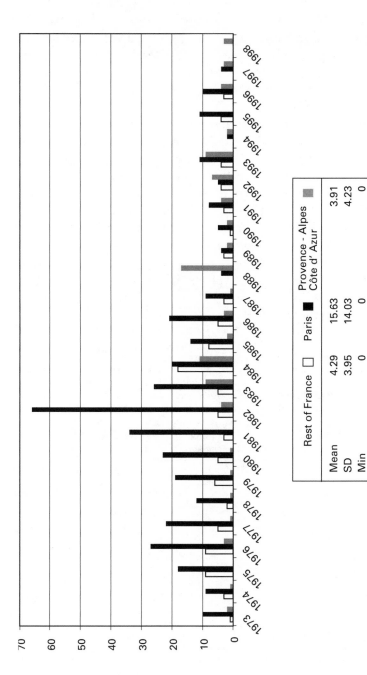

Figure 12.1
Number of terrorist incidents in France, 1973–1998. Source: Frey, Luechinger, and Stutzer 2007b.

This effect is approximately one-fifth that of being unemployed instead of employed. A frequently used indicator for terrorism, therefore, correlates with people's subjective well-being to a considerable degree.

The estimated coefficients can be used to calculate the hypothetical willingness to pay for a discrete change in the level of terrorism. For the purpose of comparison, the difference between living in the region of Ile-de-France (Paris) and living in the rest of France (except Provence-Alpes-Côte d'Azur) is considered with regard to terrorism. A resident of Paris (with average household income) would be willing to pay approximately 14 percent of his income for a reduction in terrorist activity to a level that prevails in the more peaceful parts of the country. This implicit willingness to pay is comparable with the one identified by Blomquist, Berger, and Hoehn (1988) on the labor and housing markets for individuals living in the county with the highest rate of violent crime in the United States. This exploratory application demonstrates that life-satisfaction data are well suited to assess the utility loss in a population that is due to terrorism.

Table 12.1
Terrorism and life satisfaction in France, 1973–1998. Dependent variable: Life satisfaction [1–4]. Least-squares estimations; standard errors adjusted for clustering within regions per year. Significance level: ** $p < 0.01$. Source: Frey, Luechinger, and Stutzer 2007b. The data are from the Euro-Barometer Survey Series, 1970–1999, RAND–St. Andrews Chronology of International Terrorism, 1968–2000, provided by the Oklahoma City National Memorial Institute for the Prevention of Terrorism (www.mipt.org) and the Terror Attack Database of the International Institute for Counter-Terrorism (www.ict.org.il).

	Coefficient	t value
Number of terrorist incidents (in 10s)	−0.028**	−4.03
ln(income)	0.218**	17.22
Control variables[a]	Yes	
Regional fixed effects	Yes	
Time fixed effects	Yes	
Number of observations	43,231	
Number of clusters	70	
Prob > F	0.000	
R^2 adj.	0.07	

a. Control variables include size of household, sex, age, age squared, level of educational achievement, number of children, marital status, employment status, and type of community.

Conclusions

Using life-satisfaction data to measure the value that individuals attribute to public goods is an interesting new approach that overcomes some of the major weaknesses of the prevalent techniques.

The method is particularly suited for macroeconomic evaluations of the value of public goods and bads such as the natural environment or terrorism. It tends to be more difficult to apply when a specific public good is to be evaluated—for instance, in the context of a benefit-cost analysis of a particular microeconomic project. The reason is the reliance of the life-satisfaction method on statistical relationships for which a sufficient number of observations are crucial.

Our empirical application shows that the Life Satisfaction Approach is well suited to capture the social costs of terrorism. The social costs of terrorism are both economically and statistically significant. The social costs of terrorism exceed the purely economic ones.[2] Hence, psychic costs of terrorism such as fear and grief of the bereaved are likely to be large.

---

2. For a survey of the economic costs of terrorism, see Frey, Luechinger, and Stutzer 2007a.

III   Policy Consequences

Happiness research has considerable consequences for policy, especially economic policy. In comparison with theoretical and empirical research, policy has received less attention among scholars. However, the results of happiness research are important. After all, happiness is a major goal in life—for many individuals, the ultimate goal.

Chapter 13 looks first at the advice offered in the literature derived from research on happiness. The popular media have drawn several far-reaching conclusions, and the new branch of "Positive Psychology" has evolved.

The advice based on happiness research in economics can draw on a large number of well-established results. Concrete suggestions for economic policy can be offered, such as changing preferences, increasing leisure time, or reducing unemployment by raising inflation. The proposals advanced by some scholars that the government should maximize a National Happiness Indicator and that taxes should be raised to reduce positional externalities are critically discussed.

Chapter 14 looks at the relationship between happiness and political institutions. The first section considers the evidence that citizens are made happier when the institutions of direct democracy strengthen political participation rights. The second section discusses the finding that more decentralized decision making increases individual happiness. A new form of federalism, Functional Overlapping Competing Jurisdictions, is proposed as an institution that would overcome the major disadvantages of current forms of federalism.

Chapter 15 draws conclusions and argues that happiness research constitutes a revolution in economics with respect to method, theory, and policy.

13   Happiness Policies

13.1   Popular Media

Many different conclusions have been drawn from the modern research on happiness. A popular literature has emerged seeking to give readers personal advice on "how to become happy." Some of the advice is of little value, but some of it is soundly based on research. For example, an article in the journal *New Scientist* (2003) identifies ten essential elements to a happy life.[1] The importance of each item of advice is evaluated by a group of happiness researchers, whose evaluations are used by *New Scientist* in a survey that grades the proposals on a scale ranging from 0 ("very unimportant") to 5 ("very important"). The ten keys to personal happiness are arranged in ascending order of importance to personal happiness:

1. "Don't worry if you aren't a genius." (weight 0) Intelligence as measured by IQ does not make you much happier, if at all. The reason may be that brighter people tend to have higher expectations.

2. "Earn more money (up to a point)." (weight 0.5) Chapter 3 showed that higher relative income does indeed buy happiness, but only to a small degree and only up to a specific income, which varies by country and period.

3. "Grow old gracefully." (weight 0.5) On average, increasing age tends to increase life satisfaction, as demonstrated in chapter 3. This is true if health and other factors (e.g., income) are not deteriorating. This insight contradicts the often-heard claim that elderly people tend to be depressive. An important reason for elderly people's happiness is that

---

1. Most of these determinants are dealt with in this book. On others, see Diener and Seligman 2004.

the realization that their time is running out teaches them to regulate their emotions: they concentrate on features that make them happy and circumvent those that don't.

4. "Stop comparing your looks with others." (weight 1) Good-looking people tend to be happier, perhaps because life is easier for them. Individuals wanting happiness should avoid comparing themselves in particular with models and movie stars. They should appreciate that the media project unrealistic images of such people.

5. "Be religious, or believe in some other system." (weight 1.5) Belief in God and an afterlife gives people meaning and purpose, and reduces the feeling of being alone. Religion therefore serves as a powerful way to cope with adversity.

6. "Provide help to others." (weight 1.5) There is a strong relationship between happiness and altruism, as in chapter 7. Generous people and those who do voluntary work are more satisfied with their lives.

7. "Desire less." (weight 2) As has been documented in chapter 3, an "aspirations gap" prevents people from becoming much happier when their income increases. Those who aspire to less than that which they already have as income, friends, family, work, and health are more satisfied with life. Lowering one's aspirations is an effective way to increase one's happiness.

8. "Make friends and value them." (weight 2.5) People with few material possessions but intensive social relationships do much better than those who lack such relationships (chapter 3). Making friends takes time and effort, and it is not easy.

9. "Get married." (weight 3) Chapter 8 summarizes the evidence that married people have consistently been shown to be happier than single people. Interestingly, cohabitation does not provide the same benefits as marriage, perhaps because of the lesser degree of certainty.

10. "Make the most of your genes." (weight 5) Research by psychologists reveals that a "set point" of happiness strongly influences life satisfaction. To a large extent, the genes one inherits determine this "setpoint." To achieve happiness, it is useful to develop personality traits and life styles that support happiness. For people with high opportunity costs, that may entail, for example, a commitment to watching less television (chapter 9). Extroverts tend to be happier than introverts, as they are more likely to do things that bring happiness—e.g., enjoying time with friends, or marrying.

More basic is the advice that happiness should come as a side product and cannot be achieved by aiming at being happy. This has long been known as the "hedonic paradox." (See, e.g., Mill 1909.) The idea here is that the singular pursuit of happiness makes it more distant, whereas pursuing something else may inadvertently bring happiness closer.

13.2 "Positive Psychology"

A group of respected scholars led by Martin Seligman and Mihaly Csikszentmihalyi founded a movement with the intention of developing psychological research about valued subjective experiences such as well-being, contentment, hope, optimism, and the experience of flow (Csikszentmihalyi 1990; Seligman and Csikszentmihalyi 2000; Seligman 2002; Frederickson 2001, 2003; Carr 2003). Little is known about how normal people flourish under benign conditions. Psychology has neglected to study how the lives of "healthy" people can be improved. Instead, much of psychology has focused on how people survive and endure situations of adversity. It has become possible to understand, and provide therapy for, a large number of mental disorders.

Positive Psychology has three main elements. The first concerns positive experience, or the determinants of why one moment is better than another. Kahneman (1999) emphasizes the hedonic quality of current experience as a major determinant of happiness. Second, Positive Psychology refers to aspects of personality as self-organizing, self-directed, and adaptive entities. Self-determination theory (Deci and Ryan 2000; Ryan and Deci 2000) focuses on three related human needs: competence, a sense of belonging, and autonomy. When these needs are satisfied, high personal well-being is achieved. People experiencing such well-being are intrinsically motivated and are able to fulfill their potentialities and to engage in personal growth. Under suitable conditions, a person can maintain this intrinsic motivation even under external pressures. However, not all scholars view autonomy as a way to achieve happiness. Schwartz (2000) argues that the emphasis on autonomy results in a psychological tyranny. Too much autonomy leads to dissatisfaction, because autonomous choices become burdensome and lead to insecurity and regrets. A restriction of choice under these conditions raises rather than lowers personal happiness. This view stands in stark contrast to the rational-choice view of economics, which is that greater choice is always desirable because it allows everyone to choose what he or she prefers and to discard undesired alternatives at no cost. The third element of Positive Psychology is

based on the recognition that people and experiences are embedded in a
social context. Positive communities such as the church or the family are
considered important factors for achieving happiness.

On the basis of the aforementioned ideas, three kinds of deliberate
manipulations have been proposed which intend to result in a psychological change toward greater happiness (Nettle 2005, p. 145):

Reduce the impact of negative emotions, which are very potent.

Increase positive emotions.

Change the subject to avoid the hedonic paradox.

The question, of course, is "How can these manipulations be undertaken?"
It may well be that unhappy persons are precisely those who are incapable
of undertaking them, in which case the advice does not really help.

The suggestions brought forward by Positive Psychology to maintain
and increase one's happiness are often taken up and discussed in the
popular literature. However, the approach is not undisputed, mainly
because at its fringes it has become a quasi-religious movement that does
not always meet the stringent requirements of scientific discourse.

13.3   Economic Policies

Economists' research on happiness has produced a substantial number
of interesting insights into the determinants and the nature of happiness. These are some of the major results:

• Most people, during most periods, in most countries, are satisfied
with their lives.

• Economic conditions—income, employment, price stability, fair
income distribution—are important determinants of happiness.

• Non-material aspects—family, friendships, other social ties—matter
greatly for happiness.

• People tend to adjust to their basic level of happiness after positive and
negative life events, but the speed and the extent of such adjustment differ
depending on whether it relates to income, employment or other areas.

• People are status seekers and always compare themselves to others.

• Marriage makes people happy—but not for long.

• Children lower parents' life satisfaction, but make them happy once
they leave the household.

• Extensive television viewing makes active people less happy.

• Helping others by volunteering and by giving financial support increases happiness.

• People make systematic errors about their happiness with respect to both the past and the future (misprediction); they are subject to weakness of will.

• Procedural utility matters to happiness above and beyond outcome utility.

• Culture has little effect on the marginal effect of the various determinants of happiness.

• Political institutions—in particular, opportunities for citizens to participate via democracy and federalism—are significant determinants of life satisfaction.

• The value of public goods can be measured (using the Life Satisfaction Approach).

On the basis of these insights economists have suggested various areas for policy reforms. Several such policies are discussed below.

Changing Preferences

Standard economic theory takes preferences to be constant, and therefore does not envisage a policy to change preferences. Even the few standard economists who accept that preferences may change still assume that each individual is the best judge of his or her interests. In contrast, Happiness Research demonstrates that preferences are endogenous (chapter 3) and that individuals may make systematic errors in their decisions (chapter 11). Easterlin (2003) argues, therefore, that serious attention should be paid to decision-making measures as contributing to more informed preferences. However, Easterlin is mute on the question of how this can be achieved, as is Layard (1980, 2006, 2007). They rely on education, but historical experience tells us that it is difficult, and sometimes impossible, to induce people to change their preferences in the desired direction.

It is rather bland merely to advise individuals that they should take into account the effects of hedonic adaptation and social comparison on their aspirations. Indeed, people could be offered courses devoted to "Education for Life" (Layard 2005). But, as was argued in chapter 11, individuals do not find it easy to correct their prediction of their own future preferences. There is no simple learning process, and therefore it is not clear to what extent such a policy would work. If the suggested policy intervenes with individuals' rights to make their own decisions, major difficulties arise. Many people would agree with the suggestion that advertisements aimed at children should be banned (Layard 2005), but other, more invasive government interventions have also been suggested as part of happiness policy. (See section 13.4.)

More Leisure Time

Developed economies are characterized by strong inequalities between employed and unemployed people. In the European Union, approximately 10 percent of the work force is unemployed; in Eastern Germany this figure is closer to 20 percent, and in some areas it is above 30 percent. Most unemployed people would like to work. As was noted in chapter 4, people suffer a very high loss of life satisfaction while unemployed, even when compensated for their loss of income. Similarly, a substantial share of retired people would like to continue working in some way but are forced to stop. This happens particularly in the public sector, with its rigid employment rules. On the other hand, a large number of employed people would like to work fewer hours per week and per year, even if they had to forgo some of their income (Sousa-Posa 2002). Often a person must take a full-time job with narrowly prescribed working hours. Because these restrictions strongly impair their choices, individuals are unable to reach the best possible arrangement of working hours (Di Tella and MacCulloch 2005). Many employees feel systematically overworked, stressed, and tired. This is particularly true in the United States (Schor 1991). Increased flexibility in choosing work time is therefore likely to increase life satisfaction. One way this flexibility can be achieved is by offering more part-time jobs. Among the major impediments to such a move are the present taxation and social security arrangements. Because many of the same social security and employment burdens are imposed on part-time workers as on full-time ones, both firms and workers find partial employment disadvantageous.

Although life satisfaction would increase if work could be distributed better, this is not an easy goal to achieve. Work cannot simply be redistributed in a mechanical way from those who are overworked to those who are seeking jobs or more work. The outcome depends greatly on how wage rates are affected and on how closely the many different intentions of those trying to reduce their work harmonize with the intentions of those seeking work. (This is known as the "matching problem.") Moreover, the reduction in work time of the overworked persons should not result in so great an increase in labor productivity that no additional jobs can be offered to the unemployed.

Reducing Unemployment by Increasing Inflation

One of the most consistent results identified by happiness research is the devastating effect of unemployment on happiness. A 1-percentage-point increase in the rate of inflation reduces happiness less than it is reduced by a 1-percentage-point increase in unemployment. The question is by how much, on average, a country must increase its inflation to achieve a 1-percentage-point reduction in unemployment. The aforementioned study by Di Tella et al. (2001), which is based on Euro-Barometer data, addresses this question. Di Tella et al. assume that, over the relevant range, reported life satisfaction can be assumed to depend linearly on the two economic factors. In their estimate, they control for country fixed effects, year effects, and country-specific time trends. It is calculated that a 1-percentage-point increase in the unemployment rate is compensated for by a 1.7-percentage-point decrease in the inflation rate. For example, if unemployment rises by 5 percentage points (say, from 3 percent to 8 percent), the inflation rate must decrease by 8.5 percentage points (say, from 10 percent to 1.5 percent per year) to keep the population equally satisfied. The so-called Misery Index, which simply adds the unemployment rate to the inflation rate, distorts the picture by attributing too little weight to the effect of unemployment, relative to inflation, on self-reported happiness.

According to the proponents of this macroeconomic policy (Di Tella and MacCulloch 2006), efforts to reduce unemployment increase the subjective well-being of the population as long as the rate of inflation increases by less than 8.5 percent when the rate of unemployment is reduced by 5 percent. Such an approach is somewhat misleading, for it suggests that economic policy makers can freely choose any position on the tradeoff between unemployment and inflation. This kind of choice is not possible, because expectations of inflation change as the tradeoff shifts. Moreover, it is not likely that policy instruments can be steered precisely enough to allow such a policy, especially in small open economies.

Other Policies

The policies discussed above are certainly not the only ones. In principle, all the factors systematically influencing happiness, as identified in the micro- and macroeconometric happiness function discussed in this book, are candidates for policy intervention. If a determinant has a positive influence on well-being, policy should foster it; if it has a negative influence, policy should restrict it. Some examples follow.

• Marriage contributes strongly to happiness whereas separation and divorce reduce it greatly, as shown in chapter 8. A policy that supports family values tends to increase life satisfaction.

• Curbing advertising on television, or restricting the content of television in other ways, may be a good way to increase happiness, because it reduces the unrealistic comparisons typical for that medium (chapter 9 above; Layard 2005). If television did not exist, we would be less frequently confronted with much richer, much more beautiful, much more successful, and much "cooler" individuals, and would therefore be more satisfied with what we have.

• Environmental degradation negatively affects happiness. A policy safeguarding and improving environmental conditions increases people's subjective well-being.

• The emphasis on mobility can be reduced, for it tends to lower happiness by ending important social relationships. Instead, reliability and loyalty should be fostered (Layard 2005; Osterloh et al. 2001, 2002; Frey and Osterloh 2002).

• Terrorism and crime lower life satisfaction, as was argued and empirically shown in chapter 12. Curbing terrorist activities is, therefore, important to making the population happier. Different anti-terrorism policies will have quite different effects on welfare. A coercive anti-terrorism policy based on deterrence (i.e., killing or incarcerating terrorists) has many negative effects on a country's own population. In particular, human rights are curtailed and traveling becomes more cumbersome. In contrast, a positive anti-terrorism policy tries to lead terrorists back into civil society (Frey 2004). It is not only more effective, but also has fewer negative side effects. It can be expected to yield higher returns in life satisfaction.

13.4   Should Government Maximize a National Happiness Indicator?

This section deals with the question of whether government should be given the task of achieving the highest possible value of an aggregate, or national, happiness index.

The Concept of National Happiness

The standard measure of aggregate economic activity, gross national product (GNP), is a well-defined standard that international organizations such as the Organization for Economic Cooperation and Development or the United Nations have imposed. Nevertheless, measuring aggregate economic activity by GNP has many well-known shortcomings from the point of view of welfare. The five most important of the defects are the following:

• Consumer surplus on intra-marginal units of consumption is disregarded.

• It is not possible to aggregate from the level of the individual consumer to the whole economy in welfare terms, because of distributional considerations.

• Social activities not exchanged on markets, such as services performed without pay in private households, are disregarded. (A major exception is government activity, which is measured by its cost.)

• Shadow market activities (i.e., value-adding production outside the scope of the national accounts system) are disregarded. (This applies particularly to illegal transactions such as drug dealing.)

• Some activities measured as productive, such as the activities resulting from road accidents, are "regrettables" and therefore welfare-reducing.

Because of these shortcomings, GNP is a bad indicator of the well-being of the population. Nevertheless, it is used regularly, both in scholarly treatises and in popular discussions, as a measure of welfare.

A group of outsiders, including development economists and "post-autistic economists" (Bakshi 2004), tries to counteract the orthodox GNP measure by proposing "Gross National Happiness" (GNH). This approach has been strongly supported in the Himalayan Kingdom of Bhutan. Gross National Happiness seeks to describe prosperity in "holistic" terms and to identify actual well-being rather than consumption. "Basic happiness" is measured by the quality of nutrition, housing, education, health care, and community life. A major practical shortcoming of Gross National Happiness is that there is no consensus on how it should be constructed and measured (Ura and Gatay 2004).

Recently, several leading scholars in happiness research[2] proposed an alternative "National Happiness Indicator" (NHI)—a set of indicators

---

2. See Diener 2000; Di Tella et al. 2001; Kahneman et al. 2004a; Diener and Seligman 2004; Di Tella and MacCulloch 2005.

for capturing the overall well-being of the population of a country—based on measurements of subjective well-being discussed in chapter 2.

Kahneman et al. (2004a, p. 433) argue that "the goal of public policy is not to maximize measured GNP, so a better measure of well-being could help to inform policy" and propose "measuring national well-being by weighing the time allocated to various activities by the subjective experiences associated with these activities." Such a measure summarizes the average affective well-being of a population. Kahneman et al. expect three potential uses for such a National Happiness Indicator:

• Changes in the well-being in a country over time can be identified, in particular the role of changes in affect for a given set of situations.

• The same can be done for differences in well-being between groups of people—for instance, between high-income and low-income earners.

• Differences in well-being between nations can be identified and decomposed.

Diener and Seligman (2004) also start by criticizing economic indicators for capturing only part of what is relevant for human happiness. Instead of economic indicators, they propose a "national system of well-being indicators." The system should go far beyond the present systems of measuring life satisfaction (e.g., the Euro-Barometer and the World Values Survey). It consists of "a full scale of measures, including experience sampling of certain sub-samples, that will be sensitive to changes of well-being and ill-being in the major domains of life, such as work and health, as well as narrower measures of trust, stress, meaning, and other components of well-being" (ibid., p. 21). According to Diener and Seligman, well-being includes positive emotions and moods ("The Pleasant Life"), engagement ("The Good Life"), and having meaning in life ("The Meaningful Life"). They expect the set of indicators of national well-being to provide answers to important questions and to ensure that the corresponding issues are brought to citizens' attention and addressed by policy makers. Among the questions are these: "How does economic growth influence well-being?" "How does governance influence well-being?" "Does income inequality affect well-being?" "What makes a job enjoyable and engaging?" (ibid., p. 22)

The proponents are well aware that establishing a National Happiness Indicator would require huge resources and certainly would not be easy. They argue, however, that the benefits would warrant the large costs.

Advantages

An obvious temptation in economic policy is to consider happiness functions as a reasonably good—or at least the best existing—approximation of a social-welfare function, and to maximize them. The optimal values of the determinants so derived are, according to this view, the goals that economic policy should achieve. To maximize social welfare as the ultimate goal of economic policy is an old dream in economics, dating back to Bentham (1789) and Edgeworth (1881) and introduced into contemporary economics by Tinbergen (1956) and Theil (1964). This dream is closely associated with the effort to turn economics into a natural science comparable to physics. Consistent with this view, Edgeworth titled his 1881 book *Mathematical Psychics*. A major shortcoming of this approach was that the social-welfare function to be maximized could not be measured empirically. It seems that the (so far empirically empty) social-welfare maximum of the quantitative theory of economic policy has at long last been filled with content. Di Tella, MacCulloch, and Oswald (2001) open their influential 2001 paper with the following statement:

Modern macroeconomics textbooks rest upon the assumption of a social welfare function defined on inflation, π, and unemployment, U. To our knowledge, no formal evidence for such a function W (π, U), has ever been presented in the literature.... Although an optimal policy rule cannot be chosen unless the parameters of the presumed W (π, U) function are known, that has not prevented the growth of a large amount of theoretical literature in macroeconomics. (p. 2)

Maximizing a National Happiness Indicator (NHI) can be considered a sensible policy for several reasons:

• A National Happiness Indicator includes *non-material* aspects of human welfare, such as the influence of social relations, autonomy, and self-determination on subjective well-being. In an important way, it goes beyond existing extensions of GNP such as the "Measure of Economic Welfare" designed by Nordhaus and Tobin (1972), "Economic Aspects of Welfare" (Zolotas 1981), and the "Index of Sustainable Economic Welfare" devised by Daly and Cobb (1989), all of which endeavor to count as losses all resources used to prevent crime or to repair damage.[3]

• A National Happiness Indicator looks at *outcome* aspects of components already included in GNP via input measures. In particular, this holds for

---

3. For a fuller treatment of the various empirical welfare measures, see Michalos 2005.

the vast area of government activity (measured in GNP by the costs of material and of labor). It is also directly relevant to (public) health and educational expenditures. "Social Indicators" such as the "Index of Social Progress" (Estes 1988) mostly measure the input side, such as numbers of hospital beds and doctors or numbers of classrooms and teachers.

• A National Happiness Indicator looks at *subjectively* evaluated outcomes. In contrast, the capabilities approach (which has led to the World Bank's "Human Development Index") looks at observable capabilities and functionings (Sen 1985, 1992, 1999; Nussbaum 1999, 2000; Anand, Hunter, and Smith 2005; Comim 2005).

• A National Happiness Indicator provides a *new vision* for government—a vision that goes beyond GNP and that serves as a signal that government really cares for people's well-being.

• A National Happiness Indicator augments the possibility that citizens will evaluate the government's general performance according to the criterion of individual well-being.

• A National Happiness Indicator is *democratic* in the restricted sense of attributing equal weight to every person. In contrast, the prices relevant to assessment of the value of goods in the GNP are determined by the purchasing power, and thus the income and wealth, of market participants. The preferences of individuals without income to spend are disregarded.

Despite these arguments in favor of maximizing social welfare by using a National Happiness Indicator, the following subsections argue that this approach should be rejected for a number of reasons.

Welfare Economics' Objections to Maximization of a Social-Welfare Function

Classical welfare economics[4] has long raised fundamental arguments against using the concept of aggregate social welfare rather than the concept of individual welfare. There are two highly important and partially interconnected objections to the concept of aggregate social welfare (Sen 1970).

The Impossibility Theorem
Since Arrow (1951), it has been widely accepted that, under a number of "reasonable" conditions, no social-welfare function exists that

---

4. Decisive influence was exerted by Robbins (1932) and by Hicks and Allen (1934).

generally and consistently ranks outcomes, except a dictatorship. This result derived from the assumption of impossibility spawned a huge literature (categorized by the term "social choice") that analyzed the robustness of this impossibility result when the assumptions are modified. Theorem after theorem demonstrated that nearly all changes in the axiomatic structure left unchanged the result pertaining to dictatorship. (See e.g. Sen 1970, 1995; Slesnick 1998.) It has been concluded that "there is no way we can use empirical observations on their own to produce an ethically satisfactory cardinalization, let alone an ethically satisfactory social welfare ordering" (Hammond 1991, pp. 220–221). This verdict applies to happiness functions in their capacity as social-welfare functions.

Cardinality and Interpersonal Comparisons
The ordinalist revolution in economics, on which classical microeconomics is firmly based, takes it for granted that individual welfare can be measured only in an ordinal, not a cardinal, way, and that interpersonal comparisons of utility make no sense. Even if an ideal measure of individual welfare were possible, the fundamental philosophical issues in judging social welfare for the purpose of public policy could not be avoided. For example, should people with more refined tastes, who are able to make distinctions between minute differences in quality, be accorded greater weight in social choice?[5] Interestingly, psychologists (who are usually very demanding about measurement) seem to be more comfortable with comparing indicators of feelings or utility across individuals (Kahneman et al. 2004a, p. 432). Evidence has been accumulated to show that both cardinality and interpersonal comparability may be less problematic on a practical level than on a theoretical level (Ng 1996; Kahneman 1999). Ordinal and cardinal treatments of satisfaction scores generate quantitatively quite similar results in microeconometric happiness functions (as was argued in chapter 2). This is consistent with validation results of the income-evaluation approach, which focuses on the translation of verbal evaluations into numerical figures in a context-free setting (van Praag 1991). The meaning of a sequence of verbal labels is approximately the same for all the people in the sample and the verbal scale is used efficiently because the underlying intervals are of approximately equal length.

---

5. See Stigler 1950. For an extensive recent discussion, see Kimball and Willis 2005.

Happiness Research's Objections to Maximization of a National Happiness Indicator

Within Happiness Research, two concerns have been raised regarding the use of a National Happiness Indicator as an objective of public policy.

Is Happiness the Ultimate Goal?

As was discussed in chapter 1, to achieve happiness (in its various forms) might not be people's ultimate goal. Other goals may be loyalty, responsibility, self-esteem, freedom, or personal development, for instance. Procedural aspects are also important, as was argued in chapter 10. Social-welfare measures either exclude such aspects or fail to capture them sufficiently (Lane 2000; Kimball and Willis 2005). Whether happiness is the ultimate goal of individuals, or whether it is only one of several goals, constitutes a deep and much-discussed question in philosophy. In any case, the maximization of a National Happiness Indicator is not the obvious ultimate goal of public policy.

Short-Run Effects versus Sustainable Happiness

One of the central findings of Happiness Research is that many effects of life circumstances have only a short-lived effect on reported life satisfaction (Kahneman and Krueger 2006, pp. 14–15). Extreme and well-known examples are paraplegics who, after experiencing very low subjective well-being after the accident, report themselves to be in the long run only slightly less happy than before. In contrast, lottery winners, after a short period of elation, report themselves to be little happier than before (Brickman, Coates, and Janoff-Bulman 1978). A more recent study based on longitudinal data finds that average life satisfaction decreases when a person is subjected to a moderate disability but fully recovers to the pre-disability level after 2 years. Only in the case of a severe disability, the recovery is less complete (Oswald and Powdthavee 2006). As was shown in chapter 8, average happiness increases significantly in the period leading up to marriage, but over the course of a marriage the happiness level declines to only slightly above the pre-marriage level. Most importantly for economics, chapter 3 emphasized the hedonic or "aspiration treadmill" effect, which has been used to explain the Easterlin Paradox (Easterlin 1974, 1995, 2001): people adapt quite rapidly to increases in their income, and two-thirds or more of the benefits of the increase in income wear off after about a year.

The aspiration treadmill has great consequences for social-welfare maximization, depending on how it is treated. It may well be argued that an individual who adapts quickly to higher income should be taxed very heavily, because his utility is barely and only briefly increased, whereas an individual whose utility is permanently raised by higher income should be taxed lightly. But does the small and brief increase in utility justify such a decision? And might taxpayers not react to foreseeing such a consequence in taxation by wrongly reporting a permanently higher happiness level? Alternatively, the whole issue of adaptation may be disregarded, which boils down to assuming no adaptation at all. Another possibility is to rely on remembered utility once the effects of the increase in income have been assimilated. However, it is well established that an individual's memory of the past is severely biased because of duration neglect.[6]

It must be concluded that the approach of maximizing social welfare on the basis of a National Happiness Indicator does not deal with the above-mentioned aspects of sustainable happiness. The role to be attributed to adaptation and aspiration as elements of social welfare must be discussed and decided on a more fundamental level. We need a social decision-making mechanism to indicate how adaptation effects (and similar effects) are to be taken into account.

Political Economy's Objections to Maximization of a Social-Welfare Function

The social-welfare-maximization approach disregards existing political institutions and processes and tries to substitute for them. This is the "benevolent dictator" view that is castigated in Constitutional Political Economy (Buchanan and Tullock 1962; Frey 1983; Brennan and Buchanan 1985; Mueller 1996, 1997; Vanberg 2005). The essential message is that in a democracy constitutionally designed rules and institutions allow citizens to reveal their preferences and provide politicians (the government) with an incentive to put them into reality. The maximization of a social-welfare function does not serve this process. Even if the government were to take notice, it has no incentive to follow it. The social-welfare-maximizing approach, based on empirically

---

6. According to the concept of duration neglect, retrospective evaluations of episodes are radically insensitive to variations in duration but are shaped by the most extreme moment and its end. This is the "peak/end rule" (Kahneman et al. 1993; Schreiber and Kahneman 2000).

estimated happiness functions, disregards the institutions on which democracy is based. Citizens are reduced to "metric stations." The interaction between citizens and politicians, the representation of interests by organized groups, and the concomitant information and learning processes (Bohnet and Frey 1994) are all disregarded.

Induced Incentive Distortions

So far, it has been assumed that the decision to use aggregate social welfare captured by an empirically estimated happiness function does not influence the measurement of happiness. This assumption must be doubted. Indeed, the political use of the happiness function will certainly generate strategic interactions between the government and the individuals. Two kinds of distortions should be taken into account.

Manipulation
Once the happiness function has become politically relevant, the government, the public bureaucracy, and interest groups have incentives to manipulate it. This has proved true for GNP and for other economic indicators declared to be goals of government. Since the rate of unemployment has become a politically important indicator, governments have started to influence it to suggest a better picture of the state of the labor market than is true in reality. For instance, people who have been unemployed for a long time are defined as no longer belonging to the work force and so no longer contributing to any increase in the official rate of unemployment. It is also well known that the measure of budget deficit were strongly manipulated by some European countries when the rules for the European Monetary Union required that budget deficits not exceed 3 percent of GDP and that public debt not exceed 60 percent of GDP. Many EU member countries (most notably Greece and Italy) resorted to "creative accounting" (Jameson 1988) to meet these requirements, although in reality they clearly violated them (Brück and Stephan 2006; von Hagen and Wolff 2006; Forte 2001). Such distortions of indicators were so widespread that some observers stated that "the determining factor for achieving membership of the planned European Monetary Union (EMU) seems to rely on widespread use of public-sector creative accounting measures" (Dafflon and Rossi 1999, pp. 59–60). In the (rare) case in which a government is unable to manipulate a particular indicator to its benefit, it has an incentive to create new indicators. This is certainly possible in the case of happiness. As was

pointed out in chapter 2, a variety of indicators may capture individual well-being. Governments and pressure groups will choose those most beneficial to their respective interests or will even create new ones to suit themselves.

Misrepresentation
The second systematic distortion stems from the reaction by respondents to happiness surveys. When individuals become aware that the happiness level they report influences the behavior of political actors, they have an interest in misrepresenting it. They try to "play the system."

The two systematic distortions discussed represent a basic phenomenon that applies even in the natural sciences. The Heisenberg Uncertainty Principle states that observation of a system fundamentally disturbs it. In the social sciences, both observation and public reporting can change the observed behavior of the persons involved. This reaction is similar to what is known in macroeconomics as Goodhart's Law and the Lucas Critique.[7] Goodhart's Law (1975) states that any observed statistical relationship—such as the happiness function—will tend to collapse once pressure is placed upon it for control purposes. The Lucas Critique (1976) refers more specifically to econometric modeling: different policy-making behaviors influence the expectations of private agents, and this changes behavior in a rational-expectations model.

How to Use Happiness Research for Policy

The preceding discussion has endeavored to show that the maximization of a social-welfare function measured by happiness is a dubious approach for several reasons:

• Problems of cardinality and interpersonal comparability are not fully overcome.

• Governments are not composed of purely benevolent politicians who want to make the population as happy as possible; the personal interests of politicians also matter.

• The essential elements of democratic governance are disregarded: it does not simply consist in recording the reported well-being of the citizens.

---

7. See Chrystal and Mizen 2003.

• The government has an incentive to manipulate the happiness indicators and to create new ones to suit its goals. The individuals have the incentive to influence government policy in their favor by strategically misrepresenting their happiness levels.

Of course, these arguments do not mean that the maximization of GNP would be preferable to maximizing social welfare. Rather, they suggest that the insights provided by happiness research should be used in a different way.

The fundamental social institutions shape the incentives of the policy makers. Once these basic institutions are in place and the incentives have been set, little can be done to influence the current politico-economic process. This is the fundamental message of Constitutional Economics. Economic policy must, therefore, help to establish the fundamental institutions that lead to the best possible fulfillment of individuals' preferences. Research in Constitutional Economics helps us to identify the institutions that serve this goal. Happiness Research gives us insights into how and to what extent institutions systematically affect individual well-being. The results gained from happiness research should be taken as *inputs* into the political process. These inputs have to prove themselves in political competition and in the discourse among citizens, and between citizens and politicians. This vision differs fundamentally from an approach that seeks to maximize a social-welfare function.

Happiness research has already produced many insights that can be brought into the political discussion process. As will be argued in the next chapter, results from estimates of microeconometric happiness functions for Switzerland are pertinent. They suggest that institutions of direct democracy, such as popular initiatives, referenda, and federalism, increase the life satisfaction of the population. In direct democracies and federal countries, individuals experience a higher level of autonomy—an important factor in happiness (Ryan and Deci 2001).

Conclusions

The objective of this section is to demonstrate that Happiness Research has become most useful for public policy and that it helps us to increase social welfare. However, the appropriate approach is not to maximize aggregate social welfare directly. The insights provided by Happiness Research should serve more as *inputs into the political process*, in which deliberations on the various views and results play a major role. Citizens can choose for themselves which insights they might want to consider for their own lives. The danger of state paternalism is evaded and individuals are given the chance to determine for themselves in what way they choose to raise their well being.

13.5   Should Taxes Be Raised to Reduce Positional Externalities?

This section discusses a practical proposal directly derived from one of the major results of economic happiness research: that people do not value the absolute level of their income but always compare themselves to others. This tends to lead to a socially wasteful race for ever higher income and consumption, at the end of which no one is better off than before.

The Taxation Proposal

Positional externalities occur when the rise in one person's rank decreases the utility of other persons. Some economists, notably Layard (2005, 2006) and Robert Frank (1999), are strongly impressed by the zero-sum nature of social status. When one person's position rises, the *relative* status of other persons falls correspondingly and the group as a whole, or society, is no better off. When status comes through income and someone is made happier as the result of a salary increase, other persons' incomes automatically decrease in relative terms. A higher level of income cannot increase overall happiness if people do not value absolute income but value only the relative position. The same happens for specific goods and services important to one's position in society. Someone owning such a good (for instance, a fancy sports car) imposes so strong a negative external effect on all those who do not own such a good that overall happiness stays constant (Frank 2003). As a result, the expenditure of resources to produce and sell such goods is socially wasteful, because it does not increase social well-being. It then appears beneficial to impose a high tax on higher income and on the consumption of positional goods, to discourage people from engaging in such zero-sum status competition.

The externality may be produced by differences in income or by differences in consumption. In the extreme, the utility gain by the person rising in rank is completely compensated by the utility loss of the other persons. In that case, there is a "positional treadmill" where the effort of any particular person to rise relative to the others does not produce any gain for society overall. It may even be possible that such effort reduces total individual welfare. The research on happiness discussed in chapter 3 has indeed found empirical evidence that an individual's happiness level is reduced when the average income of other persons increases. There is also convincing circumstantial evidence suggesting the same externality with respect to consumption, especially of luxury goods (Frank 1985a, 1997, 1999).

According to standard welfare economics, a tax may be warranted when an activity (here the rise in income or consumption) imposes negative external effects on other people. The government should intervene to undo the welfare-decreasing differences in income or consumption. The proposal to (highly) tax positional externalities has been advanced in particular by Frank (1999) and Layard (2006). Layard bases his proposal directly on the results of econometrically estimated happiness functions. In its simplest formulation, an individual's happiness H(i) may be seen to depend on his or her own income $Y(i)$, on the average income of others Y^*, and on a large set X of other socio-demographic, economic, cultural, and institutional determinants:

$$H(i) = H(Y(i) - \alpha Y^*, X).$$

The optimal tax arising from the positional externality is derived to be α. Its size can be approximated by econometric estimates, as has been done for various countries and periods. For the United States, Blanchflower and Oswald (2004b), using the General Social Survey based on almost 33,000 individuals and the period 1972–1998, find that α is about 0.3; Luttmer (2005), using the National Survey of Families and Households of 10,000 adults and the periods 1987–88 and 1992–1994, estimates α to be between 0.23 and 0.28. For Switzerland, Stutzer (2004), using the Swiss Poverty Study of 6,000 individuals in 1992–1994, estimates α to be around 0.33 provided that the indirect effect of the rise in induced aspirations is taken into account. The proposed tax is substantial, although it must be taken into account that part of the existing tax may already serve the same purpose. This evidence suggests that the negative effect on other persons of the rise in rank of a particular person should be taken seriously.

However, the idea of taxing positional externalities has severe limits.

Ineffective Taxation

The government may be unable or unwilling to tax high-income earners or consumption according to the positional externalities produced. It may

well happen that the distribution is made even worse because the rich may
be induced to exploit the larger opportunities to evade taxation they have
compared to the middle and lower classes. Moreover, increased tax reve-
nues may increase waste in the government bureaucracy and may induce
politicians to spend more money on welfare-decreasing purposes.[8]

Welfare-Decreasing Effects of Taxation

The higher tax induces distorting effects in the economy. According to
the proposal, at first a negative-incentive effect on work effort of the
higher taxation of income or consumption is desired because it internal-
izes status externalities. However, raising taxes is likely to induce individuals not only to supply less labor in the official economy, but also to
evade taxes by switching to the shadow economy (Schneider and Enste
2000, 2002). In addition, cheating on taxes may increase. The induced
distortions in resource allocation undermine the internalization of status externalities and may even cause overall welfare to decrease.

The two aspects just described have been treated extensively in the
economic literature and will not be discussed further here. The emphasis here is on a third aspect addressing an entirely different issue.

Individuals as Status Seekers

As a result of evolution, man is genetically disposed to seek differences
in position. That striving for status has been inherited from the early
humans (Henrich and Gil-White 2001) is well supported by evolutionary
anthropology (Chapais 1991; de Waal 1989) and by various sociological
theories (Bales 1953; Blau 1964; Stryker and Stratham 1985; Ridgeway
and Walker 1995; de Botton 2004). In economics, the importance of status effects has been emphasized by Frank (1985a, 1997), Layard (2005,
2006), and others.[9]

The scholars advocating taxes on positional externalities disregard
an important consequence of the general desire for status differences:
when one outlet for status is blocked, individuals actively seek other
ways to differentiate themselves from others. Even if the taxation of
income and consumption were successful in undoing the negative positional externalities, individuals would try to distinguish themselves
from other individuals in other ways. The crucial question is whether

8. For summaries of the literature on public choice, see Mueller 1997, 2003.
9. Hirsch 1976; Sen 1983; Bolton and Ockenfels 2000; Fehr and Schmidt 1999. For more
specific analyses relating to work status, see Nicholson 1998; Loch, Huberman, and Stout
2000; Huberman, Loch, and Önçüler 2004.

the positional externalities in these other dimensions are weaker or stronger. If they are weak, the taxation of income and consumption differences may be warranted. On the other hand, if the negative external effects produced by differences in other dimensions are strong, the taxation of income and consumption differences may be ineffective or even counterproductive. If individuals find a way in which one person's rise in rank appreciably reduces the utility of those of lower rank, the proposed taxation decreases welfare.

The Behavior of Status Seekers

Individuals actively seek new dimensions for distinction, often in creative and imaginative ways. As was discussed above, when the income and consumption dimensions are blocked by high taxation, individuals endeavor to differentiate themselves on other dimensions. Here are a few of the most important ones:

Political power   The difference in rank with respect to political position is probably as old as mankind. There have always been "ins" and "outs," "powerful" and "powerless" persons.

Awards   Some people acquire distinction by receiving orders, titles, medals, and other conferred signs of distinction (Frey 2005, 2006); others receive none.

Education   The better educated clearly have higher status.

Other activities   Individuals can seek distinction by engaging in activities outside economics and politics. Important ways to acquire distinction are sports, the arts, scholarship, social and voluntary activities, and merely being a "celebrity."

Leisure   Frank and Layard assume that when either income or consumption is taxed, individuals take more time for leisure. It is interesting to note that the evaluation of work time and leisure has changed dramatically over recent centuries. In the eighteenth century and in much of the nineteenth century, upper-class people distinguished themselves by having substantially more leisure time than lower-class people, who had to work extremely long hours. Veblen (1899) therefore spoke of the "leisure class." Today, the opposite seems to be true: being overworked is taken as a sign of being important or "in demand," whereas having time free is considered close to being unemployed.

Happiness   Individuals may seek to distinguish themselves by leading a "good life." They may engage in meditation or other philosophical, religious, and esoteric endeavors. Buddhism and other Eastern philosophies have recently become popular, and of course there is also a long Christian tradition exemplified by religious orders (Cistercians, Trappists, Carthusians, et al.). In contrast with some of the other dimensions mentioned above, individuals who practice these philosophies or religions rarely consider themselves to be of "higher rank," but they are certainly aware that they distinguish themselves from other individuals. Indeed, the latter are often willing to accept that those leading a "good life" are superior, and they rarely express any misgivings about this. Few positional externalities appear to be created by resorting to a "good life."

Determinants of Positional Externalities

To assess the welfare consequences of substituting other dimensions when the positional externalities due to income and consumption are successfully blocked by taxation, one needs to know the factors determining the extent of external effects produced by the various ranking dimensions. A great many such determinants exist. For the purpose of our inquiry, it suffices to concentrate on two: acceptance and visibility.

Acceptance of Differences
In traditional societies, people are taught and have learned to accept differences in positions of many kinds, including economic, political, and social. This attitude is strengthened by religions which proclaim that it is God's will that one should stay in the position into which one was born. When people see no way to alter this allocation of positions, they find it preferable to accept it.

Individuals committed to modern market societies[10] accept economic inequalities insofar as they result from differences in ability and hard work. High incomes and high consumption then have no negative external effects on other individuals. To some extent, the market ideology is also transferred to success in other areas. For example, successful

---

10. For an extensive survey, see Lane 1991.

athletes do not impose any positional externalities on others, because their rank is seen to be due to their own effort. The same does not hold to the same extent for political positions and awards (such as orders and medals), because many feel that these are obtained not by ability and effort but by illegitimate means.

Differences in status are resented by societies strongly committed to equality as it is propagated by the Enlightenment, by the French ("égalité") and American Revolutions, and by socialism in its multiple forms. Differences in all ranks create positional externalities, but this applies most strongly to income, consumption, and political power.

Visibility

When status differences are evident, they are more likely to be resented and to create positional externalities. "Conspicuous consumption" as described by Veblen (1899) is a case in point. The modern media, in the form of tabloids and popular television stations, work in the same direction. The positional externalities created refer not only to income and consumption but also to political power, and less so, apparently, to differences in status related to scholarly, athletic, artistic, and social activities.

In some traditional and dictatorial societies, an effort is made to hide the high consumption of the leaders. This may occasionally be possible to some extent. However, in the case of the *Nomenklatura* in Communist countries, this effort largely failed; some people even believed that the consumption level of the leaders was higher than it was in reality. However, to the extent that the status differences are and remain hidden, no positional externalities are imposed.

Combining Acceptance and Visibility

The acceptance and the visibility of status differences interact and must be considered jointly. The strongest positional externalities are produced when their acceptance is low and their visibility is high; this applies, for instance, in a modern open society committed to equality. The weakest positional externalities occur when such differences are accepted and hidden; this applies, for instance, to dictatorships in a traditional society. With high acceptance and strong visibility or low acceptance and low visibility, there are countervailing effects and the extent of positional externalities is not certain.

Conclusions

We can now turn back to the initial question: Should positional externalities due to differences in income and consumption be (highly) taxed?

The answer depends on the two well-known effects of taxation on work incentives and the capacity and willingness of the government to attain the desired reduction in the inequality of income via higher taxation: the larger the induced distorting effects of taxation, and the lower the government's ability and willingness, the more damage is done by intervening in the economy via such taxation.

Even if these two conditions were fulfilled, the normative case against taxing positional externalities would depend on whether individuals seek to re-establish their ingrained desire for status differences by substituting with dimensions that are subject to high positional externalities. The externalities created may even be higher than those for income and consumption. Positional externalities that relate to political positions, to awards, to education, to achievements in sports, the arts, and academia, to leisure, and to happiness itself also matter. The normative case for the taxation of positional externalities in income and consumption becomes weak if people transfer their drive for status to these other dimensions. On the other hand, taxing positional externalities is well taken if additional income taxes affect work incentives only weakly and if people react by resorting to dimensions with low positional externalities.

The present extent of empirical knowledge in happiness research does not allow us to determine whether positional income externalities should be taxed. Moreover, no general answer applying to all countries and all periods is warranted.

The policy approaches discussed so far share a common thread: they are based on the idea that government acts like a benevolent dictator. The next chapter argues that this approach takes a mistaken view of the politico-economic process. Instead, a constitutional approach should be followed in setting the institutions so that people can pursue their own way to happiness. Provided these institutions are well set, the ensuing processes among consumers, citizens, interest groups, organizations, and the government lead to outcomes in which individuals reap a high level of happiness.

14   Happiness and Political Institutions

The fundamental social institutions shape the incentives of the policy makers. Once these basic institutions are in place and the incentives set, little can be done to influence the current politico-economic process. This is the fundamental message of Constitutional Economics. Economic policy therefore must help to establish fundamental institutions that enable individuals to reach the level of happiness to which they aspire. Research in positive Constitutional Economics helps us to identify which institutions serve this goal, and whether they do in fact systematically affect happiness.

Two basic institutions that affect happiness significantly are direct democracy and federalism. Section 14.1 analyzes how the direct political participation rights of the citizens via popular initiatives and referenda affect their well-being. These rights constitute a major step above and beyond the right of citizens to vote, which is restricted to selecting their representatives in the legislature. Section 14.2 looks at the effects on citizen's well-being of having decentralized, and therefore often small, political units. These decentralized units—such as provinces, states, or political communes—can affect outcomes only if they have a substantial amount of power to decide for themselves. For that reason, federal decentralization requires that the sub-units have taxation power.

14.1   Direct Political Participation Rights

Institutional conditions in the form of democracy, in addition to demographic and economic factors, have systematic and sizable effects on individual well-being. Based on extensive survey data for Switzerland, the analysis in chapter 6 reveals that individuals' life satisfaction varies with how well developed the institutions of direct democracy are in their area of residence. (For a full account, see Frey and Stutzer 2000.)

An important policy conclusion, therefore, is that elements of direct democracy should be introduced.

Direct Democratic Decision Making and Its Diffusion

There are many different meanings, conceptions and misunderstandings about what "direct democracy" is. Here the term "direct democracy" (see e.g. Butler and Ranney 1994; Kriesi 2005) has the following important aspects.

Direct democracy (more precisely, semi-direct democracy) shifts the final rights in determining issues to the citizens. It does not substitute for a legislative body, a government, courts, and all the other features known in representative democracies. The extent of the right to direct participation may vary, but it always includes the power to change the constitution, normally by an obligatory referendum. Optional referenda and initiatives (allowing citizens to put issues on the political agenda) require a predetermined number of signatures by the citizens before they can take place.

From a historical perspective, three main stages of democracy may be distinguished:

• Classical democracy, which was first developed in Athens and other Greek city-states. Participation rights were restricted to male citizens and extended over only a small area. Nevertheless, the principles of democracy revered and used today were developed there.

• The French Revolution, which extended democracy over a large area. The principle of representation made it possible to introduce indirect political participation to the nation-state.

• Direct democracy, which combines the two earlier types of democracy by giving every citizen the right to decide on certain issues. The extreme (classical) form of having citizens decide on each and every issue is not practiced anywhere today, but the number of issues on which citizens may vote varies widely between countries.

Referenda are a right given to the citizens by the constitution. Government and the legislature are bound by these rights: they are not free to ask the opinion of the citizens only when it suits them. This distinguishes referenda from plebiscites undertaken by governments to sanction *ex post* a decision already made by them. With plebiscites, the citizens are not asked to decide on an issue, but only to express their support of the government. Referenda also fundamentally differ from on-the-spot opinion surveys, which do not entail any consequences for the government: it can choose to act in accordance with the results or disregard them. In contrast, when citizens have made a decision in a referendum, the constitution obliges the government to put the corresponding policy into practice.

No fewer than 405 popular referenda on the national level were held in the years 1990–2000 (Gross and Kaufmann 2002). Of these, 248 took place in Europe (half of them in Switzerland), 78 in the United States, 37 in Africa, 26 in Asia, and 16 in Oceania. In the period 1980–1990 there were only 129 national referenda. Before August 2002, issues of European integration led to no fewer than 30 national referenda. There are a large number of popular referenda at lower levels of government, particularly in Switzerland, where thousands of referenda are held at the local, cantonal, and federal levels of government.

Most democracies do not allow the general electorate to participate in important decision making. Except in Switzerland and Liechtenstein, popular referenda are not used anywhere in a regular and systematic way at the national level. In the United States, despite the many local popular decisions and the frequent use of referenda in some states, such as California and Oregon, there are no national referenda. Many important decisions likely to affect a country's fate for decades are not subject to popular referenda. A telling example is Germany, where citizens had no say with respect to either the terms or the conditions for the integration of the former GDR, the abolition of the Deutsche Mark in favor of the Euro, or the adoption of the proposed European Constitution. The politicians in power often do not take direct democratic decisions seriously, because that would restrain their power.

Direct Democracy Prevents a Cartel among Politicians

Politicians versus Voters
People acting within the confines of the political system have incentives to exploit it to their advantage. Politicians are not any worse than other people, but they may be as self-serving as other people. They strive to further their own interests, which include material wealth, recognition, and prestige.

In a democracy, politicians have three different main ways to exploit the general population and gain rents at the citizens' expense:

• Politicians may take actions that they know deviate from the voters' preferences. Political actors may do so because they follow their own ideology and want to reap material and non-material advantages, or because they have insufficient information. For instance, politicians systematically prefer direct interventions in the economy to employing the price system, because regulations generally allow them to derive larger rents.

• Politicians may secure excessive privileges for themselves or their parties in the form of direct income, pensions, or fringe benefits such as cars, houses, and lavish expense accounts.

• Exploitation of citizens may take the form of corruption (i.e., direct payments to politicians for special services provided to the payers but not to others).

Politicians have a common interest in protecting and extending these rents where possible. This means that they have an incentive to form a cartel. The politicians in many countries form a close-knit group of people clearly differentiated from the rest of the population. Their main interactions remain within the group, so that the social disapproval of the few who dare to break out of the cartel is acutely felt and carries high costs. Moreover, party leaders manage cartels, so that, in most countries and time periods, only a limited number of members are involved. As a result, the other members of the cartel will quickly and effectively sanction any defecting politician. Access to legislative positions (in particular, membership in powerful commissions), or the monetary support provided by the state, may be curtailed.

Constitutional Provisions
All the actors involved, in particular the voters, are well aware that there are strong and ubiquitous incentives for the politicians to form a cartel and to exploit the voters. This awareness has led to the establishment of three quite different forms of institutions in democratic constitutions, which are designed to keep such exploitation in check:

• Rules prohibiting excessive appropriation of rents by politicians, the most stringent ones designed to prevent corruption. Such rules are effective only if they cannot easily be circumvented and if they are well enforced. Such provisions are completely useless to prevent the first type of exploitation mentioned, namely the systematic deviation from citizens' preferences. Since the privileges the politicians accord themselves are extremely varied and are difficult to detect (especially with respect to pensions), experience shows that politicians' rent seeking can hardly be prevented. Only the most blatant cases of corruption are revealed. It must be concluded that, although such rules are of some use, they certainly do not prevent exploitation of citizens to any significant extent.

• Special courts can be established with the task of to prevent exploitation of citizens. All democratic countries have courts of account, but they fulfill their role only to a limited extent. The more directly the courts depend on the politicians they are supposed to control (Feld and Voigt 2005; Voigt 2005), the less effective they are. In this respect, it does not help much if the members of the courts of account must answer to the legislature (instead of to the government), because the cartel includes politicians inside and outside the government. Even courts of account, which are formally independent of the government and the legislature, have little incentive to, and little ability to, check exploitation of citizens by politicians. This applies particularly to deviation from citizens' preferences; it may indeed be argued (Frey 1994b) that non-directly-elected courts of account, which necessarily have to focus on the formal correctness of politicians' and administrators' behavior, tend in some respects to widen the gap between what politicians provide and what the people want.

• Competition between parties is the classical institution in representative democracies to prevent politicians from pursuing their own goals at the population's expense. Constitutions include various devices to promote competition and make a coalition among the politicians more difficult. One is the division of power among executive, legislative, and jurisdictional branches. Another is the establishment of two legislative houses. Because of the many types of existing interactions, and the well-defined gains to be expected, these devices are rather ineffective in checking the interests of the political class. An important constitutional provision for stimulating competition between parties is to guarantee, and to facilitate, the entry of new politicians and parties into the political system. Although this certainly forces the established parties in a democracy to take better care of the people's wishes and to be more careful with regard to privileges and corruption, the effects tend to be short-lived. The previous outsiders quickly realize that many advantages are to be gained by tolerating the politicians' cartel, and even more by participating in it. The experience witnessed in many countries supports this theoretical proposition. An example is Germany's Green Party, which at first fought the political establishment but which learned in a surprisingly short time to take advantage of the taxpayers' money for its own purposes.

These arguments suggest that constitutional rules, courts, and party competition are not particularly successful in reducing the possible exploitation of the general population by politicians. The constitutional features that have been elaborated are not useless, but they do not provide sufficient safeguards against politicians' rent-seeking. It is therefore desirable to search for, and to seriously consider, other constitutional means for fighting the politicians' cartel.

A referendum in which all citizens have the right to participate gives decision-making power to people outside the politicians' cartel. The ordinary citizens making the decision are not integrated into the political class and therefore oppose the cartel formed by politicians. In an *initiative*, the demands are explicitly directed against the political establishment represented in the legislature and the government. *Optional* and *obligatory* referenda serve a controlling function because, if successful, they overrule the decisions made by the executive and the legislative bodies.

A popular referendum (in the widest sense of the word) can serve its purpose only if the political class cannot block it. In many countries, the Supreme Court or, even worse, the legislature has the power to decide whether a referendum is admissible. The criteria appear to be purely formal, but in fact the members of the political class have a considerable number of opportunities and incentives to block referenda that threaten the position of the politicians' cartel. Often vague concepts, based on what *they* consider to be the "raison d'état," are employed. In Switzerland, no such possibilities exist, and therefore issues that are not desired, and sometimes even strongly disliked by the politicians, may be brought to a vote.

Historical Evidence

Referenda are indeed able to break the politicians' cartel by forcing passage of constitutional provisions and laws that are wholly against the interests of the political class. The following cases refer to Switzerland (the nation of referenda *par excellence*) and concern important historical episodes (Blankart 1992):

• During the nineteenth century, the house of representatives (the Nationalrat) was elected according to the majority rule. The largest party benefited greatly. Through seven decades, the Radical-Democratic Party secured the majority of seats. When the idea was raised that the elections should follow proportional representation to allow small parties to enter the Nationalrat, the political class strongly rejected this proposal for obvious reasons of self-interest. Nevertheless, in 1918 the majority of the population and the majority of the cantons accepted the corresponding referendum. In the subsequent elections, the Radical-Democratic Party lost no less than 40 percent of its seats.

• Until World War II, Urgent Federal Laws (*dringliche Bundesbeschluesse*) were not subject to (optional) referenda. To avoid having to seek the people's approval, and to pursue policies in their own interests, the political class in the government and the Nationalrat often declared federal laws "urgent" even if that was not in fact the case. In 1946, an initiative was started with the objective of preventing this disregard of the interests of the population. Again, the executive and legislative bodies urged the voters to reject the initiative, which was clearly one of self-interest for the politicians. However, the voters accepted the initiative. The politicians are now forced to take the citizens' interests into account when they decide on federal laws.

The history of Swiss voting provides many more examples of such clashes between the opinions of the leaders and the citizens. Moreover, the politicians have to make great efforts to endorse as quickly as possible any movements originating from outside the cartel. Sometimes established parties (but usually those at the fringes of the cartel) or associated interest groups initiate referenda. If this strategy is to be successful, the politicians have to take the population's preferences into account at least partially, and have to reduce the extent of their rent seeking. The *institution* of the referendum in this case leads indirectly to the desired outcome in which the politicians' cartel has less discretion. Citizens' initiatives also allow "unbundling" of issues, in contrast with the bundling that is typical of representative democracies. This induces policy outcomes that have a closer relationship with popular preferences (Besley and Coate 2000; Besley 2006).

Politicians are well aware that the institution of popular referendum severely restricts their opportunity to exploit the citizens/taxpayers, and therefore they oppose the introduction of elements of direct democracy. Once out of power, politicians tend to consider direct democracy more favorably—but they immediately revert to opposing it once they are back in power.

Referendum as a Process

A referendum is not merely a vote. Two important processes before and after the vote are important.

Pre-Referendum Process

The constitutional setting determines to a large extent which issues are put on the political agenda and which are prevented from appearing. In representative democracies, politicians are often skilled in preventing discussion of issues in the legislature which they dislike or which are to their disadvantage. As has been shown both theoretically and empirically, such agenda-setting power has a significant effect on voting outcomes (Romer and Rosenthal 1978, 1982; Weingast and Moran 1983).

An important feature of referenda is the *discussion process* stimulated among the citizens, and between politicians and citizens (Frey and Kirchgässner 1993, Bohnet and Frey 1994).[1] Pre-referendum discussions may be interpreted as an exchange of arguments among equals. This institutionally induced discussion meets various conditions of the "ideal discourse process," as envisaged by Habermas (1983). Citizens are encouraged to participate in politics, depending on how important the issue in question is considered to be. The experience of Switzerland shows indeed that some referenda (e.g., the referendum on whether to join the European Economic Space, whose participation rate was almost 80 percent compared with an average of roughly 40 percent) motivate intense and far-reaching discussions. Other referenda are considered to be of little importance by the voters and engender little discussion and low participation rates (as low as 25 percent). This variability in the intensity of discussion and participation overrides the much-studied "paradox of voting" (Tullock 1967; Riker and Ordeshook 1973).

The main function of the pre-referendum process is to raise the level of information of the participants. (For empirical evidence, see the next section.) It may be hypothesized that the exchange of arguments also forms the participants' preferences. What matters most is that this preference formation can be influenced, but not controlled, by the political class.

A further important aspect of the referendum process is that of moving beyond outcome considerations. Citizens may benefit from the process itself, for it is well established that individuals have a preference for participation in decision making because it enhances their perception of self-determination (Pateman 1970).[2] With regard to direct democracy, Cronin (1989, p. 11) notes that "giving the citizen more of a role in governmental processes might lessen alienation and apathy." Moreover, the political discussion stimulated by initiatives and referenda helps citi-

---

1. On the general role of discourse in democracy, see Dryzek 1990.
2. For an extensive survey, see chapter 13 of Lane 2000.

zens to understand different political opinions and positions. The social contract based on consensus is strengthened and motivates people to go beyond actions of narrow self-interest. Direct political participation possibilities are thus an important source of perceived procedural fairness, which shapes individual behavior.

Post-Referendum Adjustments
Although a political decision is formally made in a referendum, this does not necessarily mean that the government and the public administration take the appropriate action to implement it. Ultimately the extent of implementation depends on whether the persons in power obey the constitutional rules. The more legitimacy is accorded to the constitution in a political system, the higher are the costs of not following the rules. The politicians may also be persuaded to act legitimately by the threat of not being re-elected.

Which side gets a majority in a referendum is not the only thing that matters. A referendum also reveals how the population feels about a matter, and where and how large the minorities are. Groups dissenting from the majority are identified, and their preferences become visible and are integrated into the political agenda (Gerber 1997).

Empirical Literature on the Consequences of Direct Democracy

The results or consequences of having direct democratic rights are difficult to measure empirically: to do so, a frame of reference is needed. A comprehensive comparison across countries is impossible because there is essentially only one country, Switzerland, where voters take all major decisions via initiatives and compulsory or optional referenda. Scholars have therefore turned to analyses that compare the situations within the United States and Switzerland, where the extent of direct democratic rights differs between states and cantons (and sometimes between municipalities and communes).[3] Mentioning some of the most important insights will suffice to convey a general impression of the nature of this research. In the case of the United States, econometric studies reveal that the more directly democratic states (*ceteris paribus*) have lower total public expenditures, spent mostly at the county level, but tend to spend more on education.[4]

---

3. No systematic account of this line of research need be given here. For reviews, see Kirchgässner, Feld, and Savioz 1999; Matsusaka 2004; Kriesi 2005; Frey and Stutzer 2006a.
4. On general expenditures, see Matsusaka 2004; on public education expenditures, see Santerre 1989, 1993.

For Switzerland, econometric analyses suggest that (*ceteris paribus*) the more extended the direct democratic rights are in a canton, the higher is tax morale, the lower are the tax burden and public deficits, the less citizens evade taxes, and the higher per-capita incomes are.[5] In all these studies, jurisdictions within a common institutional framework are compared, and influences independent of direct democratic institutions are carefully controlled for. As a whole, with the evidence on reported life satisfaction also taken into account, econometric research leads to the conclusion that the preferences of the citizens are better observed in jurisdictions with more direct participation rights.

Introducing Direct Participation Rights

Preconditions

Institutions of direct democracy cannot function successfully unless certain conditions are met in a society. Direct democracy works well when the same group of people does not always find itself in the minority and therefore feel exploited. Citizens must have sufficient trust that the politicians will turn the decisions of referenda into reality, and the politicians must trust that the citizens will take reasonable decisions when voting on issues. This mutual trust must develop over time and cannot simply be instilled from outside. The "grand" solution of jumping from a representative democracy to a fully developed direct democracy is both unrealistic and undesirable. Instead, direct participation rights for the citizens should be introduced gradually, to enable a learning process for the citizens, the legislature, and the government.

The use of initiatives and referenda by the citizens is a major factor in raising social capital, especially in the form of citizens' trust in the government. In this way, direct democracy helps to create the necessary conditions for its own functioning, provided that learning does indeed take place.

Gradual Procedure

These are five ways in which directly democratic rights can be introduced gradually:

---

5. On the effects of direct democracy on general government expenditures, self-financing ratios, taxes, and debt, see Schneider and Pommerehne 1983; Feld and Kirchgässner 1999, 2000. On the effects on tax morale and tax evasion, see Pommerehne and Weck-Hannemann 1996; Frey 1997a; Feld and Frey 2002, 2007a,b; Torgler 2004, 2005, 2007; Torgler et al. 2003; Torgler and Frey 2007. On per-capita gross domestic product, see Feld and Savioz 1997.

Decision level   Direct democratic rights can be restricted by initially assigning them only at a particular level of the state. One possibility is to start at the local level, giving citizens the right to launch initiatives and vote in referenda in political communes. This allows the citizens to use everyday information to form a reasoned opinion. Moreover, the issues are often of immediate relevance to the population. But this procedure makes sense only if the political communes have a sufficient amount of autonomy. Preferably, they should be able to decide on both taxes and public expenditures. Another possibility is to start at the national level when major issues are at stake. In several countries, the decision whether to join the European Union, or the decision whether to accept the proposal for a European Constitution, has been relegated to the citizenry as a whole. Since these decisions are of great importance, citizens are well aware of their relevance and will certainly be inclined to participate in the vote.

Issue domain   Some questions can be excluded from direct voting for fear of "irresponsible" or "uncontrollable" outcomes. Basic provisions of the constitution, such as those referring to human, political, and civil rights, can be excluded. Supposedly sensitive issues may be removed from citizens' voting. This may refer to problems important to particular minorities, ethnic or religious groups, but also, for example, to the death penalty.

Citizens' competence   Some issues are thought to be beyond the competence of the citizens. This may be assumed to hold for taxation, for instance. Whether this is indeed true is another matter. (The example of Switzerland's referenda suggests otherwise.)

Time   A sufficient amount of time may be required to pass between the start of an initiative or referendum process, the vote, and the decision's becoming effective. This is a move toward the constitutional idea (Brennan and Buchanan 1985; Mueller 1996) of putting people behind the veil of uncertainty and thereby influencing them to take a more "objective" position. A more innovative idea is first to have an informative vote and then, after sufficient time to allow a discussion of the outcome, to have a decisive vote.

Size of majority   Passing a proposal in a popular vote may require a supermajority, for instance two-thirds of the participants. Alternatively, one may require a simple majority but of the whole electorate, including those abstaining. A stronger restriction on popular initiatives and optional referenda is the number of signatures required. A balance is needed between having a low required number (and therefore many referenda) and a high required number (and therefore few referenda).

Co-determination   The citizens' decision may become effective only if it is supported by a corresponding vote in the legislature (and perhaps even in its two houses). Another possibility would be to accord a veto right to either the citizens or to the legislature. One may also consider a double majority in the form of the vote of the whole citizenry and that of the regions (cantons or states). The latter requirement applies in Switzerland, where both the majority of all voters and the majority of the cantons must approve a constitutional referendum.

Governing Gradual Introduction
Some of the restrictions just discussed constitute a considerable danger for direct democracy. Most importantly, the restrictions introduced may stay for good. For several restrictions, this would amount to a destruction of the whole idea of citizens' participation in political decision making. The institutions of direct democracy cannot then develop their full strength. Moreover, the citizens are unable to learn the special features of direct democracy effectively. If only unimportant issues are put to the vote, for instance, or if the number of signatures required for an initiative or optional referendum is too high, the citizens cannot experience the advantages of direct democracy. On the other hand, the politicians can always claim that they gave direct democracy a chance, but that it did not work. In the case of tight restrictions, a vicious circle may develop. The way in which popular participation is introduced leads to unsatisfactory results and experiences, which provide the opponents of direct democracy (in particular, the politicians in power) with a good reason to introduce even more severe restrictions. Of course, under these circumstances direct democracy cannot work.

Conclusions

The evidence allows us to draw the following conclusions:

• Direct democracy systematically increases subjective well-being (citizens' happiness).

• Direct participation possibilities increase the procedural utility produced for the voters, which is an additional source of individual well-being.

• The standard arguments against direct democracy (citizens' incompetence and lack of interest, danger of manipulation and emotionality, hindering progress and destroying civil rights, high cost) are not convincing.

• Direct democratic decisions require time and opportunity for intensive discussion.

• Elements of direct democracy can be introduced at the national and local levels and can then proceed further.

• A gradual introduction of features of direct democracy is certainly possible and advisable, since this supports a necessary learning process,

• Citizens should have the right to govern the process of introducing popular initiatives and referenda.

The institutions of direct democracy have beneficial effects on happiness by improving political outcomes as well as raising procedural utility. Direct democracy is not, of course, the only institution capable of increasing people's life satisfaction through politics. There are many other fruitful possibilities for achieving this aim. Nevertheless, it is certainly a worthwhile direction for the further development of democracies.

14.2   Decentralized Political Decision Making

Federal decentralization, and local autonomy in particular, is another constitutional feature which was shown in chapter 6 to increase citizens' happiness. Political decision making in communes is closer to relevant information about residents' preferences and also closer to direct control by citizens.

The term 'federalism' is commonly understood to refer to division of a nation's territory into smaller units. The middle units—called provinces, states, or cantons—add up to the national territory, while the political communes add up to the individual middle units. Here, a proposal is advanced that breaks drastically with this principle. A new form of decentralization is designed which allows overlapping political jurisdictions. This proposal helps to solve the important question of what jurisdiction should be considered in happiness policy. It suggests that it should be not simply the nation but more the particular functional units.

A New Proposal for Federalism

The idea developed here is based on four basic conditions that future democratic governance should meet so as to contribute to the happiness of the citizens: it should be peaceful and democratic, allow diversity, and be productive. The proposal emphasizes the role of citizens in the political process and suggests decentralization of each government function to a jurisdiction with the most appropriate size. The new concept of federalism is called *Functional, Overlapping Competing Jurisdictions.*[6] The acronym is FOCJ. (One such jurisdiction will be called a FOCUS.) FOCJ form a decentralized system of governments that is not dictated from above but rather emerges from below as a response to citizens' preferences. A constitutional decision is required, ensuring that the emergence of FOCJ is not blocked by existing jurisdictions such as direct competitors or higher-level governments. The lowest political units (the communes) must be given a certain degree of independence so that they can engage in forming FOCJ. Such local fiscal responsibility motivates the citizens to balance the benefits and cost of public expenditure and in turn motivates the politicians in the lower-level governmental units to use the scarce resources they have for the benefit of the citizens.

The vision proposed here is to some extent radical, but not outlandish:

• The proposal of democratic decentralized jurisdictions is based on concepts central to economics and to the economic theory of federalism in particular (Breton 1996; Oates 1999), e.g. "fiscal equivalence," "voting by foot" or "clubs." However, they are combined in new ways to yield a different type of federalism.

• The proposal does not require the dismantling of the national states. The nation survives insofar as it can demonstrate that it is able to well serve the demands of citizens across its territory. Some services may indeed be best provided at the national level, but these are apt to be few. Many public services are better provided at levels that bridge the existing territorial boundaries of nations and provinces.

• The proposal is realistic. Indeed, pertinent examples can be found in history. Moreover, the proposal can be introduced in marginal steps.

---

6. For more extensive treatments of FOCJ, see Frey and Eichenberger 1999 and Eichenberger and Frey 2002

Constituting Elements

The federal units proposed here have four essential characteristics:

• functional (F)—i.e., the new political units extend over areas defined by the tasks to be fulfilled

• overlapping (O)—i.e., governmental units corresponding to the many different tasks (functions) extend over different geographical areas

• competing (C)—i.e., individuals and/or communities may choose to which governmental unit they want to belong, and they have political rights to express their preferences directly via initiatives and referenda

• jurisdictions (J)—i.e., the units established are governmental; they have enforcement power, and above all they can levy taxes.

FOCJ establish a new system of governments different from the one suggested in the standard literature on federalism. Whereas the economic theory of federalism analyzes the behavior of *given* political units at the different levels of government, FOCJ *emerge* in response to the "geography of problems."

The four elements of FOCJ are now related to economic theory as well as to existing federal institutions; there are both similarities to and differences from existing concepts.

Functions

The people living in a geographical location that benefits from a particular public service should also finance it (i.e., there should be no spillovers). The various governmental units providing for different functions provide for regional differences in the populations' preferences. To minimize cost, these units have to exploit economies of scale in production where they exist. Since the latter may strongly differ between functions (e.g., schools, police, hospitals, power plants, and defense), an additional reason exists for uni-functional (or few-functional) governmental units of different sizes. This is the central idea of "fiscal equivalence," as proposed by Olson (1969) and Oates (1972). This endogeneity of the size of governmental units constitutes an essential part of FOCJ. However, fiscal equivalence theory has been little concerned with decision making within functional units. Either the supply process is left unspecified or it is assumed that the mobility of individuals (and of firms, a fact rarely mentioned) automatically induces these units to take account of individual preferences.

Overlaps

FOCJ may overlap in two respects: (a) FOCJ providing for different functions may overlap; (b) two or more FOCJ even providing for the same function may geographically intersect (e.g., a multitude of school FOCJ may exist in the same geographical area). An individual or a political community normally belongs to various FOCJ at the same time. FOCJ need not be physically contiguous, and they need not have a monopoly over a certain area of land. They are in this respect similar to Buchanan's (1965) "clubs," which may intersect. This concept differs completely from archaic nationalism committed to pieces of land.

Competition

The heads of FOCJ are motivated to conform closely to their members' preferences by two mechanisms: while the individuals' and communities' possibilities to *exit* mimics market competition (Hirschman 1970), their right to *vote* establishes political competition (Mueller 2003). It should be noted that migration is only one means of exit; often, membership in a particular FOCUS can be discontinued without changing one's location. Exit is not restricted to individuals or firms; as was noted above, political communities, or parts of them, may also exercise this option. Moreover, exit may be total or only partial. If exit is partial, an individual or a community participates in only a restricted set of FOCUS activities.

Secession has been suggested as an important ingredient for a future European constitution (Buchanan 1991; European Constitutional Group 1993). The right to secede stands in stark contrast to the prevailing concepts of nation-states and federations, according to which this is strictly forbidden and often prevented by force. Current European treaties do not provide for the secession of a nation from the European Union, and *a fortiori* they do not provide for a part of a nation to do so. For FOCJ to establish competition between governments, exit should be as unrestrained as possible. In contrast, entry need not necessarily be free. Jurisdictions and individuals may be asked to pay a price if they want to join a particular FOCUS and benefit from its public goods. The current members of the particular FOCUS have to decide democratically whether a new member is to be admitted and which is the adequate entry price to be paid.

Further, competition should be promoted by political institutions, for the exit option does not suffice to persuade governments to act efficiently. The citizens should directly elect the persons managing the

FOCJ, and should be given the right to initiate popular referenda on specific issues. These democratic institutions are known to increase efficiency in the sense of providing well for individual preferences.[7]

Jurisdictions

A FOCUS is a democratic governmental unit with authority over its citizens, including the power to tax. According to the two types of overlap, two forms of membership can be distinguished:

• The lowest political unit (normally the political community) and all corresponding citizens automatically become citizens of the FOCJ to which their community belongs. In that case, an individual can exit only via mobility.

• Individuals may choose freely whether they want to belong to a particular FOCUS, but they are subject to its authority as long as they are its citizens. Such FOCJ may be non-voluntary in the sense that one must belong to a FOCUS providing for a certain function (e.g., a school FOCUS) and must pay the corresponding taxes. (This is analogous to health insurance, which in many countries is obligatory, but for which individuals are allowed to choose an insurance company.) The citizens of such a school FOCUS may then decide that everyone must pay taxes to finance a particular school, irrespective of whether one has children. With respect to FOCJ providing functions with significant redistributive effects, a minimal regulation by the central government may be in order so that, for example, citizens without children do not join a "school FOCJ" that in fact does not offer any schooling and have correspondingly low (or zero) taxes.

Advantages and Claimed Disadvantages of FOCJ

Advantages

FOCJ compare favorably with traditional forms of federalism. One aspect concerns the governments' incentives and possibilities of satisfying heterogeneous preferences of individuals. Because of the concentration on one functional area, the citizens of a particular FOCUS have better information on its activity, and are in a better position to compare its performance with that of other governments. Because many benefits and costs extend over a rather limited geographic area, FOCJ often

---

7. On elections, see Downs 1957 and Mueller 2003. On referenda, see Kirchgässner, Feld, and Savioz 1999.

tend to be small. The exit option opened by the existence of overlapping jurisdictions is also an important means to make one's preferences known to governmental suppliers.

On the other hand, FOCJ are able to provide public services at low cost because they are formed to minimize inter-jurisdictional spillovers and to exploit economies of scale. When the benefits of a specific activity indivisibly extend over large areas, and there are decreasing costs, the corresponding optimal FOCUS may cover many communities, or several nations, or an even greater area. An example may be defense against outward aggression, where the FOCUS should be appropriately large.

The threat of dissatisfied citizens or communities leaving the FOCUS, and the benefit of new citizens and communities joining, gives an incentive to take individuals' preferences into account and to provide the public services efficiently. Quite another advantage of FOCJ is that they open up the politicians' cartel to functionally competent outsiders. Whereas all-purpose jurisdictions attract people with broad and non-specialized knowledge to become politicians, people with a well-grounded knowledge in a particular functional area (say, education or refuse collection) are successful in FOCJ.

Claimed Disadvantages
Up to this point, the advantages of FOCJ have been emphasized. However, there are also possible disadvantages. These will now be discussed. (See also Vanberg 2000.)

• Citizens are overburdened by the voting load. In a federal system of FOCJ, each individual is a citizen of various jurisdictions. Individuals may consequently be overburdened by voting in elections and by referenda taking place in each FOCUS. However, citizens in a direct-democratic FOCUS find it much easier to participate politically, because they have to assess only one or two concrete issues at a time.

• Citizens are cognitively overburdened. An individual is confronted with a multitude of suppliers of public services, which arguably makes life difficult. However, FOCJ do not cause the dimensionality of politics to grow: they make it explicit instead. The evidence from private consumer markets tells us that citizens are able to cognitively master a broad array of supplies if they have the appropriate information. FOCJ provide stronger incentives and opportunities for the citizens to be politically informed than do traditional forms of government. Membership in FOCJ is decided on the local or even the private level, and the performance of functional units can be easily monitored by comparison and benchmarking. To help citizens, an independent advisory service offering information can be established.

• Coordination is needed. While co-ordination is obviously often needed, coordination between governments is not necessarily beneficial. It sometimes serves to build cartels among the members of the political class, who then evade or even exploit the population's wishes (CEPR 1993; Vaubel 1994; Frey 1994a). Where welfare-increasing coordination is concerned, its need is reduced because the FOCJ emerge to minimize externalities. If major spillovers exist between FOCJ, new FOCJ will be founded and will take care of these externalities.

• Income needs to be redistributed. It is sometimes claimed that all forms of federalism—including FOCJ—undermine redistribution. FOCJ are also said to emerge on the basis of income. To the extent that redistribution is based on the citizens' solidarity or on insurance principles, this fear is not warranted. A problem may arise only where redistribution is a pure public good and so must be enforced to prevent free-riding. Even then, FOCJ compare favorably with traditional forms of federalism: they lead to less geographical segregation because the citizens can select their supplies without migrating. However, recent empirical research (Gold 1991; Kirchgässner and Pommerehne 1996; Ashworth, Heyndels, and Smolders 2002) suggests that substantial redistribution is feasible in federal systems. To the extent that redistribution is a pure public good, it will be delegated to higher-level governments or perhaps to specialized redistribution FOCJ at the national or international levels.

Existing Functional Political Units

History
Decentralized, overlapping political units have been an important feature in European history. The competition was intensive between governments in the Holy Roman Empire of German Nations, especially in what is known today as Italy and Germany. Many of these governments were small. Many scholars attribute the rise of Europe to this diversity and competition of governmental units, which fostered technical, economic, and artistic innovation.[8] The unification of Italy and Germany in the nineteenth century, although often praised as a major achievement, partially ended

---

8. On this competitive aspect of European history, see Hayek 1960; Jones 1981; Rosenberg and Birdzell 1986; Weede 1993.

the stimulating competition between governments and led to deadly struggles between nation-states. Some smaller states escaped unification: Liechtenstein, Luxembourg, Monaco, San Marino, and Switzerland stayed politically independent, and at the same time grew rich.

The above-mentioned governmental units were not FOCJ in the sense that is outlined here, but they shared the characteristic of competing for labor and capital. History also reveals examples of jurisdictions even closer to FOCJ. The highly successful Hanse prospered from the twelfth century to the sixteenth, and comprised *inter alia* Lübeck, Bremen, Köln (today German), Stettin and Danzig (today Polish), Kaliningrad (today Russian), Riga, Reval, and Dorpat (today parts of the Baltic republics), and Groningen and Deventer (today Dutch). Furthermore, London (England), Bruges and Antwerp (today Belgian), and Novgorod (today Russian) were *Handelskontore* (associated members). It was clearly a functional governmental unit that provided trade rules and facilities and was not geographically contiguous.

Present-Day Cases

In the United States and in Switzerland, functional, overlapping, and competing jurisdictions exist to some degree. They do not in all cases meet all the requirements of FOCJ specified above, but nevertheless they show that democratic functional jurisdictions are viable.

Single-purpose governments called *special districts* play a significant role in the American federalist system. They have increased in number more quickly than other types of jurisdictions (Zax 1988). There are autonomous and democratically organized districts as well as dependent special districts (e.g., for fire prevention, recreation, and parks). Empirical research suggests that the former type is significantly more efficient (Mehay 1984). Existing jurisdictions tend to oppose the formation of special districts. In order that the monopoly power of existing municipalities may not be threatened, statutes in 18 states prohibit new municipalities within a specified distance of existing municipalities; in various states, a minimum population size is required and various other administrative restrictions have been introduced (Nelson 1990). Empirical studies reveal that these barriers tend to reduce the relative efficiency of the local administration (DiLorenzo 1981; Deno and Mehay 1985) and that they tend to increase the expenditures of local governments (Martin and Wagner 1978).

Many cantons in Switzerland have overlapping and competing functional jurisdictions that share many features of FOCJ. For example, in Canton Zurich (with a population of 1.2 million and a size of 1,700 square kilometers) there are 171 political communes, which in turn have from three to six independently managed, democratically organized special communes devoted to specific functions and able to collect taxes. Examples for such types of functional communes are found not only in Canton Zurich, but also in other cantons (Casella and Frey 1992). The example of Switzerland—generally considered a well-organized and well-administered country—shows that a multiplicity of functional jurisdictions under democratic control is not a theorist's wishful thinking but an entity that has worked out well in reality.

FOCJ may also be useful for managing ethnic conflict, as Kyriacou (2006) argues for the cases of Cyprus, Kosovo, and the Kurds.

Putting the Idea to the Test

In view of the major advantages of FOCJ, the economist's standard question arises: If this type of federalism is so good, why is it not more successful?

The organization of states today does not follow the model of FOCJ for two major reasons:

• An obvious and important reason is that individuals and communities are prohibited from establishing such jurisdictions, and in many countries communities are not even allowed to formally collaborate with each other without the consent of the central government (Sharpe 1993).

• A system of FOCJ could not evolve, because it violates the interests of politicians and public officials at the higher levels of government. The emergence of FOCJ reduces the public suppliers' power and increases citizens' influence.

FOCJ would be useful for the integration of Europe. At present, the European Union insists that new members fully accept the *acquis communautaire*, even though their economic and institutional development may differ drastically from those of the present member states. Even staunch supporters of the present European unification are aware that it is not possible to integrate these countries into the EU without creating major economic and social problems. FOCJ would also present an excellent opportunity to open up the EU constitution to overcome its "democracy deficit" and its "decentralization deficit."

Functional Overlapping Competing Jurisdictions are a progressive form of political decentralization. They can therefore be expected to strengthen the features of federalism that Happiness Research has found to increase individual well-being.

15   A Revolution in Economics

Some readers may well agree that happiness research has yielded new insights that may be called revolutionary when compared with standard economics. Other readers will not be convinced that happiness research has really extended our knowledge much beyond what was known before. They would not call this new branch of economics revolutionary.

The term 'revolutionary' has many different meanings and connotations, and its use is strongly determined by personal preferences. But most scholars would agree that it involves fundamental new insights, and the question then is "What do 'fundamental' and 'new' mean in the case of happiness research?" The skeptics will still argue that the changes introduced into economics are not really basic or new. They are right in the sense that there is nothing new under the sun and in the sense that almost everything has already been thought and argued about.

I wish to suggest, nevertheless, that happiness research has a revolutionary character in comparison with standard (textbook) economics. In the following, this claim will be illustrated by considering three aspects: method (section 15.1), theory (section 15.2), and policy (section 15.3).

15.1 Method

In the 1930s, economic theory was fundamentally changed by two ideas propagated forcefully in the "ordinalist revolution": that utility cannot be measured and that it is not necessary to measure utility to derive the major microeconomic propositions. At the time, these ideas were rightly considered to be a (successful) "revolution." Microeconomics thereafter adopted them as a major element—perhaps even the essential element. This is clearly evident in all modern textbooks of microeconomic theory.

Happiness theory reverses the two claims:

• It is possible to use measures of subjective well-being as a (reasonably) good proxy for the theoretical concept of utility as preference satisfaction.

There are five approaches to measuring subjective well-being or happiness (as was shown in chapter 3). All these approaches may be criticized. However, steady progress is being made, and the resulting measures of happiness will become more and more useful for theory and policy.

• Measurement of utility is sometimes needed to deal with important issues faced by economics.

Utility must be measured when it is known or suspected that revealed preferences do not faithfully reflect individuals' utility. As was argued in chapters 9 and 11, this holds particularly when individuals make systematic errors in decision making that are due to misprediction of the future utility of the consumption goods or to self-control problems. Utility has always been measured in order to evaluate public goods. But the willingness-to-pay method and the hedonic market method used for this purpose have serious limitations. Approaches based on happiness research at least partly overcome these shortcomings, as was illustrated in chapter 12 by the case of the welfare loss brought about by terrorism.

If the claim that utility cannot and need not be measured was considered revolutionary for economics in the 1930s, it may well be argued that the reversal of this claim is also revolutionary. Happiness in this regard is a counter-revolution to standard microeconomics.

15.2   Theory

Happiness research can be considered revolutionary for economics because it opens new avenues and suggests new aspects that have so far been disregarded or found to be unproductive. Two examples, one from microeconomics and the other from macroeconomics, may support this claim.

Public Economics

One of the most important fields of application of neoclassical economics to public finance has long been the theory of optimal taxation (Bradford and Rosen 1976.) The same approach has also been used to calculate optimal prices for goods offered by public enterprises (Bös 1981) and to derive optimal policies against tax evasion (Allingham and Sandmo 1972; Sandmo 2005). This approach proceeds by assuming certain properties of individual utility functions and derives the optimal use of the policy instruments by maximizing these utilities. Happiness research may provide important inputs into this approach, since it allows us to provide empirical support (or rejection) for the assumptions made concerning the properties of the individual utility functions. For instance, the extent to which the marginal utility of income falls with increasing income may be indicated. This knowledge is most relevant for optimal taxation theory, especially when aspects of income distributions are taken into account. It would introduce a measure of practicality sometimes missing in the optimal taxation exercises.

Economic Growth

The theory of optimal growth has been an important area in economics. It studies what share of income should be devoted to investment to attain the highest long-run utility for the individuals. If the investment share is low, economic growth is hampered and individuals will be able to consume less in the future. If the investment share is high, present consumption is low but individuals will be able to consume more in the future. To address this optimization problem, various assumptions about the properties of the welfare functions have to be made—in particular, by how much future consumption must be discounted.

Happiness research can contribute relevant insights into this optimization issue. In particular, empirical evidence can be adduced for how strongly marginal utility decreases with increasing income. But perhaps even more importantly, happiness research can point out the adaptation of individuals to higher income levels and the comparison with peer groups (as was discussed in chapter 3). These aspects of sustainable well-being were almost entirely neglected in growth theory, but happiness research shows them to be of great empirical relevance. Such knowledge opens the way to fundamental new consideration of the extent to which economic growth increases individual well-being and how it does so. Because of the rapid adaptation and strong positional effects, increasing per-capita income levels loses force as a major goal.

Again, it is an open question whether these and other inputs into economic theory are substantial enough to merit the adjective 'revolutionary'. But it is hard to deny that the new insights provided should have a considerable influence on how the optimization issues are conceived.

15.3   Policy

This book has emphasized the important consequences of the results derived from happiness research for economic policy. The reader is reminded of three aspects.

Establishing Causality

An important requirement for any economic policy is to firmly establish the influence of policy on outcomes. Correlation is not sufficient because it can be produced by a third variable or a selection effect. For example, married people are happier than unmarried ones, self-employed individuals report higher job satisfaction than dependent ones, and voluntary workers are happier than those not engaging in such work. But it would be wrong to jump to the conclusion that individual well-being would be increased if more people were married, self-employed or performing voluntary work. It may be that happier people are more likely to be married, to choose self-employment and to volunteer. The discussion in chapters 7 and 8 indicates that both causal directions are relevant. This is an insight of considerable policy consequence. It suggests *prima facie* that a policy directly or indirectly supporting marriage, self-employment and voluntary work is potentially able to increase people's happiness.

Evaluation of Tradeoffs

Happiness research provides important empirical inputs to decision makers faced with choosing between macroeconomic variables that conflict with each other. The most important one is the classical tradeoff between unemployment and inflation. In many countries, a similarly important tradeoff exists between economic growth and equality, or between growth and unemployment. Chapter 13 warns us that happiness theory should not be used to try to maximize aggregate social welfare. Instead, the insights provided by happiness research should be used as one important input into the political process of how the tradeoff between macroeconomic variables can be evaluated. In particular, the research on happiness strongly suggests that unemployment imposes high costs on individuals. It also suggests that it is not sufficient to compensate the unemployed by securing their income. It is rather that major costs in terms of psychological stress should be taken into account.

Institutional Design

Happiness research allows us to see more clearly the consequences for individuals' well-being of choosing particular institutional settings. According to the empirical evidence adduced in chapter 14, more extensive political participation rights and federalism increases the life satisfaction of individuals. There are many other institutions whose effects on individual utility can and should be studied. An example would be to determine to what extent an independent central bank and independent judiciary contribute to individual happiness.

There can be little doubt that happiness research can make new and most useful contributions to economic policy that go far beyond what was possible before its advent. It is, therefore, not far-fetched to speak of a possible revolutionary impact on policy.

15.4   Only a Beginning

If happiness research may be said to have revolutionary consequences for economics (and also for the other social sciences), the existing state of knowledge is only a first step. Our knowledge is woefully incomplete, as has been repeatedly pointed out in this book. Much is still unknown and uncertain, and many interesting issues have not been addressed at all. In particular, little is known about what results apply to exactly what settings. For instance, does the positive effect of increased political participation rights found in Switzerland carry over to other periods, types of democracy, traditions, and cultures? This question has not been studied in the context of happiness research, but I hope that it will be in the future. Another issue about which we should know more is how happiness develops over the longer term. Existing studies strongly suggest that happiness depends less on levels than on changes. For many determinants of happiness, such as income or divorce, people affected by positive or negative shocks tend to revert to a base-line level of happiness after some time. They adapt and cope to some extent. Knowing more about the characteristics of this adjustment process would help us to better understand *sustainable* happiness.

That so much is still open, and that the revolution has only started, are challenges to scholars. In particular, young economics scholars should be attracted to this field, in which so much useful and interesting work can still be done.

References

Akerlof, George, and Rachel Kranton. 2005. Identity and the Economics of Organizations. *Journal of Economic Perspectives* 19, no. 1: 9–32.

Alesina, Alberto, Rafael Di Tella, and Robert MacCulloch. 2004. Inequality and Happiness: Are Europeans and Americans Different? *Journal of Public Economics* 88: 2009–2042.

Alesina, Alberto, and Edward Glaeser. 2004. *Fighting Poverty in the US and Europe: A World of Difference*. Oxford University Press.

Alesina, Alberto, Edward Glaeser, and Bruce Sacerdote. 2001. Why Doesn't the US Have a European-Style Welfare State? *Brookings Papers on Economic Activity* 2: 187–277.

Alesina, Alberto, and Eliana La Ferrara. 2005. Preferences for Redistribution in the Land of Opportunities. *Journal of Public Economics* 89, no. 5–6: 897–931.

Allais, Maurice. 1953. Le comportement de l'homme rationnel devant le risqué, critique des postulats et axioms de l'école Americaine. *Econometrica* 21: 503–546.

Allingham, Michael, and Agnar Sandmo. 1972. Income Tax Evasion: A Theoretical Analysis. *Journal of Public Economics* 1, no. 3–4: 323–338.

Alm, James, Gary McClelland, and William Schulze. 1992. Why Do People Pay Taxes? *Journal of Public Economics* 48, no. 1: 21–38.

Anand, Paul. 2001. Procedural Fairness in Economic and Social Choice: Evidence from a Survey of Voters. *Journal of Economic Psychology* 22, no. 2: 247–270.

Anand, Paul, Graham Hunter, and Ron Smith. 2005. Capabilities and Well-Being; Evidence Based on the Sen-Nussbaum Approach to Welfare. *Social Indicators Research* 74, no. 1: 9–55.

Andreoni, James, Brian Erard, and Jonathan Feinstein. 1998. Tax Compliance. *Journal of Economic Literature* 36, no. 2: 818–860.

Andrews, Frank, and John Robinson. 1991. Measures of Subjective Well-Being. In *Measures of Personality and Social Psychological Attitudes*, ed. J. Robinson, P. Shaver, and L. Wrightsman. Academic Press.

Andrews, Frank, and Stephen Withey. 1976. *Social Indicators of Well-Being: Americans' Perceptions of Life Quality*. Plenum.

Angeletos, George-Marios. 2001. The Hyperbolic Consumption Model: Calibration, Simulation, and Empirical Evaluation. *Journal of Economic Perspectives* 15, no. 3: 47–68.

Anheier, Helmut, and Lester Salamon. 1999. Volunteering in Cross-National Perspective: Initial Comparisons. *Law and Contemporary Problems* 62, no. 4: 43–65.

Argyle, Michael. 1987. *The Psychology of Happiness*. Methuen.

Argyle, Michael. 1999. Causes and Correlates of Happiness. In *Well-Being: The Foundations of Hedonic Psychology*, ed. D. Kahneman, E. Diener, and N. Schwarz. Russell Sage Foundation.

Argyris, Chris, and Donald Schön. 1978. *Organizational Learning: A Theory of Action Perspective*. Addison-Wesley.

Arrow, Kenneth. 1951. *Social Choice and Individual Values*. Wiley.

Arrow, Kenneth, Robert Solow, Edward Leamer, Paul Portney, Ray Radner, and Howard Schuman. 1993. Report of the NOAA-Panel on Contingent Valuation. *Federal Register* 58, no. 10: 4601–4614.

Ashworth, John, Bruno Heyndels, and Carine Smolders. 2002. Redistribution as a Local Public Good: An Empirical Test for Flemish Municipalities. *Kyklos* 55: 27–56.

Atkinson, Anthony, François Bourguignon, and Christian Morrison. 1992. *Empirical Studies of Income Mobility*. Harwood.

Bakshi, Rajni. 2004. Gross National Happiness. *Post-Autistic Economics Review* 26, August, article 6.

Bales, Robert. 1953. The Equilibrium Problem in Small Groups. In *Working Papers in the Theory of Action*, ed. T. Parsons, R. Bales, and E. Shils. Free Press.

Barkow, Jerome. 1975. Strategies for Self Esteem and Prestige in Maradi, Niger Republic. In *Psychological Anthropology*, ed. T. Williams. Mouton.

Baumeister, Roy. 1998. The Self. In *The Handbook of Social Psychology*, volume 1, ed. D. Gilbert, S. Fiske, and G. Lindzey. Oxford University Press.

Becker, Gary. 1965. A Theory of the Allocation of Time. *Economic Journal* 75: 493–517.

Becker, Gary. 1973. A Theory of Marriage: Part I. *Journal of Political Economy* 81, no. 4: 813–846.

Becker, Gary. 1974a. A Theory of Marriage: Part II. *Journal of Political Economy* 82, no. 2: S11–S26.

Becker, Gary. 1974b. A Theory of Social Interactions. *Journal of Political Economy* 82, no. 6: 1063–1093.

Becker, Gary. 1981. *A Treatise on the Family*. Harvard University Press.

Benesch, Christine, Bruno Frey, and Alois Stutzer. 2006. TV Channels, Self-Control and Happiness. Working Paper 301, IEW (Institute for Empirical Research in Economics), University of Zurich.

Bentham, Jeremy. 1789 [1996]. *An Introduction to the Principles of Morals and Legislation*. Clarendon.

Benz, Matthias. 2005. The Relevance of Procedural Utility for Economics. Working Paper 256, IEW (Institute for Empirical Research in Economics), University of Zurich.

Benz, Matthias. 2005. Not for the Profit, but for the Satisfaction?—Evidence on Worker Well-Being in Non-Profit Firms. *Kyklos* 58, no. 2: 155–176.

Benz, Matthias. 2007. The Relevance of Procedural Utility for Economics. In *Economics and Psychology: A Promising New Cross-Disciplinary Field*, ed. B. Frey and A. Stutzer. MIT Press.

Benz, Matthias, and Bruno Frey 2008a. Being Independent Is a Great Thing: Subjective Evaluations of Self-Employment and Hierarchy. Forthcoming in *Economica*.

Benz, Matthias, and Bruno Frey. 2008b. The Value of Doing What You Like: Evidence from the Self-Employed in 23 Countries. Forthcoming in *Journal of Economic Behavior and Organization*.

Benz, Matthias, and Alois Stutzer. 2003. Do Workers Enjoy Procedural Utility? *Applied Economics Quarterly* 49, no. 2: 149–172.

Bertrand, Marianne, and Sendhil Mullainathan. 2001. Do People Mean What They Say? Implications for Subjective Survey Data. *American Economic Review* 91, no. 2: 67–72.

Besley, Timothy. 2006. *Principled Agents? The Political Economy of Good Government*. Oxford University Press.

Besley, Timothy, and Anne Case. 2000. Unnatural Experiments? Estimating the Incidence of Endogenous Policies. *Economic Journal* 110, no. 467: 672–694.

Besley, Timothy, and Stephen Coate. 2000. Issue Unbundling via Citizens' Initiatives. Working Paper 8036, National Bureau of Economic Research.

Bewley, Truman. 1999. *Why Wages Don't Fall during a Recession*. Harvard University Press.

Bies, Robert, and Joseph Moag. 1986. Interactional Justice: Communication Criteria of Fairness. In *Research on Negotiation in Organizations*, volume 1, ed. R. Lewicki, B. Sheppard, and M. Bazerman. JAI.

Björklund, Anders, and Tor Eriksson. 1998. Unemployment and Mental Health: A Survey of Nordic Research. *Scandinavian Journal of Social Welfare* 7: 219–235.

Björnskov, Christian. 2003. The Happy Few: Cross-Country Evidence on Social Capital and Life Satisfaction. *Kyklos* 56: 3–16.

Blanchflower, David. 2000. Self-Employment in OECD Countries. *Labour Economics* 7: 471–505.

Blanchflower, David, and Andrew Oswald. 1998. What Makes an Entrepreneur? *Journal of Labor Economics* 16, no. 1: 26–60.

Blanchflower, David, and Andrew Oswald. 1999. Well-Being, Insecurity and the Decline of American Job Satisfaction. Working paper, University of Warwick.

Blanchflower, David, and Andrew Oswald. 2004a. Money, Sex and Happiness: An Empirical Study. *Scandinavian Journal of Economics* 106: 393–415.

Blanchflower, David, and Andrew Oswald. 2004b. Well-Being over Time in Britain and the USA. *Journal of Public Economics* 88: 1359–1386.

Blanchflower, David, Andrew Oswald, and Alois Stutzer. 2001. Latent Entrepreneurship across Nations. *European Economic Review* 45, no. 4–6: 680–691.

Blankart, Charles. 1992. Bewirken Referendum und Volksinitiative einen Unterschied in der Politik? *Staatswissenschaft und Staatspraxis* 3: 509–523.

Blankart, Charles. 1998. Politische Ökonomie der Zentralisierung der Staatstätigkeit. Discussion Paper 108, Humboldt-Universität, Berlin.

Blau, Peter. 1964. *Exchange and Power in Social Life*. Wiley.

Blomquist, Glenn, Mark Berger, and John Hoehn. 1988. New Estimates of Quality of Life in Urban Areas. *American Economic Review* 78, no. 1: 89–107.

Bohnet, Iris. 2007. Why Women and Men Trust Others. In *Economics and Psychology: A Promising New Cross-Disciplinary Field*, ed. B. Frey and A. Stutzer. MIT Press.

Bohnet, Iris, and Bruno Frey. 1994. Direct Democratic Rules: The Role of Discussion. *Kyklos* 47, no. 3: 341–354.

Bolton, Gary, and Axel Ockenfels. 2000. ERC: A Theory of Equity, Reciprocity, and Competition. *American Economic Review* 90, no. 1: 166–193.

Bös, Dieter. 1981. *Economic Theory of Public Enterprise*. Springer.

Boskin, Michael, and Eytan Sheshinski. 1978. Optimal Redistributive Taxation When Individual Welfare Depends on Relative Income. *Quarterly Journal of Economics* 92, no. 4: 589–601.

Bosman, Ronald, and Frans van Winden. 2006. Global Risk, Investment and Emotions. Discussion Paper 5451, Center for Economic Policy Research.

Bowles, Samuel. 1998. Endogenous Preferences: The Cultural Consequences of Markets and Other Economic Institutions. *Journal of Economic Literature* 36: 75–111.

Bradford, David, and Harvey Rosen. 1976. The Optimal Taxation of Commodities and Income. *American Economic Review, Papers and Proceedings* 66: 94–101.

Brennan, Geoffrey, and James Buchanan. 1985. *The Reason of Rules: Constitutional Political Economy*. Cambridge University Press.

Brennan, Geoffrey, and Loren Lomasky. 1993. *Democracy and Decision*. Cambridge University Press.

Brennan, Geoffrey, and Philip Pettit. 2004. *The Economy of Esteem: An Essay on Civil and Political Science*. Oxford University Press.

Breton, Albert. 1996. *Competitive Governments: An Economic Theory of Politics and Public Choice Finance*. Cambridge University Press.

Brickman, Philip, and Donald Campbell. 1971. Hedonic Relativism and Planning the Good Society. In *Adaptation-Level Theory: A Symposium*, ed. M. Apley. Academic Press.

Brickman, Philip, Dan Coates, and Ronnie Janoff-Bulman. 1978. Lottery Winners and Accident Victims: Is Happiness Relative? *Journal of Personality and Social Psychology* 36, no. 8: 917–927.

Brockner, Joel, and Batia Wiesenfeld. 1996. An Integrative Framework for Explaining Reactions to Decisions: Interactive Effects of Outcomes and Procedures. *Psychological Bulletin* 120, no. 2: 189–208.

Brück, Tilman, and Andreas Stephan. 2006. Do Eurozone Countries Cheat with Their Budget Deficit Forecasts? *Kyklos* 59: 3–16.

Bruni, Luigino. 2006. *Civil Happiness: Economics and Human Flourishing in Historical Perspective*. Routledge.

Bruni, Luigino, and Pier Luigi Porta, eds. 2005. *Economics and Happiness: Framing the Analysis*. Oxford University Press.

Bruni, Luigino, and Pier Luigi Porta, eds. 2007. *Handbook on the Economics of Happiness*. Elgar.

Bruni, Luigino, and Luca Stanca. 2006. Income Aspirations, Television and Happiness: Evidence from the World Values Surveys. *Kyklos* 59, no. 2: 209–226.

Bruni, Luigino, and Luca Stanca. 2007. Watching Alone: Relational Goods, Television and Happiness. Forthcoming in *Journal of Economic Behavior and Organization*.

Buchanan, James. 1965. An Economic Theory of Clubs. *Economica* 32, no. 1: 1–14.

Buchanan, James. 1991. An American Perspective on Europe's Constitutional Opportunity. *Cato Journal* 10, no. 3: 619–629.

Buchanan, James, and Gordon Tullock. 1962. *The Calculus of Consent: Logical Foundations of Constitutional Democracy*. University of Michigan Press.

Burman, Bonnie, and Gayla Margolin. 1992. Analysis of the Association Between Marital Relationships and Health Problems: An Interactional Perspective. *Psychological Bulletin* 112, no. 1: 39–63.

Butler, David, and Austin Ranney, eds. 1994. *Referendums around the World: The Growing Use of Direct Democracy*. AEI Press.

Camerer, Colin. 2007. Neuroeconomics: Using Neuroscience to Make Economic Predictions. *Economic Journal* 117: C26–C42.

Camerer, Colin, Meghana Bhatt, and Ming Hsu. 2007. Neuroeconomics: Illustrated by the Study of Ambiguity Aversion. In *Economics and Psychology: A Promising New Cross-Disciplinary Field*, ed. B. Frey and A. Stutzer. MIT Press.

Camerer, Colin, George Loewenstein, and Drazen Prelec. 2005. Neuroeconomics: How Neuroscience Can Inform Economics. *Journal of Economic Literature* 43: 9–64.

Camerer, Colin, George Loewenstein, and Matthew Rabin, eds. 2003. Advances in Behavioral Economics. Russell Sage Foundation Press and Princeton University Press.

Campbell, Angus, Philip Converse, and Willard Rodgers. 1976. *The Quality of American Life: Perceptions, Evaluations, and Satisfactions*. Russell Sage Foundation.

Cantril, Hadley. 1965. *The Pattern of Human Concerns*. Rutgers University Press.

Carr, Alan. 2003. *Positive Psychology: The Science of Happiness and Human Strength*. Routledge.

Carroll, Christopher, Jody Overland, and David Weil. 2000. Saving and Growth with Habit Formation. *American Economic Review* 90, no. 3: 341–355.

Carson, Richard, Robert Mitchell, W. Michael Hanemann, Raymond Kopp, Stanley Pressers, and Paul Ruud. 2003. Contingent Valuation and Lost Passive Use: Damages from the *Exxon Valdez* Oil Spill. *Environmental and Resource Economics* 25, no. 3: 257–286.

Casella, Alessandra, and Bruno Frey. 1992. Federalism and Clubs: Towards an Economic Theory of Overlapping Political Jurisdictions. *European Economic Review* 36: 639–646.

Center for Economic Policy Research (CEPR). 1993. *Making Sense of Subsidiarity: How Much Centralization for Europe?*

Chapais, Bernard. 1991. Primates and the Origins of Aggression, Power and Politics among Humans. In *Understanding Behavior*, ed. J. Loy and C. Peters. Oxford University Press.

Chay, Kenneth, and Michael Greenstone. 2005. Does Air Quality Matter? Evidence from the Housing Market. *Journal of Political Economy* 113, no. 2: 376–424.

Chrystal Alec, and Paul Mizen. 2003. Goodhart's Law: Its Origins, Meaning and Implications for Monetary Policy. In *Central Banks, Monetary Theory and Policy: Essays in Honour of Charles Goodhart*, volume 1, ed. P. Mizen. Elgar.

Chun, Hyunbae, and Injae Lee. 2001. Why Do Married Men Earn More: Productivity or Marriage Selection? *Economic Inquiry* 39, no. 2: 307–319.

Clark, Andrew. 2001. What Really Matters in a Job? Hedonic Measurement of Quit Data. *Labour Economics* 8: 223–242.

Clark, Andrew. 2003. Unemployment as a Social Norm: Psychological Evidence from Panel Data. *Journal of Labor Economics* 21, no. 2: 323–351.

Clark, Andrew, and Andrew Oswald. 1994. Unhappiness and Unemployment. *Economic Journal* 104, no. 424: 648–659.

Clark, Andrew., and Andrew Oswald. 1996. Satisfaction and Comparison Income. *Journal of Public Economics* 61, no. 3: 359–381.

Clark, Andrew, and Andrew Oswald. 1998. Comparison-Concave Utility and Following Behaviour in Social and Economic Settings. *Journal of Public Economics* 70, no. 1: 133–155.

Clark, Andrew, Ed Diener, Yannis Georgellis, and Richard Lucas. 2006. Lags and Leads in Life Satisfaction: A Test of the Baseline Hypothesis. Working paper, CNRS and DELTA-Fédération Jourdan.

Clark, Andrew, Yannis Georgellis, and Peter Sanfey. 2001. Scarring: The Psychological Impact of Past Unemployment. *Economica* 68, no. 270: 221–241.

Cohen-Charash, Yochi, and Paul Spector. 2001. The Role of Justice in Organizations: A Meta-Analysis. *Organizational Behavior and Human Decision Processes* 86, no. 2: 278–321.

Comim, Flavio. 2005. Capabilities and Happiness: Potential Synergies. *Review of Social Economy* 63, no. 2: 161–171.

Coombs, Robert. 1991. Marital Status and Personal Well-Being: A Literature Review. *Family Relations* 40, no. 1: 97–102.

Costa, Paul, and Robert McCrae. 1988. Personality in Adulthood: A Six-Year Longitudinal Study of Self-Reports and Spouse Ratings on the NEO Personality Inventory. *Journal of Personality and Social Psychology* 54, no. 5: 853–863.

Cotter, Stéphanie, Marco Buscher, Doris Baumgartner, Beat Fux, Claudine Sauvain-Dugerdil, and Alex Gabadinho. 1995. Familie, Lebensverlauf und Geburtshäufigkeit— 1995 [maschinenlesbarer Datensatz]. Bundesamt für Statistik-BfS, Abteilung Bevölkerung und Beschäftigung, Neuchâtel; Soziologisches Institut, Universität Zürich; Laboratoire de démographie économique et sociale, Université de Genève.

Cronin, Thomas. 1989. *Direct Democracy: The Politics of Initiative, Referendum and Recall.* Harvard University Press.

Csikszentmihalyi, Mihaly. 1990. *Flow: The Psychology of Optimal Experience.* Harper and Row.

Csikszentmihalyi, Mihaly, and Jeremy Hunter. 2003. Happiness in Everyday Life: The Uses of Experience Sampling. *Journal of Happiness Studies* 4: 185–199.

Cutler, David, Edward Glaeser, and Jesse Shapiro. 2003. Why Have Americans Become More Obese? *Journal of Economic Perspectives* 17, no. 3: 93–118.

Dafflon, Bernard, and Sergio Rossi. 1999. Public Accounting Fudges towards EMU: A First Empirical Survey and Some Public Choice Considerations. *Public Choice* 101: 59–84.

Dahl, Robert, and Charles Lindblom. 1953. *Politics, Economics and Welfare: Planning and Politico-Economic Systems Resolved into Basic Social Processes*. Harper.

Daly Herman, and John Cobb. 1989. *For the Common Good: Redirecting the Economy toward Community, the Environment, and a Sustainable Future*. Green Print.

Darity, William, and Arthur Goldsmith. 1996. Social Psychology, Unemployment and Macroeconomics. *Journal of Economic Perspectives* 10, no. 1: 121–140.

Davidson, Richard. 2003. Affective Neuroscience and Psychophysiology: Towards a Synthesis. *Psychophysiology* 40: 655–665.

Davidson, Richard, John Marshall, Andrew Tomarken, and Jeffrey Henriques. 2000. While a Phobic Waits: Regional Brain Electrical and Autonomic Activity in Social Phobics during Anticipation of Public Speaking. *Biological Psychiatry* 47, no. 2: 85–95.

Davis, James, Tom Smith, and Peter Marsden. 2001. *General Social Survey, 1972–2000: Cumulative Codebook*. Roper Center for Public Opinion Research.

De Botton, Alain. 2004. *Status Anxiety*. Hamish Hamilton.

De Waal, Frans. 1989. *Chimpanzee Politics*. Johns Hopkins University Press.

Deaton Angus. 2005. Measuring Poverty in a Growing World. *Review of Economics and Statistics* 87:1–19.

Deci, Edward. 1971. Effects of Externally Mediated Rewards on Intrinsic Motivation. *Journal of Personality and Social Psychology* 18: 105–115.

Deci, Edward. 1975. *Intrinsic Motivation*. Plenum.

Deci, Edward, and Richard Ryan. 2000. The "What" and "Why" of Goal Pursuits: Human Needs and the Self-Determination of Behavior. *Psychological Inquiry* 11, no. 4: 227–268.

DellaVigna, Stefano, and M. Daniele Paserman. 2005. Job Search and Impatience. *Journal of Labor Economics* 23, no. 3: 527–588.

DellaVigna, Stefano, and Ulrike Malmendier. 2006. Paying Not to Go to the Gym. *American Economic Review* 96, no. 33: 694–719.

DeNeve, Kristina, and Harris Cooper. 1998. The Happy Personality: A Meta-Analysis of 137 Personality Traits and Subjective Well-Being. *Psychological Bulletin* 124, no. 2: 197–229.

Deno, Kevin, and Stephen Mehay. 1985. Institutional Constraints on Local Jurisdiction. *Public Finance Quarterly* 13: 450–463.

Di Tella, Rafael, and Robert MacCulloch. 1996. An Empirical Study of Unemployment Benefit Preferences. Economic Series Working Paper 99179, Department of Economics, Oxford University.

Di Tella, Rafael, and Robert MacCulloch. 2005. Gross National Happiness as an Answer to the Easterlin Paradox? Working Paper, Harvard Business School.

Di Tella, Rafael, and Robert MacCulloch. 2006. Some Uses of Happiness Data in Economics. *Journal of Economic Perspectives* 20: 25–46.

Di Tella, Rafael, Robert MacCulloch, and Andrew Oswald. 2001. Preferences over Inflation and Unemployment: Evidence from Surveys of Happiness. *American Economic Review* 91, no. 1: 335–341.

Di Tella, Rafael, Robert MacCulloch, and Andrew Oswald. 2003. The Macroeconomics of Happiness. *Review of Economics and Statistics* 85, no. 4: 809–827.

Diener, Ed. 1984. Subjective Well-Being. *Psychological Bulletin* 95, no. 3: 542–575.

Diener, Ed. 2000. Subjective Well-Being—the Science of Happiness and a Proposal for a National Index. *American Psychologist* 55, no. 1: 34–43.

Diener, Ed, and Robert Biswas-Diener. 2002. Will Money Increase Subjective Well-Being? *Social Indicators Research* 57: 119–169.

Diener, Ed, Marissa Diener, and Carol Diener. 1995. Factors Predicting the Subjective Well-Being of Nations. *Journal of Personality and Social Psychology* 69, no. 5: 851–864.

Diener, Ed, Carol Gohm, Eunkook Suh, and Shigehiro Oishi. 2000. Similarity of the Relations Between Marital Status and Subjective Well-Being across Cultures. *Journal of Cross Cultural Psychology* 31, no. 4: 419–436.

Diener, Ed, and Shigehiro Oishi. 2000. Money and Happiness: Income and Subjective Well-Being across Nations. In *Culture and Subjective Well-Being*, ed. E. Diener and E. Suh. MIT Press.

Diener, Ed, and Martin Seligman. 2002. Very Happy People. *Psychological Science* 13: 81–84.

Diener, Ed, and Martin Seligman. 2004. Beyond Money: Toward an Economy of Well-Being. *Psychological Science in the Public Interest* 5: 1–31.

Diener, Ed, Eunkook Suh, Richard Lucas, and Heidi Smith. 1999. Subjective Well-Being: Three Decades of Progress. *Psychological Bulletin* 125, no. 2: 276–303.

DiLorenzo, Thomas. 1981. Special Districts and Local Public Services. *Public Finance Quarterly* 9: 353–367.

Dorn, David, Justina Fischer, Gebhard Kirchgässner, and Alfonso Sousa-Poza. 2007. Is It Culture or Democracy? The Impact of Democracy, Income and Culture on Happiness. *Social Indicators Research* 82, no. 3: 505–526.

Downs, Anthony. 1957. *An Economic Theory of Democracy*. Harper and Row.

Driffill, John, Grayham Mizon, and Alistair Ulph. 1990. Costs of Inflation. In *Handbook of Monetary Economics*, volume II, ed. B. Friedman and F. Hahn. North-Holland.

Dryzek, John. 1990. *Discursive Democracy: Politics, Policy and Political Science*. Cambridge University Press.

Duesenberry, James. 1949. *Income, Savings and the Theory of Consumer Behavior*. Harvard University Press.

Easterlin, Richard. 1974. Does Economic Growth Improve the Human Lot? Some Empirical Evidence. In *Nations and Households in Economic Growth: Essays in Honour of Moses Abramowitz*, ed. P. David and M. Reder. Academic Press.

Easterlin, Richard. 1995. Will Raising the Incomes of All Increase the Happiness of All? *Journal of Economic Behaviour and Organization* 27, no. 1: 35–48.

Easterlin, Richard. 2000. The Worldwide Standard of Living since 1800. *Journal of Economic Perspectives* 14, no. 1: 7–26.

Easterlin, Richard. 2001. Income and Happiness: Towards a Unified Theory. *Economic Journal* 111: 465–484.

Easterlin, Richard., ed. 2002. *Happiness in Economics*. Elgar.

Easterlin, Richard. 2003. Building a Better Theory of Well-Being. Presented at conference on Paradoxes of Happiness in Economics, University of Milano-Bicocca.

Easterlin, Richard. 2004. Explaining Happiness. *Proceedings of the National Academy of Sciences* 100:1176–1183.

Easterlin, Richard. 2005. Building a Better Theory of Well-Being. In *Economics and Happiness: Framing the Analysis*, ed. L. Bruni and P. Porta. Oxford University Press.

Edgeworth, Francis. 1881. *Mathematical Psychics: An Essay on the Application of Mathematics to the Moral Sciences*. Kegan Paul.

Ehrhardt, Joop, Willem Saris, and Ruut Veenhoven. 2000. Stability of Life-Satisfaction over Time. *Journal of Happiness Studies* 1, no. 2: 177–205.

Eichenberger, Reiner. 2003a. Economic Innovations Depend on Political Innovations: On Deregulating the Political Process. In *Innovation Clusters and Interregional Competition*, ed. J. Bröcker, D. Dohse, and R. Soltwedel. Springer.

Eichenberger, Reiner. 2003b. Towards a European Market for Good Politics: A Politico-Economic Reform Proposal. *Jahrbuch für Neue Politische Oekonomie*. 22: 221–237.

Eichenberger, Reiner, and Bruno Frey. 2002. Democratic Governance for a Globalized World. *Kyklos* 55: 265–287.

Eichenberger, Reiner, and Mark Schelker. 2005. Controlling Government by Democratically-Elected, Competing Political Bodies. Working paper, University of Fribourg.

Eichenberger, Reiner, and Mark Schelker. 2007. Independent and Competing Agencies: An Effective Way to Control Government. *Public Choice* 130: 79–98.

Ellsberg, Daniel. 1961. Risk, Ambiguity and the Savage Axiom. *Quarterly Journal of Economics* 75: 643–669.

Elster, Jon. 1998. Emotions and Economic Theory. *Journal of Economic Literature* 36, no. 1: 47–74.

Espe, Hartmut, and Margarete Seiwert. 1987. Television Viewing Types, General Life Satisfaction, and Viewing Amount: An Empirical Study in West-Germany. *European Journal of Communication* 13: 95–110.

Estes, Richard. 1988. *Trends in World Social Development: The Social Progress of Nations, 1970–1987*. Praeger.

European Constitutional Group. 1993. A European Constitutional Settlement (draft). London.

Falk, Armin, and Markus Knell. 2004. Choosing the Joneses: Endogenous Goals and Reference Standards. *Scandinavian Journal of Economics* 106, no. 3: 417–435.

Fang, Hanming, and Dan Silverman. 2007. Time-Inconsistency and Welfare Program Participation: Evidence from the NLSY. Discussion Paper 1465, Cowles Foundation for Research in Economics, Yale University.

Feather, Norman. 1990. *The Psychological Impact of Unemployment*. Springer.

Fehr, Ernst, and Simon Gächter. 1998. Reciprocity and Economics. The Economic Implications of "Homo Reciprocans." *European Economic Review* 42: 845–859.

Fehr, Ernst, and Simon Gächter. 2000. Fairness and Retaliation: The Economics of Reciprocity. *Journal of Economic Perspectives* 14: 159–181.

Fehr, Ernst, and Lorenz Götte. 2005. Robustness and Real Consequences of Nominal Wage Rigidity. *Journal of Monetary Economics* 52, no. 4: 779–804.

Fehr, Ernst, Urs Fischbacher, and Michael Kosfeld. 2005. Neuroeconomic Foundations of Trust and Social Preferences. *American Economic Review* 95, no. 2: 346–351.

Fehr, Ernst, and Klaus Schmidt. 1999. A Theory of Fairness, Competition, and Cooperation. *Quarterly Journal of Economics* 114, no. 3: 817–868.

Fehr, Ernst, and Klaus Schmidt. 2003. Theories of Fairness and Reciprocity—Evidence and Economic Applications. In *Advances in Economics and Econometrics—8th World Congress*, ed. M. Dewatripont, L. Hansen, and S. Turnovsky. Cambridge University Press.

Fehr, Ernst, and Tania Singer. 2005. The Neuroeconomics of Mind Reading and Empathy. *American Economic Review. Papers & Proceedings* 95: 340–345.

Feld, Lars, and Bruno Frey. 2002. Trust Breeds Trust: How Taxpayers Are Treated. *Economics of Governance* 3: 87–99.

Feld, Lars, and Bruno Frey. 2007a. Tax Compliance as the Result of a Psychological Tax Contract: The Roles of Incentives and Responsive Regulation. *Law & Policy* 29, no. 1: 102–120.

Feld, Lars, and Bruno Frey. 2007b. Tax Evasion in Switzerland: The Role of Deterrence and Tax Morale. In *Tax Evasion, Trust and State Capacity*, ed. N. Hayoz and S. Hug. Peter Lang.

Feld, Lars, and Gebhard Kirchgässner. 1999. Public Debt and Budgetary Procedures: Top Down or Bottom Up. Some Evidence from Swiss Municipalities. In *Fiscal Institutions and Fiscal Performance*, ed. J. Poterba and J. von Hagen. University of Chicago Press.

Feld, Lars, and Gebhard Kirchgässner. 2000. Direct Democracy, Political Culture and the Outcome of Economic Policy: A Report on the Swiss Experience. *European Journal of Political Economy* 16, no. 2: 287–306.

Feld, Lars, and Marcel Savioz. 1997. Direct Democracy Matters for Economic Performance: An Empirical Investigation. *Kyklos* 50, no. 4: 507–538.

Feld, Lars, and Stefan Voigt. 2006. Judicial Independence and Economic Growth: Some Proposals Regarding the Judiciary. In *Democratic Constitutional Design and Public Policy: Analysis and Evidence*, ed. R. Congleton and B. Swedenborg. MIT Press.

Fernández-Dols, José-Miguel, and Maria-Angeles Ruiz-Belda. 1995. Are Smiles a Sign of Happiness? Gold Medal Winners at the Olympic Games. *Journal of Personality and Social Psychology* 69, no. 6: 1113–1119.

Ferrer-i-Carbonell, Ada. 2005. Income and Well-Being: An Empirical Analysis of the Comparison Income Effect. *Journal of Public Economics* 89, no. 5–6: 997–1019.

Ferrer-i-Carbonell, Ada, and Paul Frijters. 2004. How Important Is Methodology for the Estimates of the Determinants of Happiness? *Economic Journal* 114, no. 497: 641–659.

Fischer, Stanley. 1981. Towards an Understanding of the Costs of Inflation: II. *Carnegie-Rochester Conference Series on Public Policy* 15: 5–41.

Fong, Christina. 2001. Social Preferences, Self-Interest, and the Demand for Redistribution. *Journal of Public Economics* 82: 225–246.

Fong, Christina. 2006. Prospective Mobility, Fairness, and the Demand for Redistribution. Working paper, Carnegie Mellon University.

Fordyce, Meredith. 1988. A Review of Research on Happiness Measures: A Sixty Second Index of Happiness and Mental Health. *Social Indicators Research* 20: 355–381.

Forte, Francesco. 2001. The Maastricht "Excessive Deficit" Rules and Creative Accounting. In *Rules and Reason*, ed. R Mudambi, P. Navarra, and G. Sobbrio. Cambridge University Press.

Frank, Robert. 1985a. *Choosing the Right Pond*. Oxford University Press.

Frank, Robert. 1985b. The Demand for Unobservable and Other Nonpositional Goods. *American Economic Review* 75, no. 1: 101–116.

Frank, Robert. 1988. *Passions within Reason: The Strategic Role of the Emotions*. Norton.

Frank, Robert. 1997. The Frame of Reference as a Public Good. *Economic Journal* 107, no. 445: 1832–1847.

Frank, Robert. 1999. *Luxury Fever: Why Money Fails to Satisfy in an Era of Excess*. Free Press.

Frank, Robert. 2003. Are Positional Externalities Different from Other Externalities? Presented at conference on "Why Inequality Matters: Lessons for Policy from the Economics of Happiness," Brookings Institution, Washington.

Frederick, Shane, and George Loewenstein. 1999. Hedonic Adaptation. In *Well-Being: The Foundations of Hedonic Psychology*, ed. D. Kahneman, E. Diener, and N. Schwarz. Russell Sage Foundation.

Frederick, Shane, George Loewenstein, and Ted O'Donoghue. 2002. Time Discounting and Time Preference: A Critical Review. *Journal of Economic Literature* 40, no. 2: 351–401.

Fredrickson, Barbara. 2001. The Role of Emotions in Positive Psychology. *American Psychologist* 56: 218–226.

Fredrickson, Barbara. 2003. The Value of Positive Emotions. *American Scientist* 91: 330–335.

Freeman, A. Myrick, III. 2003. *The Measurement of Environmental and Resource Values: Theory and Methods*. Resources for the Future.

Frey, Bruno. 1983. *Democratic Economic Policy.* Blackwell.

Frey, Bruno. 1994a. Direct Democracy: Politico-Economic Lessons from Swiss Experience. *American Economic Review* 84 , no. 2: 338–348.

Frey, Bruno. 1994b. Supreme Auditing Institutions: A Politico-Economic Analysis. *European Journal of Law and Economics* 1: 169–176.

Frey, Bruno. 1997a. A Constitution for Knaves Crowds Out Civic Virtues. *Economic Journal* 107, no. 443: 1043–1053.

Frey, Bruno. 1997b. *Not Just for the Money: An Economic Theory of Personal Motivation.* Elgar.

Frey, Bruno. 2004. *Dealing with Terrorism—Stick or Carrot?* Elgar.

Frey, Bruno. 2005. Knight Fever: Towards an Economics of Awards. Working Paper 239, IEW (Institute for Empirical Research in Economics), University of Zurich.

Frey, Bruno. 2006. Giving and Receiving Awards. *Perspectives on Psychological Science* 1: 377–388.

Frey, Bruno , Christine Benesch, and Alois Stutzer. 2007. Does Watching TV Make Us Happy? *Journal of Economic Psychology* 28, no. 3: 283–313.

Frey, Bruno, and Matthias Benz. 2004. From Imperialism to Inspiration: A Survey of Economics and Psychology. In *The Elgar Companion to Economics and Philosophy,* ed. J. Davis, A. Marciano, and J. Runde. Elgar.

Frey, Bruno, and Matthias Benz. 2007. Being Independent Is a Great Thing: Subjective Evaluations of Self-Employment and Hierarchy. Forthcoming in *Economica.*

Frey, Bruno, Matthias Benz, and Alois Stutzer. 2004. Introducing Procedural Utility: Not Only What, but Also How Matters. *Journal of Institutional and Theoretical Economics* 160, no. 3: 377–401.

Frey, Bruno, and Reiner Eichenberger. 1994. Economic Incentives Transform Psychological Anomalies. *Journal of Economic Behavior and Organization* 23: 215–234.

Frey, Bruno, and Reiner Eichenberger. 1999. *The New Democratic Federalism for Europe: Functional Overlapping and Competing Jurisdictions.* Elgar.

Frey, Bruno, and Lars Feld. 2002. Deterrence and Morale in Taxation: An Empirical Analysis. CESifo Working Paper Series no. 760, Center for Economic Studies, University of Munich.

Frey, Bruno, and Reto Jegen. 2001. Motivation Crowding Theory: A Survey of Empirical Evidence. *Journal of Economic Surveys* 15, no. 5: 589–611.

Frey, Bruno, and Gebhard Kirchgässner. 1993. Diskursethik, Politische Ökonomie und Volksabstimmungen. *Analyse und Kritik* 15, no. 2: 129–149.

Frey, Bruno, and Simon Luechinger. 2003. How to Fight Terrorism: Alternatives to Deterrence. *Defence and Peace Economics* 14, no. 4: 237–249.

Frey, Bruno, Simon Luechinger, and Alois Stutzer. 2007a. Calculating Tragedy: Assessing the Costs of Terrorism. *Journal of Economic Surveys* 21, no. 1: 1–24.

Frey, Bruno, Simon Luechinger, and Alois Stutzer. 2007b. The Life Satisfaction Approach to Valuing Public Goods: The Case of Terrorism. Mimeo, University of Zurich.

Frey, Bruno, and Felix Oberholzer-Gee. 1997. The Cost of Price Incentives: An Empirical Analysis of Motivation Crowding-Out. *American Economic Review* 87, no. 4: 746–755.

Frey, Bruno, and Margit Osterloh, eds. 2002. *Successful Management by Motivation: Balancing Intrinsic and Extrinsic Incentives*. Springer.

Frey, Bruno, and Margit Osterloh. 2005. Yes, Managers Should Be Paid Like Bureaucrats. *Journal of Management Inquiry* 14, no. 1: 96–111.

Frey, Bruno, and Werner Pommerehne. 1993. On the Fairness of Pricing—An Empirical Survey among the General Population. *Journal of Economic Behavior and Organization* 20: 295–307.

Frey, Bruno, and Alois Stutzer. 1999. Measuring Preferences by Subjective Well-Being. *Journal of Institutional and Theoretical Economics* 155, no. 4: 755–788.

Frey, Bruno, and Alois Stutzer. 2000. Happiness, Economy and Institutions. *Economic Journal* 110, no. 446: 918–938.

Frey, Bruno, and Alois Stutzer. 2001. Economics and Psychology: From Imperialistic to Inspired Economics. *Revue de philosophie économique* 4: 5–22.

Frey, Bruno, and Alois Stutzer. 2002a. *Happiness and Economics: How the Economy and Institutions Affect Well-Being*. Princeton University Press.

Frey, Bruno, and Alois Stutzer. 2002b. What Can Economists Learn from Happiness Research? *Journal of Economic Literature* 40, no. 2: 402–435.

Frey, Bruno, and Alois Stutzer. 2004a. Economic Consequences of Mispredicting Utility. Working Paper 218, IEW (Institute for Empirical Research in Economics), University of Zurich.

Frey, Bruno, and Alois Stutzer. 2004b.Reported Subjective Well-Being: A Challenge for Economic Theory and Economic Policy. *Schmollers Jahrbuch* 124: 191–231.

Frey, Bruno, and Alois Stutzer. 2005a. Testing Theories of Happiness. In *Economics and Happiness: Framing the Analysis*, ed. L. Bruni and P. Porta. Oxford University Press.

Frey, Bruno, and Alois Stutzer. 2005b. Happiness Research: State and Prospects. *Review of Social Economy* 62: 207–228.

Frey, Bruno, and Alois Stutzer. 2005c. Beyond Outcomes: Measuring Procedural Utility. *Oxford Economic Papers* 57:90:111.

Frey, Bruno, and Alois Stutzer. 2006a. Direct Democracy: Designing a Living Constitution. In *Democratic Constitutional Design and Public Policy: Analysis and Evidence*, ed. R. Congleton and B. Swedenborg. MIT Press.

Frey, Bruno, and Alois Stutzer. 2006b. Mispredicting Utility and the Political Process. In *Behavioral Public Finance*, ed. E. McCaffery and J. Slemrod. Russell Sage Foundation.

Frey, Bruno, and Alois Stutzer. 2007. *Economics and Psychology: A Promising New Cross-Disciplinary Field*. MIT Press.

Frijters, Paul, John Haisken-DeNew, and Michael Shields. 2003. Investigating the Patterns and Determinants of Life Satisfaction in Germany Following Reunification. *Journal of Human Resources* 39, no. 3: 649–674.

Frijters, Paul, John Haisken-DeNew, and Michael Shields. 2004. Money Does Matter! Evidence from Increasing Real Income and Life Satisfaction in East Germany Following Reunification. *American Economic Review* 94: 730–740.

Gächter, Simon. 2007. Conditional Cooperation: Behavioral Regularities from the Lab and the Field and Their Policy Implications. In *Economics and Psychology: A Promising New Cross-Disciplinary Field*, ed. B. Frey and A. Stutzer. MIT Press.

Gardner, Jonathan, and Andrew Oswald. 2001. Does Money Buy Happiness? A Longitudinal Study Using Data on Windfalls. Mimeo, Warwick University.

Gardner, Jonathan, and Andrew Oswald. 2004. How Is Mortality Affected by Money, Marriage, and Stress? *Journal of Health Economics* 23: 1181–1207.

Gardner, Jonathan, and Andrew Oswald. 2006. Do Divorcing Couples Become Happier by Breaking Up? *Journal of the Royal Statistical Society, Series A* 169, no. 2: 319–336.

Gerber, Elisabeth. 1997. *The Populist Paradox: Interest Group Influence and the Promise of Direct Legislation*. Princeton University Press.

Gerlach, Knut, and Gesine Stephan. 1996. A Paper on Unhappiness and Unemployment in Germany. *Economics Letters* 52, no. 3: 325–330.

Gold, Steven. 1991. Interstate Competition and State Personal Income-Tax Policy in the 1980s. In *Competition among States and Local Governments*, ed. D. Kenyon and J. Kincaid. Urban Institute Press.

Goldsmith, Arthur, Jonathan Veum, and William Darity Jr. 1996. The Impact of Labor Force History on Self-Esteem and Its Component Parts, Anxiety, Alienation and Depression. *Journal of Economic Psychology* 17, no. 2: 183–220.

Goodhart, Charles. 1975. Problems of Monetary Management: The UK Experience. In *Inflation, Depression and Economic Policy in the West*, ed. A. Courakis. Marshall.

Graham, Carol. 2005. Insights on Development from the Economics of Happiness. *World Bank Research Observer*, August 11: 1–31.

Graham, Carol, and Stefano Pettinato. 2002a. *Happiness and Hardship: Opportunity and Insecurity in New Market Economies*. Brookings Institution Press.

Graham, Carol, and Stefano Pettinato. 2002b. Frustrated Achievers: Winners, Losers, and Subjective Well-Being in Emerging Market Economies. *Journal of Development Studies* 38: 100–140.

Greenberg, Jerald. 1990a. Employee Theft as a Reaction to Underpayment Inequity: The Hidden Cost of Pay Cuts. *Journal of Applied Psychology* 75, no. 5: 561–570.

Greenberg, Jerald. 1990b. Organizational Justice: Yesterday, Today, and Tomorrow. *Journal of Management* 16, no. 2: 399–432.

Grob, Alexander. 2000. Perceived Control and Subjective Well-Being across Nations and across the Life Span. In *Culture and Subjective Well-Being*, ed. E. Diener and E. Suh. MIT Press.

Gross, Andreas, and Bruno Kaufmann. 2002. *IRI Europe Country Index on Citizen Lawmaking 2002*. IRI (Initiative and Referendum Institute Europe).

Gruber, Jonathan, and Sendhil Mullainathan. 2005. Do Cigarette Taxes Make Smokers Happier? *Advances in Economic Analysis and Policy* 5, no. 1: 1–43.

Gui, Benedetto, and Robert Sugden. 2005. *Economics and Social Interaction*. Cambridge University Press.

Güth, Werner und Hannelore Weck-Hannemann. 1997. Do People Care about Democracy? An Experiment Exploring the Value of Voting Rights. *Public Choice* 91, no. 1: 27–47.

Habermas, Jürgen. 1983. Diskursethik—Notizen zu einem Begründungsprozess. In *Moralbewusstsein und kommunikatives Handeln*, ed. J. Habermas. Suhrkamp.

Hamermesh, Daniel. 1977. Economic Aspects of Job Satisfaction. In *Essays in Labor Market Analysis*, ed. O. Ashenfelter and W. Oates. Wiley.

Hamilton, Barton. 2000. Does Entrepreneurship Pay? An Empirical Analysis of Returns to Self-Employment. *Journal of Political Economy* 108, no. 3: 604–632.

Hammond, Peter. 1991. Interpersonal Comparisons of Utility: Why and How They Are and Should Be Made. In *Interpersonal Comparisons of Well-Being*, ed. J. Elster and J. Roemer. Cambridge University Press.

Hayek, Friedrich A. von. 1960. *The Constitution of Liberty*. Routledge.

Hayo, Bernd, and Wolfgang Seifert. 2003. Subjective Well-Being in Eastern Europe. *Journal of Economic Psychology* 24: 329–348.

Headey, Bruce, and Alexander Wearing. 1991. Subjective Well-Being: A Stocks and Flows Framework. In *Subjective Well-Being: An Interdisciplinary Perspective*, ed. F. Strack, M. Argyle, and N. Schwarz. Pergamon.

Heinrich, Jürgen. 1994. *Medienökonomie*. Westdeutscher Verlag.

Helliwell, John. 2003. How's Life? Combining Individual and National Variables to Explain Subjective Well-Being. *Economic Modelling* 20, no. 2: 331–360.

Helliwell, John. 2006a. Well-Being and Social Capital: Does Suicide Pose a Puzzle? *Social Indicators Research* 81: 455–496.

Helliwell, John. 2006b. Well-Being, Social Capital and Public Policy: What's New? *Economic Journal* 116, no. 510: C34–C45.

Helliwell, John, and Haifang Huang. 2007. How's Your Government? International Evidence Linking Good Government and Well-Being. Forthcoming in *British Journal of Political Science*.

Helliwell, John, and Robert Putnam. 2005. The Social Context of Well-Being. In *The Science of Well-Being*, ed. F. Huppert, N. Baylis, and B. Keverne. Oxford University Press.

Henrich, Joseph, and Francisco Gil-White. 2001. The Evolution of Prestige: Freely Conferred Deference as a Mechanism for Enhancing the Benefits of Cultural Transmission. *Evolution of Human Behavior* 22: 165–196.

Hermalin, Benjamin, and Alice Isen. 1999. The Effect of Affect on Economic and Strategic Decision-Making. CLEO Research Paper No. C01-5, University of California, Berkeley.

Hicks, John, and Roy Allen. 1934. A Reconsideration of the Theory of Value. *Economica* 1: 52–75.

Hirsch, Fred. 1976. *The Social Limits to Growth*. Harvard University Press.

Hirschman, Albert. 1970. *Exit, Voice and Loyalty*. Harvard University Press.

Holländer, Heinz. 2001. On the Validity of Utility Statements: Standard Theory versus Duesenberry's. *Journal of Economic Behavior and Organization* 45, no. 3: 227–249.

Hsee, Christopher, Jiao Zhang, Fang Yu, and Yiheng Xi. 2003. Lay Rationalism in Decision Making. *Journal of Behavioral Decision Making* 16: 257–272.

Huberman, Bernarda, Christoph Loch, and Ayse Önçüler. 2004. Status as a Valued Resource. *Social Psychology Quarterly* 67, no. 1: 103–114.

Hudson, John. 2006. Institutional Trust and Subjective Well-Being across the EU. *Kyklos* 59: 43–62.

Hughes, Michael, Carolyn Kroehler, and James Vander Zanden. 1999. *Sociology: The Core.* McGraw-Hill.

Hundley, Greg. 2001. Why and When Are the Self-Employed More Satisfied with Their Work? *Industrial Relations* 40, no. 2: 293–317.

Huppert, Felicia, Nick Baylis, and Barry Keverne, eds. 2004. The Science of Well-Being—Integrating Neurobiology, Psychology and Social Science. *Philosophical Transactions of the Royal Society B: Biological Sciences* 359, no. 1449: 1331–1332.

Inglehart, Ronald. 1990. *Culture Shift in Advanced Industrial Society.* Princeton University Press.

Inglehart, Ronald, Miguel Basanez, Jaime Diez-Medrano, Loek Halman, and Ruud Luijks. 2000. World Values Surveys and European Values Surveys, 1981–1984, 1990–1993, and 1995–1997. Computer file, ICPSR study no. 2790. Distributed by Inter-university Consortium for Political and Social Research.

Intriligator, Michael. 1973. A Probabilistic Model of Social Choice. *Review of Economic Studies* 40, no. 4: 553–560.

IP International Marketing Committee. 2004. *International Key Facts: Television 2004.*

Irwin, Francis. 1944. The Realism of Expectations. *Psychological Review* 51: 120–126.

Isen, Alice. 2000. Positive Affect and Decision Making. In *Handbook of Emotions*, ed. M. Lewis and J. Haviland-Jones. Guilford.

Isen, Alice, Kimberley Daubman, and Gary Nowicki. 1987. Positive Affect Facilitates Creative Problem Solving. *Journal of Personality and Social Psychology* 52: 1122–1131.

Isen, Alice, and Paula Levin. 1972. Effect of Feeling Good on Helping: Cookies and Kindness. *Journal of Personality and Social Psychology* 21, no. 3: 384–388.

James, William. 1890. *Principles of Psychology*, volume II. Henry Holt.

Jameson, Michael. 1988. *Practical Guide to Creative Accounting.* Kogan Page.

Jegen, Reto, and Bruno Frey. 2004. TV-Konsum und Rationalität. In *Zwischen Marktversagen und Medienvielfalt. Medienmärkte im Fokus neuer medienökonomischer Anwendungen*, ed. G. Siegert and F. Losig. Nomos.

Johnson, David, and Jian Wu. 2002. An Empirical Test of Crisis, Social Selection, and Role Explanations of the Relationship between Marital Disruption and Psychological Distress: A Pooled Time-Series Analysis of Four-Wave Panel Data. *Journal of Marriage and the Family* 64, no. 1: 211–224.

Jones, Eric. 1981. *The European Miracle.* Cambridge University Press.

Kahneman, Daniel. 1994. New Challenges to the Rationality Assumption. *Journal of Institutional and Theoretical Economics* 150, no. 1: 18–36.

Kahneman, Daniel. 1999. Objective Happiness. In *Well-Being: The Foundations of Hedonic Psychology*, ed. D. Kahneman, E. Diener, and N. Schwarz. Russell Sage Foundation.

Kahneman, Daniel. 2003. Experienced Utility and Objective Happiness: A Moment-Based Approach. In *The Psychology of Economic Decisions*, volume 1: *Rationality and Well-Being*, ed. I. Brocas and J. Carrillo. Oxford University Press.

Kahneman, Daniel. 2004. Towards a Science of Well-Being. Talk given at Würzburg University.

Kahneman, Daniel, Ed Diener, and Norbert Schwarz, eds. 1999. *Well-Being: The Foundations of Hedonic Psychology*. Russell Sage Foundation.

Kahneman, Daniel, Barbara Fredrickson, Charles Schreiber, and Donald Redelmeier. 1993. When More Pain Is Preferred to Less: Adding a Better End. *Psychological Science* 4: 401–405.

Kahneman, Daniel, and Jack Knetsch. 1992. Valuing Public Goods: The Purchase of Moral Satisfaction. *Journal of Economics and Management* 22, no. 1: 57–70.

Kahneman, Daniel, Jack Knetsch, and Richard Thaler. 1986. Fairness as a Constraint on Profit Seeking: Entitlements in the Market. *American Economic Review* 76, no. 4: 728–741.

Kahneman, Daniel, Alan Krueger, David Schkade, Norbert Schwarz, and Arthur Stone. 2004a. Toward National Well-Being Accounts. *American Economic Review* 94, no. 2: 429–434.

Kahneman, Daniel, Alan Krueger, David Schkade, Norbert Schwarz, and Arthur Stone. 2004b. A Survey Method for Characterizing Daily Life Experience: The Day Reconstruction Method. *Science* 306, no. 5702: 1776–1780.

Kahneman, Daniel, and Jason Riis. 2005. Living and Thinking about It: Two Perspectives on Life. In *The Science of Well-Being*, ed. F. Huppert, N. Baylis, and B. Keverne. Oxford University Press.

Kahneman, Daniel, and Richard Thaler. 2006. Anomalies: Utility Maximization and Experienced Utility. *Journal of Economic Perspectives* 20, no. 1: 221–234.

Kahneman, Daniel, and Carol Varey. 1991. Notes on the Psychology of Utility. In *Interpersonal Comparisons of Well-Being: Studies in Rationality and Social Change*, ed. J. Elster and J. Roemer. Cambridge University Press.

Kahneman, Daniel, Peter Wakker, and Rakesh Sarin. 1997. Back to Bentham? Explorations of Experienced Utility. *Quarterly Journal of Economics* 112, no. 2: 375–405.

Karatnycky, Adrian, ed. 2000. *Freedom in the World: The Annual Survey of Political Rights and Civil Liberties 1999–2000*. Freedom House.

Kasser, Tim. 2002. *The High Price of Materialism*. MIT Press.

Kasser, Tim, and Richard Ryan. 1993. A Dark Side of the American Dream: Correlates of Financial Success as a Central Life Aspiration. *Journal of Personality and Social Psychology* 65, no. 2: 410–422.

Kasser, Tim, and Richard Ryan. 1996. Further Examining the American Dream: Differential Correlates of Intrinsic and Extrinsic Goals. *Personality and Social Psychology Bulletin* 22, no. 3: 280–287.

Kasser, Tim, and Richard Ryan. 2001. Be Careful What You Wish For: Optimal Functioning and the Relative Attainment of Intrinsic and Extrinsic Goals. In *Life Goals and Well-Being:*

Towards a Positive Psychology of Human Striving, ed. P. Schmuck and K. Sheldon. Hogrefe and Huber.

Kaufman, Bruce. 1999. Emotional Arousal as a Source of Bounded Rationality. *Journal of Economic Behavior and Organization* 38: 135–144.

Keeney, John, and Ralph Raiffa. 1976. *Decisions with Multiple Objectives*. Wiley.

Kenny, Charles. 1999. Does Growth Cause Happiness, or Does Happiness Cause Growth? *Kyklos* 52, no. 1: 3–26.

Kiefer, Marie Luise. 2001. *Medienökonomik. Einführung in eine ökonomische Theorie der Medien*. R. Oldenbourg.

Kiefer, Marie Luise. 2003. Medienfunktionen als meritorische Güter. *Medien Journal. Zeitschrift für Kommunikationskultur* 27, no. 3: 31–46.

Kimball, Miles, and Robert Willis. 2006. Utility and Happiness. Working paper, University of Michigan.

Kirchgässner, Gebhard, Lars Feld, and Marcel Savioz. 1999. *Die direkte Demokratie: Modern, erfolgreich, entwicklungs- und exportfähig*. Helbing & Lichtenhahn and Vahlen.

Kirchgässner, Gebhard, and Werner Pommerehne. 1996. Tax Harmonization and Tax Competition in the European Community: Lessons from Switzerland. *Journal of Public Economics* 60: 351–371.

Kitayama, Shinobu, and Hazel Markus. 2000. The Pursuit of Happiness and the Realization of Sympathy: Cultural Patterns of Self, Social Relations, and Well-Being. In *Culture and Subjective Well-Being*, ed. E. Diener and E. Suh. MIT Press.

Koivumaa-Honkanen, Heli-Tuuli, Risto Honkanen, Heimo Viinamaeki, Kauko Heikkilae, Jaakko Kaprio, and Markku Koskenvuo. 2001. Life Satisfaction and Suicide: A 20-Year Follow-up Study. *American Journal of Psychiatry* 158, no. 3: 433–439.

Konovsky, Mary. 2000. Understanding Procedural Justice and Its Impact on Business Organizations. *Journal of Management* 26, no. 3: 489–511.

Konow, James. 2001. Fair and Square: The Four Sides of Distributive Justice. *Journal of Economic Behavior and Organization* 46, no. 2: 137–164.

Konow, James. 2003. Which Is the Fairest One of All? A Positive Analysis of Justice Theories. *Journal of Economic Literature* 41, no. 4: 1188–1239.

Korpi, Tomas. 1997. Is Well-Being Related to Employment Status? Unemployment, Labor Market Policies and Subjective Well-Being among Swedish Youth. *Labour Economics* 4, no. 2: 125–147.

Kraft, Kornelius. 2001. Unemployment and the Separation of Married Couples. *Kyklos* 54, no. 1: 67–88.

Kriesi, Hanspeter. 2005. *Direct Democratic Choice: The Swiss Experience*. Lexington.

Kubey, Robert, and Mihaly Csikszentmihalyi. 1990. *Television and the Quality of Life: How Viewing Shapes Everyday Experience*. Erlbaum.

Kubey, Robert, and Mihaly Csikszentmihalyi. 2002. Television Addiction Is No Mere Metaphor. *Scientific American* 286, no. 2: 74–80.

Kunreuther, Howard, and Paul Kleindorfer. 1986. A Sealed-Bid Auction Mechanism for Siting Noxious Facilities. *American Economic Review* 76, no. 2: 295–299.

Kuttner, Robert. 1997. *Everything for Sale: The Virtues and Limits of Markets.* Knopf.

Kyriacou, Andreas. 2006. Functional, Overlapping, Competing Jurisdictions and Ethnic Conflict Management. *Kyklos* 59, no. 1: 63–83.

Ladner, Andreas. 1994. Finanzkompetenzen der Gemeinden—Ein Überblick über die Praxis. In *Finanzföderalismus*, ed. F. Eng, A. Glatthard, and B. Koenig. ESG (Emissionszentrale der Schweizer Gemeinden).

Laibson, David. 1997. Golden Eggs and Hyperbolic Discounting. *Quarterly Journal of Economics* 112, no. 2: 443–477.

Lalive, Rafael. 2005. Social Interactions in Unemployment. Mimeo, University of Zurich.

Lancaster, Kevin. 1966. A New Approach to Consumer Theory. *Journal of Political Economy* 74, no. 2: 132–157.

Lane, Robert. 1991. *The Market Experience.* Cambridge University Press.

Lane, Robert. 1998. The Joyless Market Economy. In *Economics, Values, and Organization*, ed. A. Ben-Ner and L. Putterman. Cambridge University Press.

Lane, Robert. 2000. *The Loss of Happiness in Market Economies.* Yale University Press.

Larsen, Randy, and Barbara Fredrickson. 1999. Measurement Issues in Emotion Research. In *Well-Being: The Foundations of Hedonic Psychology*, ed. D. Kahneman, E. Diener, and N. Schwarz. Russell Sage Foundation.

Layard, Richard. 1980. Human Satisfaction and Public Policy. *Economic Journal* 90: 737–750.

Layard, Richard. 2005. *Happiness: Lessons from a New Science.* Penguin.

Layard, Richard. 2006. Happiness and Public Policy: A Challenge to the Profession. *Economic Journal* 116: C24–C33.

Layard, Richard. 2007. Happiness and Public Policy: A Challenge to the Profession. In *Economics and Psychology: A Promising New Cross-Disciplinary Field*, ed. B. Frey and A. Stutzer. MIT Press.

Lebergott, Stanley. 1993. *Pursuing Happiness: American Consumers in the Twentieth Century.* Princeton University Press.

Lechner, Michael, and Friedhelm Pfeiffer. 1993. Der Weg in die Selbständigkeit am Beginn der Marktwirtschaft. *ZEW Wirtschaftsanalysen* 1: 45–65.

Lepper, Heidi 1998. Use of Other-Reports to Validate Subjective Well-Being Measures. *Social Indicators Research* 44, no. 3: 367–379.

Leu, Robert, Stefan Burri, and Tom Priester. 1997. *Lebensqualität und Armut in der Schweiz.* Haupt.

Lewin, Kurt, Tamara Dembo, Leon Festinger, and Pauline Sears. 1944. Level of Aspiration. In *Personality and the Behavior Disorders*, volume I, ed. J. McVicker Hunt. Ronald.

Lewin, Shira. 1996. Economics and Psychology: Lessons for Our Own Day from the Early Twentieth Century. *Journal of Economic Literature* 34, no. 3: 1293–1323.

Lind, E. Allan, and Tom Tyler. 1988. *The Social Psychology of Procedural Justice*. Plenum.

Lind, E. Allan, Carol Kulik, Maureen Ambrose, and Maria de Vera Park. 1993. Individual and Corporate Dispute Resolution: Using Procedural Fairness as a Decision Heuristic. *Administrative Science Quarterly* 38, no. 2: 224–251.

Lindenberg, Siegwart. 1986. The Paradox of Privatization in Consumption. In *Paradoxical Effects of Social Behavior*, ed. A. Diekmann and P. Mitter. Physica.

Lindenberg, Siegwart. 1990. Homo Socio-oeconomicus: The Emergence of a General Model of Man in the Social Sciences. *Journal of Institutional and Theoretical Economics* 146: 727–748.

Lindenberg, Siegwart. 2001. Intrinsic Motivation in a New Light. *Kyklos* 54: 317–342.

Lindenberg, Siegwart, and Bruno Frey. 1993. Alternatives, Frames and Relative Prices: A Broader View of Rational Choice Theory. *Acta Sociologica* 36: 191–205.

Loch, Christoph, Bernardo Huberman, and Suzanne Stout. 2000. Status Competition and Performance in Work Groups. *Journal of Economic Behavior and Organization* 43, no. 1: 35–55.

Loewenstein, George. 1996. Out of Control: Visceral Influences on Behavior. *Organization Behavior and Human Decision Processes* 65: 272–292.

Loewenstein, George. 1999. Because It Is There: The Challenge of Mountaineering…for Utility Theory. *Kyklos* 52, no. 3: 315–343.

Loewenstein, George. 2000. Emotions in Economic Theory and Economic Behavior. *American Economic Review, Papers and Proceedings* 90: 426–432.

Loewenstein, George, and Daniel Adler. 1995. A Bias in the Prediction of Tastes. *Economic Journal* 105: 929–937.

Loewenstein, George, Ted O'Donoghue, and Matthew Rabin. 2003. Projection Bias in Predicting Future Utility. *Quarterly Journal of Economics* 118: 1209–1248.

Loewenstein, George, and David Schkade. 1999. Wouldn't It Be Nice? Predicting Future Feelings. In *Well-Being: The Foundation of Hedonic Psychology*, ed. D. Kahneman, E. Diener, and N. Schwarz. Russell Sage Foundation.

Lucas, Richard, Andrew Clark, Yannis Georgellis, and Ed Diener. 2003. Reexamining Adaptation and the Set Point Model of Happiness: Reactions to Changes in Marital Status. *Journal of Personality and Social Psychology* 84, no. 3: 527–539.

Lucas, Richard, Andrew Clark, Yannis Georgellis, and Ed Diener. 2004. Unemployment Alters the Set-Point for Life Satisfaction. *Psychological Science* 15: 8–13.

Lucas, Richard, Ed Diener, and Eunkook Suh. 1996. Discriminant Validity of Well-Being Measures. *Journal of Personality and Social Psychology* 71, no. 3: 616–628.

Lucas, Robert, Jr. 1976. Econometric Policy Evaluation: A Critique. *Carnegie-Rochester Conference Series on Public Policy* 1: 19–46.

Lucas, Robert, Jr. 1981. Discussion of Stanley Fischer, "Towards an Understanding of the Costs of Inflation: II." *Carnegie-Rochester Conference Series on Public Choice* 15: 43–52.

Luttmer, Erzo. 2005. Neighbors as Negatives: Relative Earnings and Well-Being. *Quarterly Journal of Economics* 120, no. 3: 923–1002.

Lyubomirsky, Sonja, Laura King, and Ed Diener. 2005. The Benefits of Frequent Positive Affect: Does Happiness Lead to Success? *Psychological Bulletin* 131, no. 6: 803–855.

Lyubomirsky, Sonja, and Heidi Lepper. 1999. A Measure of Subjective Happiness: Preliminary Reliability and Construct Validation. *Social Indicators Research* 46, no. 2: 137–155.

Lyubomirsky, Sonja, Kennon Sheldon, and David Schkade. 2005. Pursuing Happiness: The Architecture of Sustainable Change. *Review of General Psychology* 9, no. 2: 111–131.

MacLeod, W. Bentley. 1996. Decision, Contract, and Emotion: Some Economics for a Complex and Confusing World. *Canadian Journal of Economics* 29, no. 4: 788–810.

Marks, Gary, and Nicole Fleming. 1999. Influences and Consequences of Well-Being Among Australian Young People: 1980–1995. *Social Indicators Research* 46, no. 3: 301–323.

Marshall, Alfred. 1890 [1920]. *The Principles of Economics*, eighth edition. Macmillan.

Marshall, Monty, and Keith Jaggers. 2004. Polity IV Project: Political Regime Characteristics and Transitions, 1800–2004. The Polity IV Dataset. http://www.cidcm.umd.edu.

Martin, Dolores, and Richard Wagner. 1978. The Institutional Framework for Municipal Incorporation. *Journal of Law and Economics* 21: 409–425.

Mastekaasa, Arne. 1992. Marriage and Psychological Well-Being: Some Evidence on Selection into Marriage. *Journal of Marriage and the Family* 54, no. 4: 901–911.

Matsusaka, John. 2004. *For the Many or the Few: How the Initiative Process Changes American Government*. University of Chicago Press.

McIlwraith, Robert. 1998. "I, Addicted to Television": The Personality, Imagination, and TV Watching Patterns of Self-Identified TV Addicts. *Journal of Broadcasting & Electronic Media* 42, no. 3: 371–386.

McMahon, Darrin. 2006. *The Pursuit of Happiness: A History from the Greeks to the Present*. Allen Lane.

Mehay, Stephen. 1984. The Effect of Governmental Structure on Special District Expenditures. *Public Choice* 44: 339–348.

Meier, Stephan. 2006. *The Economics of Non-selfish Behaviour: Decisions to Contribute Money to Public Goods*. Elgar.

Meier, Stephan. 2007. A Survey of Economic Theories and Field Evidence on Pro-Social Behavior. In *Economics and Psychology: A Promising New Cross-Disciplinary Field*, ed. B. Frey and A. Stutzer. MIT Press.

Meier, Stephan, and Alois Stutzer. 2008. Is Volunteering Rewarding in Itself? Evidence from a Natural Experiment. Forthcoming in *Economica*.

Mellers, Barbara. 2000. Choice and the Relative Pleasure of Consequences. *Psychological Bulletin* 126, no. 6: 910–924.

Meyer, Bruce. 1995. Natural and Quasi-Experiments in Economics. *Journal of Business and Economic Statistics* 13, no. 2: 151–162.

Michalos, Alex. 1985. Multiple Discrepancies Theory (MDT). *Social Indicators Research* 16: 347–413.

Michalos, Alex. 1991. *Global Report on Student Well-Being*, volume 1: *Life Satisfaction and Happiness*. Springer.

Michalos, Alex, ed. 2005. *Citation Classics from Social Indicators Research: The Most Cited Articles*. Springer.

Mill, John Stuart. 1909. *Autobiography*. Collier.

Mitchell, Terence, Leigh Thompson, Erika Peterson, and Randy Cronk. 1997. Temporal Adjustments in the Evaluation of Events: The "Rosy View." *Journal of Experimental Social Psychology* 33, no. 4: 421–448.

Modigliani, Franco. 1949. Fluctuations in the Saving-Income Ratio: A Problem in Economic Forecasting. *Studies in Income and Wealth* 11: 371–443.

Morgan, Michael. 1984. Heavy Television Viewing and Perceived Quality of Life. *Journalism Quarterly* 61, no. 3: 499–504.

Mueller, Dennis. 1978. Voting by Veto. *Journal of Public Economics* 10, no. 1: 57–76.

Mueller, Dennis. 1996. *Constitutional Democracy*. Oxford University Press.

Mueller, Dennis, ed. 1997. *Perspectives on Public Choice: A Handbook*. Cambridge University Press.

Mueller, Dennis 2003. *Public Choice III*. Cambridge University Press.

Murphy, Gregory, and James Athanasou. 1999. The Effect of Unemployment on Mental Health. *Journal of Occupational and Organizational Psychology* 72, no. 1: 83–99.

Myers, David. 1993. *The Pursuit of Happiness: Who Is Happy and Why?* Avon.

Myers, David. 1999. Close Relationship and Quality of Life. In *Well-Being: The Foundations of Hedonic Psychology*, ed. D. Kahneman, E. Diener, and N. Schwarz. Russell Sage Foundation.

Myers, David. 2000. The Funds, Friends, and Faith of Happy People. *American Psychologist* 55, no. 1: 56–67.

Nelson, Michael. 1990. Decentralization of the Subnational Public Sector: An Empirical Analysis of the Determinants of Local Government Structure in Metropolitan Areas in the U.S. *Southern Economic Journal* 57, no. 2: 443–457.

Nettle, Daniel. 2005. *Happiness: The Science Behind Your Smile*. Oxford University Press.

Neumark, David, and Andrew Postlewaite. 1998. Relative Income Concerns and the Rise in Married Women's Employment. *Journal of Public Economics* 70, no. 1: 157–183.

New Scientist. 2003. Reasons to Be Cheerful. October 4–10: 44–47.

Ng, Yew-Kwang. 1978. Economic Growth and Welfare: The Need for a Complete Study of Happiness. *Kyklos* 31:575–587.

Ng, Yew-Kwang. 1996. Happiness Surveys: Some Comparability Issues and an Exploratory Survey Based on Just Perceivable Increments. *Social Indicators Research* 38, no. 1: 1–27.

Ng, Yew-Kwang. 1997. A Case for Happiness, Cardinalism, and Interpersonal Comparability. *Economic Journal* 107, no. 445: 1848–1858.

Ng, Yew-Kwang. 2001. From Preference to Happiness: Towards a More Complete Welfare Economics. *Social Choice and Welfare* 20, no. 2: 307–350.

Nicholson, Nigel. 1998. How Hardwired Is Human Behavior? *Harvard Business Review* 76, no. 4: 135–147.

Nieboer, Anna, Siegwart Lindenberg, Anne Boomsma, and Alinda Van Bruggen. 2005. Dimensions of Well-Being and Their Measurement: The SPF-IL Scale. *Social Indicators Research* 73, no. 3: 313–353.

Nordhaus, William, and James Tobin. 1972. *Is Growth Obsolete?* Columbia University Press.

Nozick, Robert. 1974. *Anarchy, State, and Utopia*. Basic Books.

Nussbaum Martha. 1999. *Sex and Social Justice*. Oxford University Press.

Nussbaum, Martha. 2000. *Women and Human Development: The Capabilities Approach*. Cambridge University Press.

Nussbaum, Martha. 2007. Mill between Aristotle and Bentham. In *Economics and Happiness*, ed. L. Bruni and P. Porta. Oxford University Press.

Nussbaum, Martha, and Amartya Sen. 1993. *The Quality of Life*. Oxford University Press.

O'Donoghue, Ted, and Matthew Rabin. 1999. Doing It Now or Later. *American Economic Review* 89, no. 1: 103–124.

Oates, Wallace. 1972. *Fiscal Federalism*. Harcourt Brace Jovanovich.

Oates, Wallace. 1999), An Essay on Fiscal Federalism. *Journal of Economic Literature* 37: 1120–1149.

Oberholzer-Gee, Felix. 2007. The Helping Hand—A Brief Anatomy. In *Economics and Psychology: A Promising New Cross-Disciplinary Field*, ed. B. Frey and A. Stutzer. MIT Press.

Oberholzer-Gee, Felix, Bruno Frey, Albert Hart, and Werner Pommerehne. 1995. Panik, Protest und Paralyse. Eine empirische Untersuchung über nukleare Endlager in der Schweiz. *Schweizerische Zeitschrift für Volkswirtschaft und Statistik* 13, no. 2: 147–177.

OECD (Organization for Economic Cooperation and Development). 2001. *The Well-Being of Nations: The Role of Human and Social Capital*.

Okun, Arthur. 1970. *The Political Economy of Prosperity*. Brookings Institution.

Olson, Mancur. 1969. The Principle of "Fiscal Equivalence": The Division of Responsibilities among Different Levels of Government. *American Economic Review* 59, no. 2: 479–487.

Osterloh, Margit, and Bruno Frey. 2000. Motivation, Knowledge Transfer, and Organizational Forms. *Organization Science* 11, no. 5: 538–550.

Osterloh, Margit, and Bruno Frey. 2004. Corporate Governance for Crooks? The Case for Corporate Virtue. In *Corporate Governance and Firm Organization*, ed. A. Grandori. Oxford University Press.

Osterloh, Margit, and Bruno Frey. 2006. Shareholders Should Welcome Knowledge Workers as Directors. *Journal of Management and Governance* 10, no. 3: 325–345.

Osterloh, Margit, Bruno Frey, and Jetta Frost. 2001. Managing Motivation, Organization and Governance. *Journal of Management and Governance* 5, no. 3–4: 231–239.

Osterloh, Margit, Bruno Frey, and Jetta Frost. 2002. The Dynamics of Motivation in New Organizational Forms. *International Journal of the Economics of Business* 9: 61–77.

O'Sullivan, Arthur. 1993. Voluntary Auctions for Noxious Facilities: Incentives to Participate and the Efficiency of Siting Decisions. *Journal of Environmental Economics and Management* 25, no. 1: 12–26.

Oswald, Andrew. 1997. Happiness and Economic Performance. *Economic Journal* 107, no. 445: 1815–1831.

Oswald, Andrew, and Nattavudh Powdthavee. 2006. Does Happiness Adapt? A Longitudinal Study of Disability with Implications for Economists and Judges. IZA Discussion Paper No. 2208, Institute for the Study of Labor. Parducci, Allen. 1995. *Happiness, Pleasure, and Judgment: The Contextual Theory and Its Applications*. Erlbaum.

Pateman, Carol. 1970. *Participation and Democratic Theory*. Cambridge University Press.

Pavot, William, and Ed Diener. 1993. The Affective and Cognitive Context of Self-Reported Measures of Subjective Well-Being. *Social Indicators Research* 28, no. 1: 1–20.

Pearlin, Leonard, and Carmi Schooler. 1978. The Structure of Coping. *Journal of Health and Social Behavior* 19, no. 1: 2–21.

Peterson, Christopher. 1999. Personal Control and Well-Being. In *Well-Being: The Foundations of Hedonic Psychology*, ed. D. Kahneman, E. Diener, and N. Schwarz. Russell Sage Foundation.

Pollak, Robert. 1970. Habit Formation and Dynamic Demand Functions. *Journal of Political Economy* 78, no. 4: 745–763.

Pollak, Robert. 1976. Interdependent Preferences. *American Economic Review* 66, no. 3: 309–20.

Pollak, Robert. 2002. Gary Becker's Contributions to Family and Household Economics. *Review of Economics of the Household* 1, no. 1: 111–141.

Pommerehne, Werner, and Hannelore Weck-Hannemann. 1996. Tax Rates, Tax Administration and Income Tax Evasion in Switzerland. *Public Choice* 88, no. 1–2: 161–170.

Portney, Paul. 1994. The Contingent Valuation Debate: Why Economists Should Care. *Journal of Economic Perspectives* 8, no. 4: 3–17.

Powdthavee Nattavudh, 2007. Putting a Price Tag on Friends, Relatives, and Neighbours: Using Surveys of Life Satisfaction to Value Social Relationships, Forthcoming in *Journal of Socioeconomics*.

Prelec, Drazen, and Richard Herrnstein. 1991. Preferences or Principles: Alternative Guidelines for Choice. In *Strategy and Choice*, ed. R. Zeckhauser. MIT Press.

Pugno, Maurizio. 2004a. The Happiness Paradox: A Formal Explanation from Psycho-Economics. Working paper, Department of Economics, University of Trento.

Pugno, Maurizio. 2004b. Rationality and Affective Motivations: New Ideas from Neurobiology and Psychiatry for Economic Theory? Discussion Paper 0501, Department of Economics, University of Trento.

Pugno, Maurizio. 2007. The Subjective Well-Being Paradox: a Suggested Solution Based on Relational Goods. In *Handbook on the Economics of Happiness*, ed. L. Bruni and P. Porta. Elgar.

Putnam, Robert. 2000. *Bowling Alone: The Collapse and Revival of American Community*. Simon & Schuster.

Rabin, Matthew. 1998. Psychology and Economics. *Journal of Economic Literature* 36: 11–46.

Ravallion, Martin, and Michael Lokshin. 2001. Identifying Welfare Effects from Subjective Questions. *Economica* 68, no. 271: 335–357.

Rayo, Luis, and Gary Becker. 2007. Evolutionary Efficiency and Happiness. *Journal of Political Economy* 115, no. 2: 302–337.

Ridgeway, Cecilia, and Henri Walker. 1995. Status Structures. In *Sociological Perspectives on Social Psychology*, ed. K. Cook, G. Fine, and J. House. Pearson Education.

Riis, Jason, George Loewenstein, Jonathan Baron, Christopher Jepson, Angela Fagerlin, and Peter Ubel. 2005. Ignorance of Hedonic Adaptation to Hemodialysis: A Study Using Ecological Momentary Assessment. *Journal of Experimental Psychology* 134, no. 1: 3–9.

Riker, William, and Peter Ordeshook. 1973. *An Introduction to Positive Political Theory.* Prentice-Hall.

Robbins, Lionel. 1932. *An Essay on the Nature and Significance of Economic Science.* Macmillan. Selections reprinted in *The Philosophy of Economics: An Anthology*, ed. D. Hausman. Cambridge University Press.

Robinson, John, and Geoffrey Godbey. 1999. *Time for Life: The Surprising Ways Americans Use Their Time*, second edition. Pennsylvania State University Press.

Robinson, Michael, and Gerald Clore. 2002. Belief and Feeling: Evidence for an Accessibility Model of Emotional Self-Report. *Psychological Bulletin* 128, no. 6: 934–960.

Romer, Paul. 2000. Thinking and Feeling. *American Economic Review* 90, no. 2: 439–443.

Romer, Thomas, and Howard Rosenthal. 1978. Political Resource Allocation, Controlled Agendas, and the Status Quo. *Public Choice* 33: 27–43.

Romer, Thomas, and Howard Rosenthal. 1982. Median Voters or Budget Maximizers: Evidence from School Expenditure Referenda. *Economic Inquiry* 20: 556–578.

Rosen, Sherwin. 1974. Hedonic Prices and Implicit Markets: Product Differentiation in Pure Competition. *Journal of Political Economy* 82, no. 1: 34–55.

Rosenberg, Nathan, and Luther Earl Birdzell. 1986. *How the West Grew Rich: The Economic Transformation of the Industrial World.* I.B. Tauris.

Ross, Catherine, John Mirowsky, and Karen Goldsteen. 1990. The Impact of the Family on Health: The Decade in Review. *Journal of Marriage and the Family* 52, no. 4: 1059–1078.

Ross, Michael. 1989. Relation of Implicit Theories to the Construction of Personal Histories. *Psychological Review* 96: 341–357.

Rubin, Alan. 2002. The Uses-and-Gratification Perspective of Media Effects. In *Media Effects: Advances in Theory and Research*, ed. J. Bryant and D. Zillmann. Erlbaum.

Ruhm, Christopher. 2000. Are Recessions Good for Your Health? *Quarterly Journal of Economics* 115, no. 2: 617–650.

Ryan, Richard, and Edward Deci. 2000. Self-Determination Theory and the Facilitation of Intrinsic Motivation, Social Development, and Well-Being. *American Psychologist* 55: 68–78.

Ryan, Richard, and Edward Deci. 2001. On Happiness and Human Potentials: A Review of Research on Hedonic and Eudaimonic Well-Being. *Annual Review of Psychology* 52: 141–166.

Ryff, Carol. 1989. Happiness Is Everything, or Is It? Explorations on the Meaning of Psychological Well-Being. *Journal of Personality and Social Psychology* 57: 1069–1081.

Ryff, Carol, and Burton Singer. 1998. The Contours of Positive Human Health. *Psychological Inquiry* 9: 1–28.

Sandmo, Agnar. 2005. The Theory of Tax Evasion: A Retrospective View. *National Tax Journal* 58, no. 4: 643–663.

Sandvik, Ed, Ed Diener, and Larry Seidlitz. 1993. Subjective Well-Being: The Convergence and Stability of Self-Report and Non-Self-Report Measures. *Journal of Personality* 61, no. 3: 317–342.

Santerre, Rexford. 1989. Representative versus Direct Democracy: Are There Any Expenditure Differences? *Public Choice* 60, no. 2: 145–154.

Santerre, Rexford. 1993. Representative versus Direct Democracy: The Role of Public Bureaucrats. *Public Choice* 76, no. 3: 189–198.

Schelker, Mark, and Reiner Eichenberger. 2006. Making Audit Courts Effective: Theory and Empirical Evidence. In *Essays in Fiscal Sociology II*, ed. J. Backhaus. Peter Lange.

Schelling, Thomas. 1984. Self-Command in Practice, in Policy, and in a Theory of Rational Choice. *American Economic Review* 74, no. 2: 1–11.

Schneider, Friedrich, and Dominik Enste. 2000. Shadow Economies: Sizes, Causes, and Consequences. *Journal of Economic Literature* 38, no. 1: 77–114.

Schneider, Friedrich, and Dominik Enste. 2002. *The Shadow Economy: Theoretical Approaches, Empirical Studies, and Political Implications.* Cambridge University Press.

Schneider, Friedrich, and Werner Pommerehne. 1983. Macroeconomia della crescita in disequilibrio e settore pubblico in espansione: il peso delle differenze istituzionali. *Rivista Internazionale di Scienze Economiche e Commerciali* 33, no. 4–5: 306–320.

Schooler, Jonathan, Dan Ariely, and George Loewenstein. 2003. The Pursuit and Assessment of Happiness Can Be Self-Defeating. In *The Psychology of Economic Decisions*, volume 1: *Rationality and Well-Being*, ed. I. Brocas and J. Carrillo. Oxford University Press.

Schor, Juliet. 1991. *The Overworked American: The Unexpected Decline of Leisure.* Basic Books.

Schor, Juliet. 1998. *The Overspent American: Why We Want What We Don't Need.* Basic Books.

Schreiber, Charles, and Daniel Kahneman. 2000. Determinants of the Remembered Utility of Aversive Sounds. *Journal of Experimental Psychology* 129: 27–42.

Schröder, Guido. 1997. *Die Ökonomie des Fernsehens—eine mikroökonomische Analyse.* LIT.

Schroth, Holly, and Priti Pradhan-Shah. 2000. Procedures: Do We Really Want to Know Them? An Examination of the Effects of Procedural Justice on Self-Esteem. *Journal of Applied Psychology* 85, no. 3: 462–471.

Schwartz, Barry. 2000. Self-Determination: The Tyranny of Freedom. *American Psychologist* 55: 79–88.

Schwarz, Norbert. 1990. What Respondents Learn from Scales: Informative Functions of Response Alternatives. *International Journal of Public Opinion Research* 2: 274–285.

Schwarz, Norbert, and Fritz Strack. 1999. Reports of Subjective Well-Being: Judgmental Processes and Their Methodological Implications. In *Well-Being: The Foundations of Hedonic Psychology*, ed. D. Kahneman, E. Diener, and N. Schwarz. Russell Sage Foundation.

Schwarze, Johannes, and Rainer Winkelmann. 2005. What Can Happiness Research Tell Us about Altruism? Evidence from the German Socio-Economic Panel. Discussion Paper 1487, IZA (Institute for the Study of Labor), Bonn.

Scitovsky, Tibor. 1976. *The Joyless Economy: An Inquiry into Human Satisfaction and Dissatisfaction*. Oxford University Press.

Scollon, Christie, Chu Kim-Prieto, and Ed Diener. 2003. Experience Sampling: Promises and Pitfalls, Strengths and Weaknesses. *Journal of Happiness Studies* 4, no. 1: 5–34.

Seligman, Martin. 1992. *Helplessness: On Depression, Development and Death*. Freeman.

Seligman, Martin. 2002. *Authentic Happiness*. Free Press.

Seligman, Martin, and Mihaly Csikszentmihalyi. 2000. Positive Psychology: An Introduction. *American Psychologist* 55: 5–14.

Sen, Amartya. 1970. *Collective Choice and Social Welfare*. Holden-Day.

Sen, Amartya 1982. *Choice, Welfare and Measurement*. Blackwell.

Sen, Amartya. 1983. Poor, Relatively Speaking. *Oxford Economic Papers* 35, no. 2: 153–169.

Sen, Amartya. 1985. *Commodities and Capabilities*. North-Holland.

Sen, Amartya. 1986. The Standard of Living. In *Tanner Lectures on Human Values*, volume VII, ed. S. McMurrin. Cambridge University Press.

Sen, Amartya. 1992. *Inequality Reexamined*. Russell Sage.

Sen, Amartya. 1995. Rationality and Social Choice. *American Economic Review* 85, no. 1: 1–24.

Sen, Amartya. 1996. Rationality, Joy and Freedom. *Critical Review* 10: 481–494.

Sen, Amartya. 1997. Maximization and the Act of Choice. *Econometrica* 65, no. 4: 745–779.

Sen, Amartya. 1999. *Development as Freedom*. Alfred Knopf.

Shafir, Eldar, Itamar Simonson, and Amos Tversky. 1993. Reason-Based Choice. *Cognition* 49: 11–36.

Shapiro, Jesse. 2005. Is There a Daily Discount Rate? Evidence from the Food Stamp Nutrition Cycle. *Journal of Public Economics* 89, no. 2–3: 303–325.

Sharpe, L. James, ed. 1993. *The Rise of Modern Government in Europe*. Sage.

Shiller, Robert. 1997. Why Do People Dislike Inflation? In *Reducing Inflation: Motivation and Strategy*, ed. C. Romer and D. Romer. University of Chicago Press.

Shiller, Robert, Maxim Boyocko, and Vladimir Korobov. 1991. Popular Attitudes toward Free Markets: The Soviet Union and the United States Compared. *American Economic Review* 81, no. 3: 385–400.

Sirgy, M. Joseph. 1997. Materialism and Quality of Life. *Social Indicators Research* 43, no. 3: 227–260.

Sirgy, M. Joseph, Dong-Jin Lee, Rustan Kosenko, H. Lee Meadow, Don Rahtz, Muris Cicic, Guang Xi Jin, Duygun Yarsuvat, David Blenkhorn, and Newell Wright. 1998. Does Television Viewership Play a Role in the Perception of Quality of Life? *Journal of Advertising* 27, no. 1: 125–142.

Slemrod, Joel, and Shlomo Yitzhaki. 2002. Tax Avoidance, Evasion, and Administration. In *Handbook of Public Economics*, volume 3, ed. A. Auerbach and M. Feldstein. Elsevier.

Slesnick, Daniel. 1998. Empirical Approaches to the Measurement of Welfare. *Journal of Economic Literature* 36, no. 4: 2108–2165.

Smith, Adam. 1759 [2000]. *The Theory of Moral Sentiments*. Prometheus Books.

Smith, Richard, Ed Diener, and Douglas Wedell. 1989. Intrapersonal and Social Comparison Determinants of Happiness: A Range-Frequency Analysis. *Journal of Personality and Social Psychology* 56, no. 3: 317–325.

Smith, Stephen, and Peter Razzell. 1975. *The Pool Winners*. Caliban Books.

Sobel, Joel. 2005. Interdependent Preferences and Reciprocity. *Journal of Economic Literature* 43: 392–436.

Sousa-Poza, Alfonso, and Fred Henneberger. 2002. An Empirical Analysis of Working Hour Constraints in Twenty-One Countries. *Review of Social Economy* 60, no. 2: 210–242.

Stack, Steven, and J. Ross Eshleman. 1998. Marital Status and Happiness: A 17-Nation Study. *Journal of Marriage and the Family* 60, no. 2: 527–536.

Stevens, Anthony, and John Price. 2000. *Evolutionary Psychiatry: A New Beginning*. Routledge.

Stevenson, Betsey, and Justin Wolfers. 2006. Bargaining in the Shadow of the Law: Divorce Laws and Family Distress. *Quarterly Journal of Economics* 121, no. 1: 267–288.

Stigler, George. 1950. The Development of Utility Theory. *Journal of Political Economy* 58, no. 4–5: 307–327, 373–396.

Stouffer, Samuel, Edward Suchman, Leland DeVinney, Shirley Star, and Robin Williams Jr. 1949. *The American Soldier: Adjustment during Army Life*. Princeton University Press.

Strack, Fritz, Michael Argyle, and Norbert Schwarz, eds. 1991. *Subjective Well-Being: An Interdisciplinary Perspective*. Pergamon.

Stroebe, Wolfgang, and Margaret Stroebe. 1987. *Bereavement and Health: The Psychological and Physical Consequences of Partner Loss*. Cambridge University Press.

Stryker, Sheldon, and Anne Statham. 1985. Symbolic Interaction and Role Theory. In *Handbook of Social Psychology*, ed. G. Lindzey and E. Aronson. Random House.

Stutzer, Alois. 1999. Demokratieindizes für die Kantone der Schweiz. Working Paper 23, IEW (Institute for Empirical Research in Economics), University of Zurich.

Stutzer, Alois. 2004. The Role of Income Aspirations in Individual Happiness. *Journal of Economic Behavior and Organization* 54, no. 1: 89–109.

Stutzer, Alois, and Bruno Frey. 2003. Institutions Matter for Procedural Utility. An Econometric Study of the Impact of Political Participation Possibilities. In *Economic Welfare, International Business and Global Institutional Change*, ed. R. Mudambi, P. Navarra, and G. Sobbrio. Elgar.

Stutzer, Alois, and Bruno Frey. 2007a. Stress That Doesn't Pay: The Commuting Paradox. Working Paper 151, IEW (Institute for Empirical Research in Economics), University of Zurich.

Stutzer, Alois, and Bruno Frey. 2004. Reported Subjective Well-Being: A Challenge for Economic Theory and Economic Policy. *Schmollers Jahrbuch: Zeitschrift für Wirtschafts- und Sozialwissenschaften* 124, no. 2: 191–231.

Stutzer, Alois, and Bruno Frey. 2006. Does Marriage Make Happy, or Do Happy People Get Married? *Journal of Socio-Economics* 35: 326–347.

Stutzer, Alois, and Bruno Frey. 2007b. What Happiness Research Can Tell Us about Self-Control Problems and Utility Maximization. In *Economics and Psychology: A Promising New Cross-Disciplinary Field*, ed. B. Frey and A. Stutzer. MIT Press.

Stutzer, Alois, and Rafael Lalive. 2004. The Role of Social Work Norms in Job Searching and Subjective Well-Being. *Journal of the European Economic Association* 2: 696–719.

Sugden, Robert. 1981. *The Political Economy of Public Choice*. Martin Robertson.

Sugden, Robert. 1986. *The Economics of Rights, Cooperation, and Welfare*. Blackwell.

Sugden, Robert. 2005. Correspondence of Sentiments: An Explanation of the Pleasure of Interaction. In *Economics and Happiness*, ed. L. Bruni and P. Porta. Oxford University Press.

Schweizerischer Städteverband [Swiss Association of Cities]. Various years. *Statistik der Schweizer Städte*.

Tanzi, Vito, and Ludger Schuknecht. 2000. *Public Spending in the 20th Century*. Cambridge University Press.

Tatzel, Miriam. 2002. "Money Worlds" and Well-Being: An Integration of Money Disposition, Materialism and Price-Related Behavior. *Journal of Economic Psychology* 23, no. 1: 103–126.

Thaler, Richard. 1992. *The Winner's Curse: Paradoxes and Anomalies of Economic Life*. Free Press.

Thaler, Richard. 1999. Mental Accounting Matters. In *Choices, Values and Frames*, ed. D. Kahneman and A. Tversky. Cambridge University Press.

Theil, Henry. 1964. *Optimal Decision Rules for Government and Industry*. North-Holland.

Tiebout, Charles. 1956. A Pure Theory of Local Expenditure. *Journal of Political Economy* 64, October: 416–424.

Tinbergen, Jan. 1956. *Economic Policy: Principles and Design*. North-Holland.

Tooby, John, and Leda Cosmides. 1992. The Psychological Foundations of Culture. In *The Adapted Mind*, ed. J. Barkow, L. Cosmides, and J. Tooby. Oxford University Press.

Torgler, Benno. 2004. Moral Suasion: An Alternative Tax Policy Strategy? Evidence from a Controlled Field Experiment in Switzerland. *Economics of Governance* 5: 235–253.

Torgler, Benno. 2005. Tax Morale and Direct Democracy. *European Journal of Political Economy* 21: 525–531.

Torgler, Benno. 2007. *Tax Compliance and Tax Morale: A Theoretical and Empirical Analysis*. Elgar.

Torgler, Benno, and Bruno Frey. 2007. Tax Morale and Conditional Cooperation. *Journal of Comparative Economics* 35: 136–159.

Torgler, Benno, Christoph Schaltegger, and Markus Schaffner. 2003. Is Forgiveness Divine? A Cross-Cultural Comparison of Tax Amnesties. *Swiss Journal of Economics and Statistics* 125: 375–396.

Tullock, Gordon. 1967. *Toward a Mathematics of Politics*. University of Michigan Press.

Tullock, Gordon. 1987. *Autocracy*. Martinus Nijhoff.

Tversky, Amos, and Dale Griffin. 1991. Endowment and Contrast in Judgments of Well-Being. In *Strategy and Choice*, ed. R. Zeckhauser. MIT Press.

Tyler, Tom. 1997. Procedural Fairness and Compliance with the Law. *Swiss Journal of Economics and Statistics* 133, no. 2: 219–240.

Tyler, Tom, Robert Boeckmann, Heather Smith, and Yuen Huo. 1997. *Social Justice in a Diverse Society*. Westview.

Tyler, Tom., Yuen Huo, and E. Allan Lind. 1999. The Two Psychologies of Conflict Resolution: Differing Antecedents of Pre-Experience Choices and Post-Experience Evaluations. *Group Processes and Intergroup Relations* 2, no. 2: 99–118.

Tyran, Jean-Robert, and Dirk Engelmann. 2005. To Buy or Not to Buy? An Experimental Study of Consumer Boycotts in Retail Markets. *Economica* 72, no. 285: 1–16.

Uchida, Yukiko, Vinai Norasakkunkit, and Shinobu Kitayama. 2004. Cultural Constructions of Happiness: Theory and Empirical Evidence. *Journal of Happiness Studies* 5, no. 3: 223–239.

Ura, Karma, and Karma Galay, eds. 2004. *Gross National Happiness and Development*. Centre for Bhutan Studies.

Urry, Heather Jack Nitschke, Isa Dolski, Daren Jackson, Kim Dalton, Corrina Mueller, Melissa Rosenkranz, Carol Ryff, Burton Singer, and Richard Davidson. 2004. Making a Life Worth Living: Neural Correlates of Well-Being. *Psychological Science* 15, no. 6: 367–372.

Van den Bos, Kees, Jan Bruins, Elske Dronkert, and Henk Wilke. 1999. Sometimes Unfair Procedures Have Nice Aspects: On the Psychology of the Fair Process Effect. *Journal of Personality and Social Psychology* 77, no. 2: 324–336.

Van de Stadt, Huib, Arie Kapteyn, and Sara van de Geer. 1985. The Relativity of Utility: Evidence from Panel Data. *Review of Economics and Statistics* 67, no. 2: 179–187.

Van Herwaarden, Floor, Arie Kapteyn, and Bernard van Praag. 1977. Twelve Thousand Individual Welfare Functions: A Comparison of Six Samples in Belgium and the Netherlands. *European Economic Review* 9, no. 3: 283–300.

Van Praag, Bernard. 1968. *Individual Welfare Functions and Consumer Behavior—a Theory of Rational Irrationality*. North-Holland.

Van Praag, Bernard. 1971. The Welfare Function of Income in Belgium: An Empirical Investigation. *European Economic Review* 2: 337–369.

Van Praag, Bernard. 1991. Ordinal and Cardinal Utility. An Integration of the Two Dimensions of the Welfare Concept. *Journal of Econometrics* 50: 69–89.

Van Praag, Bernard. 1993. The Relativity of the Welfare Concept. In *The Quality of Life*, ed. M. Nussbaum and A. Sen. Clarendon.

Van Praag, Bernard, and Barbara Baarsma. 2004. Using Happiness Surveys to Value Intangibles: The Case of Airport Noise. *Economic Journal* 115, no. 500: 224–246.

Van Praag, Bernard, and Ada Ferrer-I-Carbonell. 2004. *Happiness Quantified: A Satisfaction Calculus Approach.* Oxford University Press.

Van Praag, Bernard, and Paul Frijters. 1999. The Measurement of Welfare and Well-Being: The Leyden Approach. In *Well-Being: The Foundations of Hedonic Psychology*, ed. D. Kahneman, E. Diener, and N. Schwarz. Russell Sage Foundation.

Van Praag, Bernhard, Paul Frijters, and Ada Ferrer-i-Carbonell. 2003. The Anatomy of Subjective Well-Being. *Journal of Economic Behavior and Organization* 51: 29–49.

Van Praag, Bernard, and Nico van der Sar. 1988. Household Cost Functions and Equivalence Scales. *Journal of Human Resources* 23, no. 2: 193–210.

Vanberg, Viktor. 2000. Functional Federalism: Communal or Individual Rights? *Kyklos* 53: 363–386.

Vanberg, Viktor. 2005. Market and State: The Perspective of Constitutional Political Economy. *Journal of Institutional Economics* 1, no. 1: 23–49.

Vaubel, Roland. 1994. The Political Economy of Centralization and the European Community. *Public Choice* 81: 151–190.

Veblen, Thorstein. 1899. *The Theory of Leisure Class.* Modern Library.

Veenhoven, Ruut. 1993. *Happiness in Nations: Subjective Appreciation of Life in 56 Nations 1946–1992.* Erasmus University Press.

Veenhoven, Ruut. 1999. Quality-of-Life in Individualistic Society: A Comparison in 43 Nations in the Early 1990s. *Social Indicators Research* 48, no. 2: 159–188.

Veenhoven, Ruut. 2000. Freedom and Happiness. A Comparative Study in 46 Nations in the early 1990s. In *Culture and Subjective Well-Being*, ed. E. Diener and E. Suh. MIT Press.

Voigt, Stephan. 2005. The Economic Effects of Judicial Accountability—Some Preliminary Insights. Working paper, Department of Economics, University of Kassel.

Von Hagen, Jürgen, and Guntram Wolff. 2006. What Do Deficits Tell Us about Debt? Empirical Evidence on Creative Accounting with Fiscal Rules in the EU. *Journal of Banking and Finance* 30, no. 12: 3259–3279.

Waite, Linda, and Maggie Gallagher. 2000. *The Case for Marriage: Why Married People Are Happier, Healthier, and Better Off Financially.* Doubleday.

Warr, Peter. 1999. Well-Being and the Workplace. In *Well-Being: The Foundations of Hedonic Psychology*, ed. D. Kahneman, E. Diener, and N. Schwarz. Russell Sage Foundation.

Weede, Erich, and Edward Muller. 1998. Rebellion, Violence and Revolution: A Rational Choice Perspective. *Journal of Peace Research* 35, no. 1: 473–494.

Weingast, Barry, and Mark Moran. 1983. Bureaucratic Discretion or Congressional Control? Regulatory Policymaking by the Federal Trade Commission. *Journal of Political Economy* 91, no. 5: 765–800.

Welsch, Heinz. 2002. Preferences over Prosperity and Pollution: Environmental Valuation Based on Happiness Surveys. *Kyklos* 55, no. 4: 473–494.

Wilson, Chris, and Andrew Oswald. 2005. How Does Marriage Affect Physical and Psychological Health? A Survey of the Longitudinal Evidence. Mimeo, Warwick University.

Wilson, John, and Marc Musick. 1999. The Effects of Volunteering on the Volunteer. *Law and Contemporary Problems* 62, no. 4: 141–168.

Wilson, Timothy, and Daniel Gilbert. 2003. Affective Forecasting. In *Advances in Experimental Social Psychology*, volume 35, ed. M. Zanna. Elsevier.

Wilson, Timothy, and Jonathan Schooler. 1991. Thinking Too Much: Introspection Can Reduce the Quality of Preferences and Choices. *Journal of Personality and Social Psychology* 60: 181–192.

Winkelmann, Liliana, and Rainer Winkelmann. 1998. Why Are the Unemployed So Unhappy? Evidence from Panel Data. *Economica* 65, no. 257: 1–15.

Wolfers, Justin. 2003. Is Business Cycle Volatility Costly? Evidence from Surveys of Subjective Well-Being. *International Finance* 6: 1–31.

Zak, Paul. 2004. Neuroeconomics. *Transactions of the Royal Philosophical Society B* 359: 1737–1748.

Zax, Jeffrey. 1988. The Effects of Jurisdiction Types and Numbers on Local Public Finance. In *Fiscal Federalism: Quantitative Studies*, ed. H. Rosen. University of Chicago Press.

Zolotas, Xenophon. 1981. *Economic Growth and Declining Social Welfare*. Bank of Greece.

Index